LINES
OF
BATTLE

Letters from American Servicemen:

LINES OF

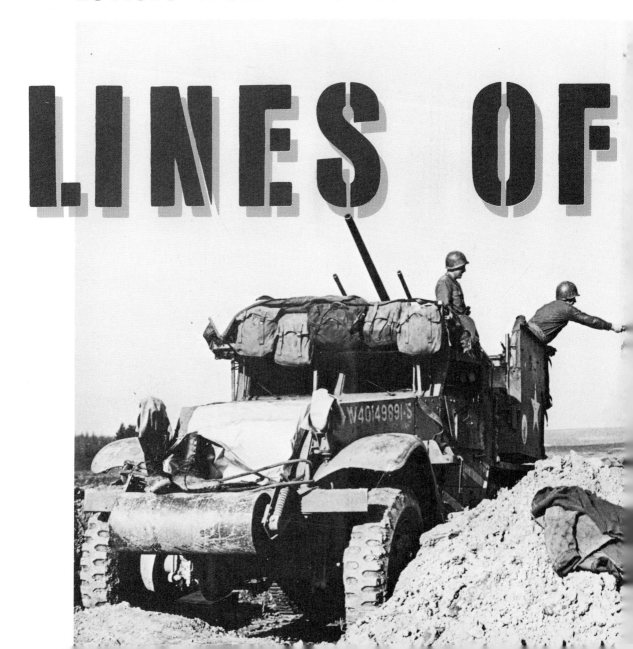

1941–1945

BATTLE

Edited by Annette Tapert

Times
BOOKS

Library of Congress Cataloging-in-Publication Data

Lines of battle.

  Bibliography: p.
  1. World War, 1939–1945—Personal narratives,
  American. I. Tapert, Annette.
D811.A2L53 1987   940.54'81'73   86-14478
ISBN 0-8129-1316-7

Designed by Robert Bull

Manufactured in the United States of America

9 8 7 6 5 4 3 2

First Edition

Page 297 is an extension of this copyright page.

ACKNOWLEDGMENTS

Most of the letters that appear in this anthology have never been published before. Some were acquired through personal solicitation, but the majority came to me in response to public appeals in regional newspapers, magazines, and military journals. I am indebted to the many publications that publicized my request for war letters. Although it was impossible for me to include all of the letters I received, I wish to thank everyone who took the time and interest to respond to my appeal.

A few of the letters I have included were selected from the outstanding collections at the Military History Institute at Carlisle Barracks in Carlisle, Pennsylvania. I want to thank Dr. Richard Sommers, Chief Archivist-Historian, and his conscientious and courteous staff for all their assistance. I am also grateful to Michael Miller, Curator of Personal Papers at the Marine Corps History Museum, and Terry Anderson at the Witness to the Holocaust Project, Emory University.

On a more personal note, I want to thank my parents, who dealt with the mountain of correspondence that arrived on their doorstep almost every day for nearly a year. And a special thank you to Jesse Kornbluth; his support and invaluable help went above and beyond the call of duty.

The last and most important acknowledgment goes to my contributors—the true authors of this book.

FOREWORD
B Y
David Eisenhower

As the years go by, the events recounted in *Lines of Battle* recede in time, but World War II remains a subject of intense interest. The fortieth anniversaries of D-Day, V-E Day, and other events have come and gone, but others approach, beginning next year with the fiftieth anniversary of Munich. Though Munich will not be celebrated, other events will be, particularly by the American people who look back on World War II as a supreme national achievement. For Americans and millions more, the war remains a living memory, a fact borne out by the recent controversies over President Reagan's visit to the military cemetery at Bitburg, West Germany, and Kurt Waldheim's election as president of Austria. Equally dramatic proof of this was the selection of Elie Wiesel as the recipient of the 1986 Nobel Peace Prize, an award tendered not for his involvement in any current crisis but in recognition of Wiesel's thirty-year effort to keep alive the memory of the Holocaust. These episodes reaffirm the universal feeling that the world dare not forget World War II.

And so the memories live on, for reasons that are self-evident. The scale of World War II was unprecedented. So was its savagery, which stands as a timeless warning about the illusions of progress. The political, military, social, and economic ramifications of the war are still deeply felt. In short, for the foreseeable future, the war looms as a unique event and its outcome remains the foundation of world politics, albeit an eroding foundation. For as time goes on, as William Jovanovich put it, "the past is always compromised by the present; many of the assurances of long ago, on reexamination, turn into questions and speculations." And as the "speculations" grow, it is crucial to recall the "assurances" accepted by the participants of the war, lest the past be forgotten altogether.

Thus, *Lines of Battle* is more than a selection of letters about a bygone period of special interest to the families of the recipients and of passing interest to the public. This book is a valuable resource, doubly so since the letters in this volume were written with no expectation that they would ever be published. *Lines of Battle* is an authentic sample of the firsthand accounts left by the servicemen who actually experienced World War II, a book of vivid descriptions and significant insights written as the war unfolded. Through these letters, a reader can transport himself back in time and imagine himself following this story as the recipients must have. In this way, a reader gains insight to the persisting question: What was the American experience like?

Annette Tapert has arranged the letters chronologically and so the story told here and the conclusions one draws from it evolve in steps. The men who wrote home individually describe episodes, rarely touching on the large aspects of the war. Philosophical passages multiply in the closing days of the war as weariness sets in, but American aims in World War II, never systematically spelled out by Roosevelt, are not articulated boldly here. Indeed, in the early years of this story, it seems as though America's war effort simply happened, that it was action preceding thought, rather than action based on firm ideas. But this is hard to reconcile with the sheer immensity of the war effort, in which eleven million servicemen crossed two oceans to fight the Axis powers at points separated by twelve thousand miles.

Why did America fight? There is no evidence here that American soil was threatened, or that an accommodation with the Axis, advocated in 1941 by the America First movement, was impossible. It becomes apparent that American motives were political, a fact that distinguishes the perspective of the American soldier from his British, French, German, or Russian counterparts, all of whom waged struggles close to home for the very existence of their countries.

As the story unfolds, the reader sees in these letters a deep appreciation for America's standing in the world and her responsibilities, a discovery which belies caricatures of the American GI as unfeeling or belatedly informed after the fact. Plainly, America did not seek direct involvement in the war; in time, however, Americans found that they could not justify abstention in a conflict in which America had the power to influence the outcome in favor of her friends. In these letters, one encounters the dismay felt by America's soldiers about home-front complacency and the tendency toward "national selfishness" which almost kept the U.S. out of war, which undermined conduct of the war and threatened to resurface as the war ended. But the soldiers in this book did not question that America had to stand up and be counted—what they wanted were weapons, support, and assurances that the life they returned to would resemble the life they left behind. This was perhaps best put in a letter by Lieutenant Charles Leiber of the 34th Infantry Division written on the eve of his death in the American advance into Bologna. " 'Why we fight' has been a topic for all of us to ponder," he wrote. "All one has to do is to look at Italy to appreciate all the good things at home. I like to feel I am fighting for the privilege of enjoying all that we as a people have been blessed with."

★　　★　　★

As the story unfolds, the experience of battle and confronting death in faraway lands predominates. These firsthand accounts are vivid for several reasons. First, the idea of global warfare was new. Compulsory Army service was also new, and the prospect of tangling with Imperial Japan and Nazi Germany was an imposing one. The story begins fittingly enough nine months before Pearl Harbor, which made war inevitable. In the opening letter, Sergeant Clarence Merson of the 557th Signal Air Warning Company describes the transit of his unit from Fort Meade, Maryland, to Fort Sam Houston, Texas, for training. As one might have expected, as he entered this strange new environment he found that the reality was less difficult than he had expected.

For Merson, the familiar stands out—he is unimpressed by his first glimpse of Texas from his Pullman car; he sees no cowboys and Indians, no Jesse James, but "trees . . . swamps . . . and darkness; nothing more." Merson goes on to describe Army life. His day begins at five, when he rises and gets into his clothes "mechanically." After cleanup, there is breakfast followed by a long, hard day of drills and marching. The routine is strenuous, but the Army is "not hard, really." Outwardly, the Army way is harsh, but Merson has found friendship and likes the invigorating pace.

The war's journey is arduous. After training, the soldiers in this book confronted separation and the ordeal of battle, which proved surprisingly easy the first time, harder than expected the second and third times out. The letters describe the confusion of combat, the pain of separation from loved ones, the peculiar horrors of modern warfare, and the timeless rituals of preparing to meet the enemy in battle. In this, the soldiers are brave and matter of fact. Private Gerald Herzfeld, as he departs with a top secret convoy across the Atlantic (his ship will be sunk) assures his family that he is sure that if he dies, then a long life for him was not meant to be. Private First Class Thomas Raulston of the 101st Airborne prepares for his drop into Normandy by praying over and over, "Give me guts." Ray Salisbury of the Ninth Air Force in North Africa proclaims his unwillingness to die, along with his confidence in his comrades, in the American method, and in American initiative, which over and over has provided "the spark . . . to do unheard of things." This is the true spirit of America, he writes, and the reason America "as a Nation will never be beaten!" What stands out in the letters is that ordinary men were capable of heroism—"Here is where you get down to bed rock," wrote Salisbury. "Here is where you discover you have pools of energy that have never been tapped."

Morale in a war fought thousands of miles from home was a constant concern at the time, and evidently, it was not a function of victory—which could, at times actually undermine morale. Morale was often bolstered by defeat. For instance, Lieutenant Colonel Herbert Blackwell at Pearl Harbor describes the soldiers and sailors in the wake of that Japanese attack as "the happiest lot you ever saw . . . itching for the Japanese to return, now that they are ready for them." Morale was shaken but not shattered by Marine combat in the jungles of the South Pacific or the hopeless situation described by Sergeant Irving Strobing in the closing days of the siege at Corregidor, a rare American defeat. But even as the garrison is about to fall, Strobing, who faces three-plus years of captivity, expresses his parting wish that his brother hasten over the Pacific and avenge his loss. Again, what sustained morale was faith in America, a belief that what each individual did was expected of him as a matter of course. Also, World War II, while necessary, was broadening as well. Perhaps the sheer wonder of it all is expressed best by General Teddy Roosevelt, Jr., in an anniversary letter to his wife. Nothing in their lives has turned out as they had expected except their children, he writes. "We never thought we'd roam the world. . . . We never thought that our thirty-third anniversary would find us deep in our second war, with me again at the front."

And so it was as the great adventure unfolded. Annette Tapert in presenting these letters chronologically also conveys the commonality of the World War II experience. It is clear that the war was a unifying and nationalizing force. For four years, men from Texas and New York served in the same units, shared similar concerns and fears, and shared a similar sense of justice and triumph, culminating perhaps in the winter battles in Belgium in 1944, in which an American Army of "soda jerks and grocers" checked the German SS and Panzers. But beneath the commonality are apparent differences. There are the contrasts between the ordinary ground soldier and the airmen and seamen who served at the cutting edge of American expertise and were the first into battle against the enemy homeland. There is a significant difference between the Asian and European theaters. These theaters were inseparable parts of one war but distinguishable in tactics, in strategy, and in different attitudes toward the enemy. Plainly, the American soldier despised the Japanese enemy, who was respected only for his ferocity. By contrast, the Americans were surprised by German ferocity. "What kind of people are these that we are fighting?" asks Private First Class Howell Iglehart of the 8th Infantry Division. The Germans are people not very unlike Americans, he concludes.

Accordingly, in Europe the ideological cast of the U.S. intervention in World War II shines clearest. Gradually, the significance of Nazi barbarism sank in as the GI was exposed to Europe's plight. Unlike the Pacific, the European campaign was fought in areas many of the Americans had visited and expected to revisit, and the scenes of desolation were sobering. The distinctions suggest that the two theaters were very different wars in fact, though not in principle. One might say that the war against Japan was less complex, a war between peoples that ultimately served as a means to the end of American participation in the most complex struggle of all time: the crusade in Europe to liberate Western Europe from the Nazi yoke and to destroy Nazism utterly.

As it proceeded, the European campaign evoked thoughtful speculation about the meaning of the war. By the winter of 1944, weariness had set in, but emotions had hardened and anger aimed at the home front again surfaced. As Colonel Herbert Enderton put it, the France of the travel posters had vanished in part because American aid had not been enough or early enough. Beauty remained, but the attractiveness was gone. Meanwhile, for the first time, the reader thinks of home. On the Belgian border in late January 1945, Lieutenant Edward Hitchin describes church services held in a hayloft shortly before his exhausted 28th Infantry Division was hurled back into action against a large German pocket holding out west of the Rhine. The hayloft was his "little barn church in the vale," and from his second floor seat, he gazed at the stream beneath him and the aged roof over him while he listened to the portable organ and the hymns of his youth.

Hitchin's ruminations are the prelude to the final act in Europe: the invasion of Germany, where the lessons of the war crystallized. In Germany, GIs witnessed firsthand the irrefutable evidence of the German barbarism that had prompted American intervention years before. The scenes evoked anger and a last spasm of determination. In a letter home, Captain Steve

Hall, an OSS officer training partisans in northern Italy, affirms the truth of widely disbelieved reports of German atrocities and describes his partisans as "the sword of God, if there has ever been one in history." Lieutenant Charles Leiber confronted death in the attack on Bologna "at peace with the world." Meanwhile, GIs entered the broken cities of Germany and the death camps, "brute testimonial to a brutality beyond comprehension." What did it mean? In this book, a German Jew confronts the American GI with the implications of what he sees. Corporal Kenneth Connelly describes his encounter with a Jewish survivor in Cologne who had wandered out of hiding to search for the American military government authorities. The survivor described the intense hatred which the Nazis had whipped up against the Jews as the source of all the mistakes in the world, but he doubted Germany was unique or that America was immune from such things. How could an insanity seize a whole nation? "I do not suppose that the American people can be expected to learn a lesson from this war," writes Howell Iglehart, "but will be satisfied to say, 'It can't happen in America.' Propaganda and indifference have certainly made it happen here in Germany."

Unanswerable questions arose as it became clear that German barbarism had been the result of choice as well as circumstance. From faraway Leyte Gulf, Combat Infantryman Jack Hogan reflected that it was a pity that anyone had viewed the war as a battle against Hitler and Hirohito. At the root of the war had been the rejection of divine authority, apathy, materialism, and moral decay, which had brought on a war "against moral anarchy, against fear and hate in men's hearts." Victory would come only with an end to racial and class divisions in America, he wrote, with a spirit of obedience to moral law, of sacrifice and the inner discipline to "root out of our national life the spirit of disunity, moral defeat and subversion and hatred that can destroy America."

With victory, there was little elation. Roosevelt's death kindled concern that the United States would succumb to "national selfishness" and apprehension about the Russians, who appear in the closing entries of this book as alien people but welcome allies in the Far East, where Russian intervention plus the A-bomb means the end of fighting. But few trust the Russians. On V-E Day, Sergeant Kenneth Board in Foggia prophetically notes that, looking ahead, "the path is beset by cross currents and undertow . . . a fine opportunity for these groups who desire another war to start laying the groundwork for it." A major war did not follow, but tensions stemming from the conflict beset the world, tensions inseparable from the stirring triumph that unfolds in this book.

Berwyn, Pennsylvania
January 1987

INTRODUCTION

E. J. Kahn, Jr., was enduring basic training at Camp Croft, South Carolina, when he had the good fortune to receive a bundle containing forty-two pieces of mail. "I was sitting in the barracks, talking to several of my buddies," he has recalled. "I was somewhat embarrassed by the size of my haul and tried to pass it off by announcing airily that some civilian friend, no doubt as a joke, appeared to have inscribed my name and address on a lot of advertisement coupons in magazines. My attitude was belied, however, by the eagerness with which I fumbled at the first tantalizing sealed envelope. The boys on the adjoining beds were impressed when the contents turned out to be another envelope. So was I. *Its* contents turned out to be an announcement of the wedding of a college classmate of mine whom I hadn't seen in four years. Feeling that some appropriate reaction to the news was required of me, I cried loudly, 'Well, upon my soul, look who old Freddie Comins married!' It became evident after a brief silence that no one cared who, so I tossed the announcement to one side, figuring that something of more general interest was bound to turn up. Half an hour later, as I reached the end of my treasure trove, I began to search anxiously for the announcement. By then I had realized sadly that the wedding announcement was, in fact, my only piece of first-class mail."

E. J. Kahn, Jr., was hardly a standard-issue Army private. At twenty-three he was already a contributor to *The New Yorker* magazine. And his account of Army life was published between hard covers in 1942, when he was still a private. But despite his precociousness and his sophistication, what E. J. Kahn, Jr., expressed was what all servicemen in World War II seemed to feel acutely from the moment of their induction—the need to keep in close touch with the world they had left behind.

This passion for letter writing is at odds with the common assumption that Americans—and American men, in particular —are inarticulate and infrequent correspondents. Having edited an anthology of letters written home by British soldiers in World Wars I and II, I was encouraged to share this assumption. In British war museums, in historical archives, and in the living rooms of war widows and still-grieving mothers, I was told, over and over again, that the letters I was collecting formed a history of those wars as valuable as the books of the most highly regarded historians. This was not to disparage the historians or the letters written by the fighting men of other nations. It was, simply, to assert a bit of common wisdom: that Britain's fighting men—in each war, the flowers of their generation—wrote letters that evoked the war and touched the heart in the richest, most eloquent language on earth.

In 1984 *Despatches from the Heart* was published in Britain, and I turned my attention to its American counterpart. As I began to collect letters from U.S. soldiers in World War II, I half expected to find that they would be terse and uncommunicative. Their real message, I thought, would be found between the lines: I miss you, I'm well, try not to worry.

In the course of my research I read thousands of letters. They came via public appeal in over two hundred regional newspapers and military journals, by searching the archives of several military institutes, and by personal solicitation. And as I read each letter, I was struck by the constant eloquence—especially the eloquence of men from the American heartland. Most had not been to college. Few had ever been exposed to the vast literature of war.

But just as the letters of their British brothers in arms had formed a parallel history of World Wars I and II, these American letters from World War II told me as much about the U.S. GIs' experience as any historical account I'd read. Indeed, these American letters told me more, for the standard texts about World War II focus mostly on the famous battles, the dates and places of the epic events, and theories on how and why they happened—in short, war from the generals' view. But in the last decade more and more historians have started to look for fresh insights in more personal stories—the stories of the men and women who actually did the fighting and dying.

For all the eloquence of their letters, U.S. soldiers didn't have a history of letter writing behind them. They'd had, in their two brief decades of life, little need to master the art of correspondence—the majority had never left their home towns before answering the call to war. Suddenly, however, these sheltered young Americans were separated from relatives, fiancées, and brides, then shipped thousands of miles across the ocean and thrust into a strange, often dangerous world for which they had no experience or preparation. This convergence of forces—loneliness, fear, the possibility of a violent death—generated an intense need for self-expression. As Henry Stimson, the U.S. secretary of war from 1940–45, has noted, U.S. servicemen were "the most homesick troops in the world."*

For these men letters were the only links with the private worlds they had left behind. As a Marine Corps captain wrote to his wife, "It seems like every chance I get to write to you, I always am brought sharply aware of how long it has been since the last letter to you. The old saying about people not appreciating things until they're deprived is so true, as so many of us have found out! And what wouldn't we give to get back to being soda jerkers, mechanics, plumbers, insurance salesmen, husbands, brothers and sons!"

That longing for personal connectedness is even seen in the letters of men trained to lend support to the GIs. An Army chaplain wrote home: "Irene, it's the foolish information I treasure. You don't know how imperative it is that I know what table cloth you are eating off today." His assistant wrote: "Tell the girls that I should love to hear particularly about the little, seemingly unimportant things that make home life so beautiful." In letter after letter I found the same beginning—an ac-

---

* Laffin, John, *Americans in Battle* (New York: Crown Publishers, Inc., 1973), p. 134.

knowledgment of the most recent letter from the United States, a request for more news from home.

Bill Mauldin, the World War II soldier–cartoonist whose sketches captured the spirit of the U.S. infantryman, has noted that "the mail is by far the most important reading matter that reaches a soldier overseas. . . . A soldier's life revolves around his mail." Letter writing quickly became the soldier's primary way to keep a grip on reality and to stay in touch with his dreams and plans; his thoughts of home kept his spirits high through the danger, loneliness, and the boredom of war.

I have tried, in choosing a hundred letters from the thousands I read, to present a cross section. The letters I chose were written by men from all ranks and branches of the armed forces. Although I have included a few letters written by men who, later in life, have become celebrated, I have not weighted the book toward those letters written by men noted for their literary gifts. I couldn't have done that if I had wanted to; more often than not, those writers' letters weren't saved by their families. On the other hand, letters written by men whose names you wouldn't recognize—or by men cut down in the war—were cherished upon arrival and preserved for future generations.

In 1942 a soldier wrote home to his family that the most important things to a soldier are food, ammunition, and mail, though not necesssarily, he said, in that order. But in the early days of the war, food and ammunition moved more rapidly to the front than mail. When letters from home arrived, they were sometimes months old.

To overcome these long delays, Army Postal Director Colonel William Rose developed the system of microfilming the mail. Victory Mail stationery—commonly known as V-Mail— was instituted in the summer of 1942. V-Mail was a special eight-and-a-half-by-eleven-inch white sheet of paper with space for approximately seven hundred words. By means of microphotography batches of sixteen hundred letters written on this paper were transferred onto ninety-foot rolls of 16-millimeter film. The film was then put into small boxes each weighing four ounces—reducing a ton of mail to twenty-five pounds. When the boxes reached their destinations, the film was developed. Finally, each letter was enlarged to a four-by-five-inch print and put into a window envelope for delivery to the stated address.

Thanks to V-Mail, a soldier at war could receive a letter from the United States—or send one home—in less than two weeks. That was a morale booster of inestimable value. As Admiral William Halsey wrote to Admiral Chester Nimitz, "Please stop the flow of Washington experts and sightseers to this area. Each expert means 200 less pounds of mail. I'll trade an expert for 200 pounds of mail at any time."

By the end of the war it was estimated that V-Mail had saved 95 percent in cubic footage of cargo space. But for all its advantages V-Mail was not initially popular. The reasons were understandable. V-Mail limited the size of a letter and did not allow for enclosures. And, like a postcard, it inhibited intimacy.

There were more substantive reasons for preferring the standard air-mail letter to V-Mail. All mail was censored—though officers, who censored one another's letters, were more inclined to approve their fellow officers' mail without reading it—but soldiers thought V-Mail was read by dozens of eyes during transmission. And some soldiers resisted V-Mail because of the myths that sprung up about it. Prominent among them was the suspicion that the film was screened in movie houses in Army camps.

V-Mail gradually grew in acceptance. According to the postmaster general's report from the war years, the number of V-Mail letters sent from the front jumped from 18,000 in June 1942 to 7.6 million in June 1943. From 1942 to September 1944 a total of 789,539,390 V-Mail letters were sent to and received from members of the armed forces overseas. By the war's end the estimated total of V-Mail letters dispatched was over one billion.

Despite that volume, I have included only a handful of V-Mail letters here. V-Mail's real contribution was as a useful morale booster; it filled the gap between longer, descriptive, more intimate letters and gave regularity and familiarity to the soldier's correspondence with family and friends. Of much greater interest, for my purposes, were letters that described military life in some detail, reflected deep emotion, or provided vivid accounts of battles.

Considering the astronomical number of letters that flowed home from the various theaters of World War II, it is tragic to think how many have been lost forever. Now that we are, however belatedly, considering World War II as a human experience, those letters would, in such volumes as this, have given us a fresh look at America's last great military campaign. For letters have the special ability to capture history in the making. They are unique in that they can recall incidents as they really were at a specific time and place and at the same time provide a human backdrop for the epic events that occurred.

It is my hope that this anthology will be a powerful reminder of war's dual nature. The movement of armies, the blackening of skies by hundreds of airplanes, the fleets of ships moving in convoys—for all the might these images suggest, they also obscure the contribution of the individual men and women in World War II. In these pages we can begin again to celebrate and memorialize those Americans who suffered, struggled, and endured the pain of separation and loss. It is, in the end, their thoughts and feelings that give reality to historical events and, in the giving, reveal another dimension in our history.

EDITOR'S NOTE

The letters have been arranged in chronological order to give the reader a sense of history. To allow the letters to speak simply for themselves, a very brief linking text provides a few background facts. In some cases information was not obtainable and I have been unable to fill in all the details. With some of the letters, I had difficulties in transcription. If, despite my efforts to check all material, mistakes have crept in, then I can only apologize to the writers of the letters. The original grammar, spelling, and punctuation remain unchanged. The letters have not been edited in any way, except that a few of them, due only to their length, have not been used in full.

PROLOGUE

Moratorium

Along with the letter, keys and such, I'll leave
My thoughts: civilian thoughts that cannot march
To military bands, that cannot breathe
In gas masks. Stored away with shirts in starch
And books in boxes, labeled neatly, rest
My restless thoughts. Assorted memories
Of certain plans, ignited and suppressed
Like fireflies. Love, a pollen on the breeze,
Inhaled on hilltops, suddenly, till breath
Had tiptoed with a shiver, and the world
Was windswept. Now inevitable Death
Or Victory advance. Our flag's unfurled.
Until the wars are won and treaties made,
I'll leave you here, my thoughts, where peace has stayed.

PRIVATE JOHN LAWRENCE SHEEHAN

★ ★ ★

Clarence Merson served as a technical sergeant with the 557th Signal Air Warning Company. Most of his service time was spent performing technical work in radar early-warning detection at Air Warning Headquarters in Seattle, Washington.

Dodd's Field, Fort Sam, Texas
[January 1941]

Dear Mother, Dad, Lee, Mollie, Sol, J.F.:

. . . To recapitulate briefly, we left Fort Mead 9 a.m. Thursday, and arrived in Fort Sam Saturday evening about 7 p.m.

Probably the most amusing incident on this entire tedious trip occurred when we crossed from Arkansas into Texas. The time was about 5:30 a.m. with everyone kicking about in their Pullman berths, dressing for chow. The colored porter walked thru the car saying "yo' now in Takes-us boys—crost d'boder 15 sens 'go."

The fellows in the upper berths jumped to the Pullman floor to look out of the window. Those in the lower berths already had their faces flattened against the glass, straining their eyes to see something of this be-you-ti-ful, rootin', Tootin' state.

The funny part about it was that everyone somehow expected to see hundreds of cowboys, slinging their lariats and yelling, "yipee, yipee, yipee" ride past. Some Indians should be behind those trees. And perhaps a Jesse James would board the train with a "Stick 'em up boys".

Hell, in the early morning darkness of January 25th, the State of Texas—at least the part we were in—was little different

3

from any other state we had crossed. There were trees and there were swamps and there was darkness; nothing more.

And the climate—it should have been stinking hot, unbearable. It was cold in Texas that morning. There was a very amusing look of disappointment on the faces of the 36 fellows who filled our car. So this is Texas! It stinks! . . .

You ask about a typical day. Well briefly, it runs something like this: You awaken about 5 a.m., swearing. Now what you swear about depends entirely upon the individual. The butt of my invective is invariably the hour, though with others it may range from the Sergeant up to the Looie or from the food down to the pay (which we haven't received.) . . .

Your clothes are slipped on mechanically. (If you wear breeches and leggins—as I do—you really have something to cuss about). You grab a towel, fumble for soap and run out of the tent into the flawless darkness of a Texas morning. And what mornings! Ten million stars an arm's length above you.

Sergeant Clarence Merson

The air is brisk, often biting. The pungent smell of wood smoke is everywhere. And as you run down a narrow boardwalk toward the bath house, your white towel piercing the darkness, an awareness of time and place creeps into your senses, and once again you remember that you are in the army and that the time is 5:15, and that you are running toward the bath house to wash, to brush your teeth, to get ready for chow. . . .

From the bath house, or rather before the bath house, comes the latrine. Though there is no S.R.O. sign outside, upon striking a match you invariably discover that there's standing room only. So you wait.

Back once more in your tent, you make your cot, sweep the floor, and roll up the sides of the tent.

By this time the Sarge is yelling: "Shake it up, boys! Shake it up, boys! All out for chow!" The tent flaps fly open like—I haven't time to think of a suitable simile—and you march with your platoon up to the mess hall. (Ours is actually a renovated airplane hangar).

Breakfast is good: two half-pint bottles of milk, corn flakes, potatoes, bread and butter. Directly from chow the company lines up fanwise and moves forward en masse, picking up match sticks, cigarette butts, etc. So now the street is clean and you run into your tent and begin packing a light pack: . . . You grab your rifle—this must all be done within three minutes—and fall in with the rest of your platoon.

The time is now 7:45 and the perfunctory hip, hup, thrup, fourp commences. You march out to the training field and drill, drill, drill. The Sarge swears to high heaven and if you don't "wake up", you're placed in the infamous 8-ball group. At 10:45 you are leg and arm weary and are quite certain that the time is at least 4:30. Then there is a short break. During this time the Sarge refrains from swearing long enough to disassemble a Browning automatic rifle or Colt pistol. He explains the parts, etc. and expects you to be able to re-assemble it. Or, he may talk about first aid or chemical warfare or about the time he slugged three men with his left arm tied behind him. After this brief respite you drill again until 11:45 and fall out for lunch. The food for lunch is consistently wretched. What food there is—

rice, chile, hot tomales—is so highly seasoned as to be most distasteful. But you eat it anyway; you're hungry. . . .

By this hour of the day the sun is usually plenty hot. . . . Your face is red and perspiring. Your pack feels like lead. The leather sling buries itself in your shoulder.

After 45 minutes the Sarge calls a halt and you flop down on your pack, the verdant grass cool about you. . . . You soon start out again, marching through woods, up hills, and across fields of high grass. Along the way the Sarge gives various alarms, air raid, tank attack, etc. Everyone dives off the road and, in the case of air attack, takes up positions and fires. There are always sufficient planes overhead to make it realistic. . . .

About 3:30 your 5 or 6 mile hike is completed and drilling commences once more. Perfection in this is merely passable. And the Sarge invariably yells: "Holy gallopn' hell, snap into it immediately, if not sooner!" The time is now your own. . . . Back in the tent again, you sweep up, study several pages of rules, and on some nights prepare a full field pack for the following day. Before you know it, it's nine o'clock. There is nothing to do but sleep or go to the post exchange.

At home you wonder how anyone can give three or more years of his life to the service. It's not hard, really. There's something about Army life that gets and sometimes keeps you. Marching up the field in full dress with rifles shouldered, a thousand legs rising as one, the band beating that boom de boom de boom, the Major an imposing figure against a perfect sky— there's something that gets you.

Sitting around a table in the smoke-filled P.X. at night, talking with fellows from Colorado, or Ohio, or perhaps Virginia, the momentary warmth of friendship flaming like a match—

Wheh y'all from? Allentown, Pa. You? Bristol, V'giny. Had a buddy went to Pennsylvania once. Got run over, both legs—

And so on into the night, these countless remembrances of things past. The whole intricate fabric of their lives is rewoven simply, sometimes naively and always without restraint. And for the moment these fellow soldiers sitting around the table smoking and drinking are the finest people you've ever known, and the bond of friendship is, perhaps, as complete and absolute as friendship can ever be.

However, in an hour, alone once more, walking under the stars, these very people become remote and their stories join the ten thousand others which clutter your brain. Ah, yes, there's something about the Army that gets you. You're in the tent, lying on your bunk, looking up into the void of night.

"What you thinkin' about, Slim?"

Silence. "Things."

"What things?"

Silence. "Just things; home."

"Bout your girl?"

"Yeh; bout Kitty and home—"

Once more it begins. Slowly the end-threads of another life begin to ravel. And what stories! From Zola to Poe and back to Balzac.

So again, the Army is not dull, not routine, but electric, every moment of it. How I shall feel about it a month from now, I don't know, though I suspect that this goggle-eyedness will disappear shortly and in its place will come an enormous desire to get away. . . .

Please write often, if only a post card. Every word is read and reread most eagerly.

     Love,

                              Clar

★ ★ ★

Lieutenant Colonel Herbert Blackwell served with the Coast Artillery Corps at Fort Shafter, Hawaii. On December 9, 1941, two days after the Japanese attack on Pearl Harbor, he wrote home to his wife. The letter was returned to him by the chief military censor because Blackwell had included too much detail regarding the military activities of December 7. The censor suggested that Blackwell rewrite the letter or retain it for the duration of the war. The following letter is Lieutenant Colonel Blackwell's censored version of the original letter.

3:15 a.m.—Dec. 9

Eloise, darling:

This is early Tuesday morning and I am on duty. The first and only sleep I have had was from 9 to 12 tonight (since early Sunday morning), yet I feel remarkably well. I was on a party Saturday night until about 2:00 a.m., thinking I could sleep late Sunday morning. However, I was rudely awakened just before 8 o'clock by the terrific noise of bombs and cannon. At first I thought it was dynamite blasting in a tunnel which is being constructed at Shafter, but when I heard the whistling sound preceding the explosion on some of the closer ones, I jumped out of bed and ran to investigate. The only reply I got to my inquiry was that "You had better get dressed and come on down to the Command Post." When I got outside I was perfectly dumbfounded. Black columns of smoke were rising from Pearl Harbor Navy Yard, about three miles distant and the sky was filled with puffs of black smoke from AA shells. It looked like war, but I just could not believe my eyes. I just could not believe that Japan could make an air attack from such a distance without our Navy having some warning. The attack caught both the Army and Navy completely by surprise. Being Sunday morning most everyone was still in bed. Our AA guns were not in firing positions, but were parked at Shafter or other posts. We were on alert against sabotage, and in a condition of readiness which allowed three hours to go into action in case of attack. We had had frequent drills on going out into battle positions and everyone had been trained thoroughly on just what to do ('thoroughly' should be qualified, however, since 80 per cent of our troops have had less than 8 mos. service, and the organization of the Brigade was not completed). We had found that this took about three hours. However, as soon as we found out that this was the real thing we cut this time in half. Speed limits were ignored. Some units began firing within 45 minutes from the time they were alerted. All units were firing before the attack was ended, and we shot down 4 or 5 planes. The AA fire I first saw was from the Navy.

★

Lieutenant Colonel Herbert Blackwell

Flames of landing ship tanks in Pearl Harbor

3:00 a.m. Wednesday, Dec. 10

Before I had time to finish this yesterday I was called, and was busy—continuously, from then until 6:00 p.m. last night, only taking out 30 min. for breakfast. No time for lunch. When I left the C.P. last night at 6:00 p.m., I had been without sleep since 6:00 a.m. Sunday, except in one instance I had laid down for three hours, fully dressed, and probably slept about one hour. This was Monday from 9 to 12 p.m. During all this time I have been existing on sandwiches, milk, coffee, and fruit juices while at work. Six o'clock last night (Tues.) I undressed and went to bed for the first time and slept until 1:00 a.m. this morning, and I feel perfectly rested. About this time in the morning everything is quiet until about 5:00 a.m., when telephones begin to ring. Each morning preparations are made for a dawn attack. I hesitate to make any further predictions after my poor guess in my last letter (I expect to get a razzing on that) but I don't believe we will have another major attack in the near future, since now we are completely on guard. However, since what

Burned landing ship tanks in Pearl Harbor

happened Sunday I am not placing much weight on expectations. . . .

You are probably wondering why I am not giving you more details about what actually happened, casualties, damage, etc. First, a very strict censorship is imposed, and second, I have been too busy to learn much about it, i.e. I haven't had much time to go out to the Navy Base, or the Air Fields, where most of the damage was done. The damage was severe. In our Brigade we had only one officer and two men killed. The Navy suffered most heavily. The telephones are beginning to ring wildly again, so I will continue this later. Signing off at 4:00 a.m.

★

3:15 a.m. Thursday Dec. 11

To continue my letter—I left the C.P. at 5:00 p.m. yesterday, and ate a good dinner at the club, went to bed about 7:00 p.m., and up at 12:30 a.m. Yesterday was comparatively quiet, and with additional officers on the staff my work has been considerably reduced. Fifteen minutes after I signed off on yesterday (at 4:15 a.m.) we had an air raid alarm. Reports began to come to my desk faster than I could read them, each one requiring immediate action. Col. Wing and a good many others were asleep nearby in various places, and they were notified. It looked like the real thing. The sequence of messages were in substance as follows:

1. Navy at Pearl Harbor sounds A.P.R. alarm, planes approaching. No friendly planes in sight.
2. Caution—these may be planes from the mainland.
3. Planes from mainland are not due to arrive at this time.
4. Friendly planes are taking off from the airfields, do not fire on them.
5. A pause of about 5 minutes.
6. Pearl Harbor has given the "all clear" signal.

As to the cause of this false alarm I have not been able to determine. It is practically impossible to get any information, except that necessary to operation. . . .

I had my first recreation yesterday. I took an hour off and

drove out to one of the Air Fields to inspect the damage from Sunday's raid. This airfield was badly bombed. Most of the hangars were destroyed, and one large three story barracks was completely demolished, killing 300 soldiers. Signing off till to-morrow.

★

11:15 p.m.—Friday Dec. 12

. . . Every night we are having a total black-out, no light, except the palest blue dot of light is allowed. This blue dot on the headlight of an automobile does not furnish the driver with any illumination but warns approaching vehicles. Autos are run at a snail's pace and you can detect an oncoming car only when within about 100 ft. We have had no moon the first part of the night and when it is cloudy you can't see a thing, it is like being totally blind. We use flashlights with blue paper over them to give a dim illumination. I tried to walk about 100 yards down the road to my house the other night over a curving road with-out a flashlight and I repeatedly found myself bumping into the curb. The first nights after the attack guards were posted every-where, and it was extremely dangerous to go out at night, for fear of being shot. Last Monday night I went to my Qts. for a few hours rest, and it sounded like a battlefield. Rifle and occa-sionally Machine Gun fire was heard on all sides, occurring about every one or two minutes. With much of the population here Japanese the threat of sabotage is great. However, these soldiers on guard were shooting on bushes when the wind would sway them, at any suspicious sounds, which may have been made by animals, etc. Whenever they heard or saw anything that did not respond to their challenge they shot at it. Only today I got a call from one of our units in the field asking what to do about removing some dead cows from the vicinity of its position, since the odor was obnoxious. I told the unit com-mander to take such action as he thought necessary, and sug-gested burial. Fortunately, as far as I know only one of our own soldiers has been shot, which I think is very remarkable. I shall be very glad when we have a little moonlight again. We have had a little excitement tonight and it is still going on. We are observing (by radio detectors) some suspicious movement of ships offshore, and every man is standing by his guns, ready for instant action. But such things as this are now routine. Nobody gets very excited any more. You would be surprised to see how our soldiers react to all this. Although they have been on duty almost continuously, with very little sleep or rest, enduring many hardships, they are the happiest lot you ever saw. They all are just itching for the Japanese to return, now that they are ready for them. You can't get one to go to sleep as long as there is any suspicion of attack. They are afraid they will miss a chance to get revenge. I will tell this little incident before I close (I may have written this before).

The other day I saw three soldiers bringing in a suspected Japanese spy which they had caught under suspicious circumstances. The Jap was sullen and slow in following directions. One soldier was behind him with his bayonet pressing against his behind, and every now and then he would give it a slight push to speed him up. On either side was a soldier with a bayonet pressed against his ribs. Whenever they wished him to change direction the bayonet was pressed into his off side, and

The 34th Infantry Division enjoying mail call in Hawaii

he would immediately respond. He could not understand English so the soldiers resorted to this method of directing him. From the expression on the faces of these soldiers I could see that they would have liked to have used the bayonets more violently. They were exercising extreme self-control. You need have no fear of the fighting spirit of our soldiers. More later. . . .

As to the further details of the raid last Sunday, I know very little more than what you have seen in the papers. We have accounted for 20 planes shot down, 8 are credited to our Air Corps and 4 to the AA, the other 8 may be due to either of the above, or to the Navy. Hangars in which our planes were parked were heavily bombed, and serious damage was inflicted. However, many of these damaged planes have been repaired. And nearly every day more planes have been arriving, and we are all set to give the Japs a fitting reception if they should return. . . .

All families on Army posts were rushed to a tunnel at Fort Shafter last Sunday morning, or some other safe place, and for several nights slept there on cots. Now they stay in buildings near the entrances to the tunnels and go into the tunnel only when the Air Raid Alarm goes off. I am so glad you and the kids are safely at home. Some of the officers here did not see their families for a day or two after the raid, and in some cases did not know where to find them. I hope you get the little gifts I sent you for Xmas, and regardless of how much I would like to be with all of you, I am glad that I am in a position to help in this fight. And every soldier here feels the same way. If we could only get a fair chance at the Japs it will be a happy lot here. Everyone over here including civilians are very cheerful, and except at night, when we have a total black-out, business is done as usual. But the whole Island is bristling with bayonets and guns. I never go outside without a pistol and gas mask. Machine guns are everywhere patrolling the streets and street corners.

Beautiful, my love to *you*, Bets, Bobs, the Robinsons and Clyde, Mitch, Less, Opie, Roy and Clifford, Cecil, Raymond, and Humps. Merry Xmas to you all. Please write to me.

Devotedly XXXX

Black

1942

Good-By to a World

So, silently, I say good-by.
And yet, I know that men will try
To catch the 8:15 as they
Did yesterday; that friends will say
The same familiar things; that I
Will thrill again to winter's sky,
To breakfast bacon, candlelight,
A faint train whistle in the night,
And all those homely, precious things
The eager joy of living brings.
The morning papers still will say:
"Continued fair and cool today";
Lovers will kiss, and after dark
Usurp the benches in the park.
But this I know is also true:
Here ends a world I lately knew.

CORPORAL LE VAN ROBERTS

Gerald Herzfeld, although an Army private, served as a machine gunner on a merchant marine vessel. Just before volunteering for the mission, he wrote home to his parents in the Bronx, New York.

January 2, 1942

Dearest Mother and Father:

Before I go into any sort of detail concerning the reasons for this letter I would like to say a word or two on several touching subjects. To a man, there isn't anything as dear to him as his parents. I, being a man, also have two very dear parents. To me, there isn't anything nor anyone that could take your places. One may fall in love, but that is a different kind of love, and it cannot compare to the filial love of which I speak. There is a gate to my heart that cannot be passed no matter what means are tried and that gate guards my love and devotion to you. Believe me when I say that no man can deny similar feelings for his parents.

Yesterday I was chosen amongst 25 others to embark upon a secret mission, under sealed orders. No one knows where we are going and no one knows when we are returning. We do not know what our job is, but you can rest assured, that no matter what it is, it will be done in the American manner and to the best of our ability. Of course you know that the American manner is the best going and cannot be stopped. I have every reason in the world to believe that I will return as I have a full life of peace to look forward to with the woman I will eventually marry. In case that I don't return, which is the reason for my writing this, I shall know in the world that waits for me, that it was not meant

17

U.S. soldiers and Army nurses wave goodbye as their transport leaves the pier at an American port on the way to a fighting front.

for me. In that case, I shall know that I have not died in vain, but to make the world safe for all the Jerry Herzfelds that are to be born in the future. Since being in the Army, I have come to realize what "responsibilty" and "matured" mean. Believe me when I say that I have passed on a much wiser and matured man. It is time for me to stop now, as I will really have both of you feeling pretty down in the dumps and that is the last reason in the world for me writing this last note. This is just a final word from your loving and obedient son,

Gerald

★

On June 7, 1942, Herzfeld was reported missing in action when his cargo ship was torpedoed.

★ ★ ★

*L*ieutenant Colonel John Sewall served in the Army Air Forces with the 27th Bombardment Group. In April, after American resistance on Bataan collapsed, he became a prisoner of war, captured by the Japanese.

In the Field, Bataan
Feb. 18, 1942

Dear Eleanor and Girls:

One of the most painful things of this whole war is our complete lack of communication. If I could only get a letter to you, or hear from you, everything would be all right. When we left Manila, we thought we would be back in a few days, so left many things undone. Since then we have been completely cut off from the outside world. Today I heard that mail was being started to the States somehow, so I shall try it.

On Feb. 12th I was promoted to Lieutenant Colonel, why or how I do not know. Living from hand to mouth as we are we do not even wear our rank because the Japs make a special effort to kill officers first.

Shortly after arriving in Manila I was given command of the Group, increased by two squadrons, nearly 1,000 men and 100 officers. We never did get any airplanes and, as all existing airplanes on Luzon were destroyed in the first few days, and we knew it was impossible to get new planes, we set to work to train as infantry, and as infantry we have functioned ever since. We were issued rifles and all the accoutrements of infantry except machine guns. For machine guns we took our air-cooled aircraft guns and made tripods for them. We evacuated Manila by boat, and had to leave all heavy gear behind. I bought a beautiful wardrobe trunk and stored everything in it except my toilet articles and one change of clothing. All that is lost to me now as it is in Jap hands. I have lost everything but what I stand up in, but so has everyone else. I have drawn no pay since the first of December, as money is not needed because there is no place to spend it.

We are living in the jungle; no tents, just a mosquito bar. We eat twice a day, at daylight and dusk. Our kitchens are five miles to the rear and food is brought forward by truck. It is mostly canned salmon and rice. Morale is high and there has been little sickness. I have lost several men and one officer, mostly killed by bombs. The officer, Captain McCorkle, was killed in ambush while out on patrol. But we have killed hundreds of Japs, too, and have suffered very little ourselves. Yesterday we were shelled for nearly two hours, but there was no damage. We have foxholes and dugouts for protection. Fortunately the Japs have not shelled at night so we usually get our rest. . . .

How or when this letter will reach you I have no idea. I am putting it in the hand of God. "A thousand shall fall at thy side, and ten thousand at thy right hand, but it shall not come Nigh thee." Psalm 91:7.

★ ★ ★

On May 6, 1942, after five months of resistance, fifteen thousand U.S. and Filipino troops surrendered to the Japanese on the island of Corregidor. Just before the fall of the fortress, Sergeant Irving Strobing tapped out this final radio message. After the surrender Sergeant Strobing became a prisoner of war, captured by the Japanese.

[May 5 or 6]

They are not yet near. We are waiting for God only knows what. How about a chocolate soda? Not many. Not here yet. Lots of heavy fighting going on. We've only got about one hour, twenty minutes before. . . . We may have to give up by noon. We don't know yet. They are throwing men and shells at us and we may not be able to stand it. They have been shelling us faster than you can count. . . .

We've got about fifty-five minutes and I feel sick at my stomach. I am really low down. They are around us now smashing rifles. They bring in the wounded every minute. We will be

U.S. soldiers and sailors surrender to Japanese forces on Corregidor Island.

waiting for you guys to help. This is the only thing I guess that can be done. General Wainwright is a right guy and we are willing to go on for him, but shells are dropping all night, faster than hell. Damage terrific. Too much for guys to take.

Enemy heavy cross-shelling and bombing. They have got us all around and from skies. From here it looks like firing ceased on both sides. Men here all feeling bad, because of terrific nervous strain of the siege. Corregidor used to be a nice place, but it's haunted now. Withstood a terrific pounding. Just made broadcast to Manila to arrange meeting for surrender. Talk made by General [Lewis C.] Beebe. I can't say much.

I can hardly think. Can't think at all. Say, I have sixty pesos you can have for this weekend. The jig is up. Everyone is bawling like a baby. They are piling dead and wounded in our tunnel. Arms weak from pounding key long hours, no rest, short rations. Tired. I know now how a mouse feels. Caught in a trap waiting for guys to come along finish it. Got a treat. Can pineapple. Opening it with a Signal Corps knife.

My name Irving Strobing. Get this to my mother. Mrs. Minnie Strobing, 605 Barbey Street, Brooklyn, New York. They are to get along O.K. Get in touch with them soon as possible. Message. My love to Pa, Joe, Sue, Mac, Carrie, Joy and Paul. Also to all family and friends. God bless 'em all, hope they be here when I come home. Tell Joe wherever he is to give 'em hell for us. My love to all. God bless you and keep you. Love.

Sign my name and tell Mother how you heard from me. Stand by. . . . . .

Strobing

★　★　★

*A*rnold Humphries MacNeil served with the Navy as chief pharmacist's mate on board the troop transport ship George Fox Elliot. *The* Elliot *was sunk during a landing operation in the Pacific.*

Dear Aunt:

Yes, the old Elliot is no more, but she did a lot of good work before she met her end, so she was not a complete loss by any means.

About a half hour before our third and fatal attack, we were standing on deck watching the landing boats. A dentist aboard remarked that during these air attacks he didn't know but what a man was safer on board one of the landing boats than on deck. He had hardly spoken when the warning came that another attack was coming.

The plane that crashed us, after we shot him down, exploded and made a flaming inferno. We were burning both below and on deck where flaming gasoline had started fires. Before we abandoned ship, flames were leaping twenty feet in the air from the stack. In fact it was getting a bit warm when a boatswain's mate broke in the movie shack, put a record on the loud-speaking system. The record's name was "Red Hot Mama."

Over the side we went, onto a life raft so loaded down that

the raft was not even in sight. We could not move an inch and as the ship was burning from stem to stern and looked as if she would go sky high any moment we agreed that anyone not wounded would get out of the raft and try to move it by thrashing hands and feet. Due to the number of wounded our progress was slow. The seriousness of it all was plainly written on each face, some looked frightened, some determined, but all were too occupied with the plight of the moment to think of anything else.

Suddenly I thought of the dentist's remark. I called to him, he spit salt water from his mouth and said, "Oh yar?" Then someone cried, "Speaking of safe places to be, I know a little beer garden in the Bronx where for a nickel you can get a beer SO BIG." We all laughed, everyone got a better grip on themselves, our progress was much better and before long we had steered the raft to a fairly safe place.

A sergeant illustrating the difference in bulk between thirty-two hundred ordinary letters and those same letters reduced to V-Mail

Thanks for your pride and faith in the Navy. So far we have been fighting against odds out here, but thank God, they are about cut down and this year will be one to remember. You wait!

Arnold

★   ★   ★

David Thomas served as a second lieutenant with the 1st Fighter Group. After several months in Britain the squadron went to North Africa. The group also participated in the Sicilian and Italian campaigns.

June 21, 1942

My dearest darling,

I bought a new cycle at one of the towns near the air base for eight pounds and six shillings [about $33]. It is a fast trim little job and is superior in many ways to the American makes. The bike comes in handy here. It is almost a necessity. I have to go anywheres from 10 to 15 miles a day and I don't want to walk that much every day. Most of the officers have cycles now and in our free time we go for rides about the countryside. In some of these countryside travels we have visited rather large cities. We have seen the results of German demolition bombs on English homes and communities. Censorship forbids me telling you any of the details, but if you can imagine whole cities the size of Elmira destroyed, you would have a vague idea of how war is affecting this place. Here people, civilians, have given their lives, their homes and their sons. They are not whimpering but bravely tell us, the American soldiers, to "keep smiling." This actually happened to me today. An old man who was standing in front of a crumbled heap which had been his home. As I saw it I gasped slightly and wrinkled my brow a bit—"Keep smiling, lad," he said.

Everlasting love,

David

★ ★ ★

Lee Merson, an Army technical sergeant attached to Radio Intelligence, wrote this letter.

Dear Dad:

What is going on there? Yesterday, my July 13 issue of Time arrived. Today, as I read it, it makes me sick and bitter, and fills my mind with unanswerable questions. The drive for scrap rubber is a "disappointing failure"; the sale of war bonds is 200 million per month below government expectations; aggressive war must wait until after the November elections; steel laborers seek a dollar-a-day increase in wages.

What kind of a game is this that is being played in those United States? Is that our invincible, our proud country? While all over the world men are being shot to pieces, other men—the steel, the aluminum, the textile, the rubber workers—are quibbling about dollars, and Washington is still activated by politicians.

Where is that common sense of which we Americans were once so proud? So they want a raise because the cost of living has risen; but isn't it evident to even the most selfish that any increase in consumer purchasing power must necessarily add still more to that cost of living? Or maybe the true fact underlying this "greatest" war effort is the very simple fact that everyone is out to get whatever he can from this unprecedented opportunity. With the aspects of inflation clearly in view, our selfish, bigoted "patriots" are willing to risk chaos and defeat—yes, defeat—because they won't believe there is a war in progress that might engulf them; they argue over something that in reality does not exist.

But those smug, complacent people are playing with human lives! The trickle of beautiful planes comes over and we look up and say to each other: "Just think of what a thousand, five thousand of them could do." You don't feel that; we do. The seamen whose ships have been blown from under them talk of the useless waste because helpless boats are not convoyed. The stunned, half-dead sailors adrift for weeks on a raft—you haven't seen them, I have. And "little steel" asks for an increase in wages.

And all the while, the young gallant sailors and Marines and soldiers are dying in the Pacific, and in Ireland the boys wait with the realization that they may be the next. And we in the outposts who feel guilty because we are so far from the actual fighting, we sit and rot in stinking, malarial jungles and have time to think—and my mind becomes corroded with what I read. Those boys who are about to die, those who may be maimed, those who may live a lingering death with tropical disease, they ask so little. They will fight for you if you but give them the weapons. They will die so that you may have pretty homes and happy families, but don't let them lose faith.

Personally, I think we shall win this war but only after tens of thousands of people have been needlessly killed, but let me offer this warning: If this generation of soldiers returns home to a collapsed and chaotic economic system due to inflation or any other cause that might easily have been prevented had the people realized the dangers of their shortsightedness, we shall not stand docilely on street corners selling apples; we shall not ashamedly wait in line to receive bread. The American soldier is not a child who can easily be fooled, Dad; he is too well informed.

Is it asking too much of civilians to give up a little of their comfort so that someone else might win security for them? The President speaks of more and more sacrifices. Sacrifices—hell! Is it a sacrifice to defend one's self against impending disaster? What a ludicrous and tragic situation that soldiers must beg, actually beg, for arms to defend people who, by their very actions, don't seem to give a damn.

Yes, Dad, tell them that my mind is sick and bitter. Tell them that I want to believe in my country but find it increasingly difficult to believe in its people. But who will listen? Who will want to listen to a solitary soldier crying out for justice? Who will be interested in mere words when big money can be made—and the boys are dying in the Pacific?

Lee

★ ★ ★

In the late summer of 1942 Private First Class Jack Blumenthal, a military policeman stationed in Australia, wrote to the member of his family most recently inducted into the armed forces—his forty-four-year-old father.

September 9, 1942

Dear Dad:

Speaking of shocks, I certainly got one when I learned you are in imminent danger of learning a new trade, i.e., soldiering. By this time in all probability, you have become quite accustomed to the G.I. zoot suit. But at any rate you can't say I didn't warn you. If you ever get into Australia be wary of bumping into your son, for he may poke a billy club at you and harshly demand that you "button those pockets."

Passing out V-Mail blanks in Australia, August 1942

If you are in the Army the only thing to do is make the best of it. By sheer experience I discovered a number of cardinal rules of behavior which I pass on to you for what they are worth; do with them as you will.

Cardinal rule number one: Mind your own business. Offer suggestions for improvement (and you will see many) only when asked. Then beware. It may be a trap. You will probably find more than half of the non-coms (and this holds true especially for corporals) are the laughing stock of the outfit.

Cardinal rule number two: Never volunteer for anything. You will increase your status in nobody's estimation and in all likelihood will be referred to as a sucker.

No. 3: Pull your own intellectual level down to that of the group. Never let it be known that you know more about any-thing than anybody. In this way you won't be set apart from the rest and treated accordingly.

No. 4: Never under any circumstances raise your voice above a conversational tone. If you have something to say to someone across the room, don't shout it but walk across to him directly and say it.

No. 5: Lend money to nobody, particularly non-coms. Nine chances out of ten you'll never get it back. If you think it wise, you can "invest" about $5 in one of the sergeants. But don't ask for its return on payday. In other words: "Neither a borrower nor a lender be."

No. 6: Always keep your shoes as shiny as possible, your uniform clean and well pressed and your face shaved. If the uniform you are issued needs alterations have it done without delay.

No. 7: Don't gamble; you can't win.

There are many more rules for behavior I could give you, but you'll find them out for yourself. The Army is very different from civilian life. Something happens to those chaps around you when they find out that they have a job they can't lose, and three meals a day without actually working too hard for them. They, of course, will all complain (in the Army it's called

V-Mail room at Base Censor's Department, Australia

"bitching"—and don't you be guilty of it; rather listen to the rest and get a laugh). They will tell you how much they think of the Army and the wonderful jobs they had in civilian life. But remember how much "poppycock" they're all singing. Probably 70 to 90% of them never had it as good before in all their lives.

Let me know every detail that happens to you. The outfit to which you are eventually assigned and your impressions of the whole thing. It may not be very funny now, but some day, perhaps not too far in the dim, distant future, we will be able to get together, swap stories and laugh like hell at the whole miserable experience and at ourselves.

Love,

Jack

★   ★   ★

*R*obert Metcalf served as a lieutenant with the Army Air Forces. He wrote this letter to his parents in Oklahoma City from North Africa.

Western Desert
Oct. 28, 1942

Dear Folks,

I hope you've heard of my good luck by now. On Oct. 26, we were hurriedly called out about three o'clock in the afternoon. We were given our vectors and told what area to patrol as we jumped into the jeep to go to our planes. We got to our planes, taxied out and then they changed the orders over the radio. There was only the flight leader and one of the rest of us, and I was in the bottom four. We were flying four abreast and stacked up. After we had passed the front lines on the ground by about twenty minutes and while we were going over one of the clear spots, we saw four Machi 202's. They were just below the clouds and headed for the front lines with bombs. We did a turn to the left and I wound up just between and behind the two on the right. I had a little better shot at the one on the inside, but just as I was ready to pull the trigger I saw one of the other P-40s coming up on my left, so I turned and got on the outside one. I gave him a burst. He started smoking and peeled off with me right on his tail. I stayed with him clearing my tail and taking short bursts. I could see parts of his plane flying off each time. The disgusting part about it was that his plane would not catch fire or go into a spin. Finally, he released his canopy and after I gave him one more burst, he bailed out. I saw his chute open and his plane went into the ground and turned into a mass of flames. Feeling all victorious, I dived and strafed everything that came in front of me. In all, I know that I got one plane, one truck and two tents. I headed for the sea, holding my speed at about 280 mph until I was about six or seven miles out when "Duke" pulled up beside me. We returned home just about ten feet off the water and land. We were among the last ones back, so you

Waist gunner of a Flying Fortress bomber trains his sights as a flight of the big American planes nears its objective during an Army Air Forces attack on Axis positions on Tunisia.

can see how quick everything happens and everyone heads for home after we've tangled with something. Oh, yes! I almost forgot to tell you that the Machi's dropped their bombs on some of their own stuff. After getting back, I found that Captain Clark, my flight leader, had sent two of them into the ground and Whittaker had sent the other one down. The boys above saw all four planes burning on the ground. Those are four less Italian planes that won't give us any trouble.

My crew was surely glad about the Machi 202. They can paint a swastika on the side of my plane now. We get to paint a small one on for each enemy we shoot down. I was one of the first to get any in our squadron. That was the first aerial gunnery that I have ever had.

Now to tell you something of an even more exciting mission. Yesterday, eight of us carried bombs over to some German fields and dropped them. Just as we were starting the bombing, enemy planes were reported at several places around us. There must have been over forty of them. I got in several shots at one of them and then one of the Me 109's got on me. He came in from the sun. I shook him right quick but I had to lose altitude doing it so I didn't go back up. I headed for home.

The sixteen of us destroyed seven of them, and several probables and damages. They didn't get any of us but put holes in two planes, not mine though. Everyone got back here O.K. and the monkeys on the other side of the line are taking a real beating. We are getting a big kick out of beating their ears back and we are more than satisfied with our planes and training.

If I can find it, I will enclose the arming pin for the first 500 lb. bomb that I dropped on them. I kept it. All in all, everything is going off as planned and I like it. Maybe I'm a bit cold-blooded, or maybe I'm still young enough to enjoy it. It just takes five to be classed as an ace in this day and age.

Lots of love,

Bob

★ ★ ★

Caleb Milne* served as volunteer stretcher bearer with the American Field Service in North Africa. The following letters were chosen from an anthology that his family privately published in 1945.

[November]

It is one of those days that, even I must admit, sometimes blurs the Egyptian climatic reputation. A fast dust is blowing continuously, not sand, but the light surface powder that flies along in the autumn wind. It seeps into my ambulance between the window cracks and the windshield drifts a bit at the corners with dry dust, like tan snow. The chief disappointment in a long-range correspondence, to me, is the fact that a letter written in

---

* Another letter from Caleb Milne appears on page 88.

one mood is read so much later by the recipient that the mood had doubtless evaporated by then. Your last letter for instance sounds a bit futile [about the war] and how natural that is! To be truthful, a thinking person, and a feeling one is hard put to find any rhyme or reason to the outcome of human actions. In my own head I can trace back cause and effect, then try to reconcile that with the sights before my eyes—but, sometimes the two don't excuse each other at all. So instead of talking war with you as I should in response, I'll skip over it as a conversation that is already stale. I just looked up and noticed the whole world was misty with dust, like a monotone study of illusion, all in beige. We had a torrential down-pour a few days ago, I was out walking toward the sea and got drenched. The mud soon was ankle deep and when I returned I found my car in the midst of a raging stream. Next day all was calm and thousands of little green plants, grasses, Jack-in-the-Pulpits and melon vines were vigorously crawling all over the deposited muck-beds.

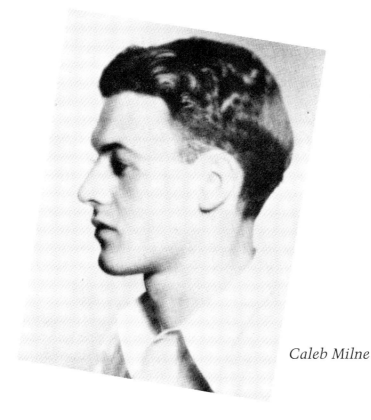

Caleb Milne

I am glad to note in your letters that you're becoming fatalistic; it is much the happiest way to be. I practice what I preach in this respect and find myself able to surmount many things that seem to bother the others a great deal. I daresay in some personal catastrophe, my fatalism would be shaken but I'd be no more unhappy, certainly, because of it. I believe one of the strongest realizations that has come to me out here is the basic simplicity of life, as it may be lived. My sense of values has opened up a whole new bottom drawer where canned meat tastes delicious, a year-old magazine is fascinating, a fresh bath is an occasion. Of course, should better things present themselves on either side, I'd resent not having them; but with everyone cut down to the same essentials, life is very tasteful, though not highly seasoned! I am not unaware of many things but I often followed the trivial trail in civilized surroundings. These months, besides providing an enormous experience of thrills, excitements, laughter and tears, has also been like an empty room wherein I can sit and listen to the noises in the rest of the crowded house. I have found it possible to get a good perspective on myself and to plan ahead. How long I'll be here is uncertain; it depends on many conditions.

★

Dawn and dusk are hours of danger as well as beauty. In the last great flush of color the bombing planes come droning across the sky. I have seen them come through the golden shaft of light each evening. Sometimes the marauders arrive in droves like mechanized bees, at other times a single plane circles overhead in the west, a deadly precursor to the black wings of night. After the long African afternoon the ground is warm and hospitable. The lowering of the sun closes in the vastness of the desert somewhat and men eat their suppers in the quiet golden wine of late afternoon. Here and there a lorry groans along a battered white road or a soldier sings over his work. But the shells are silent and the dusty queues of traffic have long since passed along the road. Cigarettes smell good in the clear air, the spilled petrol of the day has evaporated in the sand, leaving only an astringent echo to the nostrils.

Merriment, like wit, loses its vigor in the distance and becomes musical, having no meaning nor malice it floats over the ground devoid of any human quality, blending in with the soft air and the stained-glass sky. One evening I was lying on the sand cushioned by my camouflage net, the fading light having grown too dim for reading. Across the west, great copper banners were streaming from the horizon. The sun had set but its power was still triumphant pouring forth its golden radiance from beneath the rim of the earth, challenging the tender moon and the stars. Already Venus shone in the sky while in the East the first flickerings of the Pleiades and the pale emergence of Orion announced the evening. The air was very still and clear. Each long-

A Ninth Air Force sergeant in North Africa shares his package from home with his buddies.

gun, the dusty lorries, every work-a-day motor and distant tank laying in the pool of retrenchant light, assumed a touching and legendary quality spread across the vast landscape like some old caravan caught immobile against the sunset. I lay back my eyes tired from the sun. An old hymn Annie [old nurse] used to sing to me crept through my head, "Now the day is over." How sweet the melody is and the words simple and patient. I remembered her elderly Negro face droning out the verses in her soft Southern accent. My body slipped back onto the cushion and where it least seemed possible I found peace. A peace that was unknown to me in cities, and only occasionally in our New York countryside. There is a repose in flat land. No mountains lead the mind away and no roads wind out to other worlds. You are alone in the stretches of the eye, no matter how full the scene. I drifted off into my own kingdom slipping into a deepening stream of forgetfulness. I crossed over the channel of sleep lying vulnerable and naked on the sand.

A rush of chill air swept over me, I woke up violently as a bomb crashed. The ground shook, my ears winced at the sudden pressure impact, a haze of invisible sand filled the air. The sky was filled with the drone of motors. To one side the steady thudding on the earth and the terrific side-swipe of noise indicated a targetted objective. The flashes lit the night spasmodically while the whine of guns and delicate tracery of fire-bullets criss-crossed the sky. In a few seconds the ear-splitting shower of anti-aircraft barrage multiplied into a terrific din overhead. As I looked about I felt a chill of horror slide over my flesh. In the splinters of illumination no one was visible. Evidently I was the only person who had not reached a trench. Alone I lay there exposed to the bullets on all sides. With a stupid primeval impulse I tried to pull the net over my head. For some reason I was furious with myself for having fallen asleep. Only a fool would have been seduced by a sunset. This net was too clumsy to move so I shoved it back, and stretched out, hugging the sand savagely. The Olympian crash of noise was earsplitting. Now they were trying to spot the enemy overhead with shells. There was the patter of ack-ack bullets falling around the hill. My brain was numb. I was unable to move or think and lay there frozen in the vacuum of noise. Somehow I was more afraid of our own barrage falling on me than of the enemy's bombs. The German punishment was too vast, it spelled oblivion; it was the hissing bullets that endangered me the most. I clutched at the ground, my heart racing with fright; it seemed that the earth was rising up offering me to the elements, ever higher. The drone of the planes was directly overhead now. They had spent their bombs on the tracks below our hill and were moving to a new position. The throb of their motors shattered the night air. It was almost impossible to lie still beneath them—indeed I might have raced in crazy circles but some inner compulsion kept insisting to stay still, stay still! Maybe they will go away! And as I lay there engulfed in dread and horror I heard the squadron wheel off slightly to the right. If they did not circle that meant they were moving on. I held my breath, then as the minutes hung trembling in fear, the drone grew fainter. I raised my head from the ground and forced my eyes open. Against the starry sky a few bars of black climbed higher and higher, the area-guns spitting bullets and tracers after them. They were veering off to the coast!

I pulled myself up on one elbow, my body runneled with sweat. For a second I could not believe I was alive. My heart was still pounding while reactive waves of nausea choked in my throat. I heard a curious whirring noise overhead. I thought my end had come. Heading directly for me and silently advancing in a great sweep of cold air, a dark glider of black skimmed towards me, only a few feet off the ground. I stared at it, frozen, as the slow whirl bore down with relentless speed. It was almost on top of me. Suddenly in that empty crystal moment when doom confronts one, I heard the soft brush of touching wings and the secret chirrupings of a great flight. Above me, triumphant through the battle wheeled a great crescent of sand-larks, beating the night air, southward to the Transvaal Plain.

Oh, the miraculous spirit, the unquenchable force of life and liberties! Never again can I salute the heralds with so grateful a spirit as reached out to bid God-speed to that whirring rustle of birds. I jumped to my feet, my heart high and all the starred sky was filled with banners.

★ ★ ★

November 8, 1942, was the beginning of Operation Torch—the Allied invasion of French North Africa. In the early hours of the morning 500 warships, 350 transport and cargo ships convened along the coast of North Africa and began disembarking troops at Casablanca, Oran, and Algiers. Lieutenant Robert Lewin*—a member of the Western Task Force that landed at Casablanca—wrote the following letter.

[November]

Dear Mother and All America:

It is Thanksgiving—and I'm sitting at the battalion command post. We are in the basement of an old mansion. It is fine. These Moroccan nights are cold with strange yellow moons and it is very much like Thanksgiving in America.

The day we landed was pretty exciting. We went to bed at four the afternoon before and got up at ten that night and had hot cereal and got things arranged on deck. Pitch black, a lighthouse blinking on the cape at CENSORED . At daybreak the first wave of assault was scheduled to hit the beach. In the division order was the phrase, "Do not fire on mosques and minarets." The boats were loaded. A lot was messed up, and just as you could begin to see, the Navy opened up with 16-inch guns on the coastal batteries with deadly effect. The ride in was miserable, soaking wet and freezing cold. Pretty soon the shore came into sight, that shore we had studied from maps for so long, and the guns were shooting at us. My boat got lost from the wave and we were alone and shells were dropping in the water with huge geysers going up and dull booms, and the Navy answering. But they never got near our one little boat. Finally we hit the beach, and lo and behold! Everyone who had landed before us is standing around smoking and laughing, so we get

---

* Other letters from Lieutenant Lewin appear on page 49ff.

American troops on a beach in North Africa, 1942

our cart and stuff off the boat and do the same. There hadn't been any opposition on the beach. Then it came. Guns opened on us, screaming shell fragments careening around, and we get off the narrow strip of beach and dive into holes and I get covered with camel dung, actually. Then we were all clear of the enfilading fire and we get up to the command post when the planes come—bombers—and every weapon we have is fired, wasting much valuable ammunition. The men are terribly frightened and fire a great deal. The officers are running around saying: "For Christ's sake hold your fire, you God damned crazy bastards!" But we don't get over shooting first and looking later for three or four days. Then up to the attic of a house after setting up my radio, and the major says, "For Christ's sake, Lewin, can you fire on the shore battery that's shooting up our troops?" and I say, "Sure!" and I contact a destroyer and give them the co-ordinated data on the map and am just about to send "Commence firing!" when he rushes back and says, "Cut it out! Cut it out! Our own men are in there surrounding that battery!" (It was in the town of ███CENSORED███ and it held out a long time.) So I cease firing or rather my men do, and we all breathe a little easier. But it's all over now, at least right here in this area, and we have fires at night if they are small, and so on, but no one knows when or where we go next. It may be tomorrow and it may not be for the duration.

This is a land of strange ways, just like the old Bible pictures. Camels and donkeys plow together, the Arabs pray and the women do all the work.

I send this letter out, and I love all of you and God—if there is one—bless you. I have changed a little and am not as wild or careless as I used to be, and you will love me a lot better when I come back, but I mourn the fact that a lot of my pristine gayety and recklessness has forever vanished. Don't worry about me. I'm well, happy and have many friends.

Much love, keep well, and set aside a drinking fund for me so I can start off right when I return. This area is kind of dry, so to speak.

Lots of love,

Bob

★ ★ ★

*F*irst Lieutenant John Doyle served with the 5th Regiment, 1st Marine Division. On August 7, 1942, the division stormed the island of Guadalcanal and its satellite islands—Florida, Gavatu, and Tulagi. This was a battle that lasted for six months with bitter fighting on land and sea. Lieutenant Doyle received the Silver Star for gallantry at Guadalcanal on November 2, 1942. In the midst of enemy fire near the Matanikau River he courageously descended a steep hill just west of the river to attend the wounded. While under severe mortar and machine-gun fire, one of the wounded men Lieutenant Doyle was trying to carry back was killed in his arms. He successfully retrieved three men.

Guadalcanal
British Solomon Islands
11 Nov., 1942

Dear Dad:

It's relatively quiet now. Perhaps I can, without fear of violating naval censorship regulations, bring you some idea of these three months' active combat.

Green troops, and we were green although excellently trained, have a quantum of fearlessness almost approaching foolhardiness, and, well led, will accomplish their mission against veterans. This battalion of Marines (the one I was in) saw the first combat and rode roughshod over the Nips. We attached tremendous importance to our every step, and, emerging victors, thought ourselves world conquerors. Then we began to look around, at the casualties, at the defeated enemy, and finally at ourselves. We were under control only because of training. We lost many more than was necessary. We had wasted all our energy in a few hours. Nerves and excitement kept us intact from there on. There were no instances of cowardice; many of cool bravery and courage.

First Lieutenant John Doyle

The 2nd, 3rd and 4th contacts were of a different color. The second is the toughest for all leaders. You cannot doubt or mistrust yourself. Every command and order must be put so boldly that even you are almost convinced of your personal infallibility. Sometimes you must resort to cruelty. Never let a man falter. One lapse and the whole command falls through, and you're left with just a few to fight for all. In these fights men begin to show their souls.

Our 5th fight was and still is the pride of the Division. This one battalion was called upon to join in an attack when all knew that we had more than done our share, and that better than any others. Of course, there was the bitching and belly-aching from more than a few. But all went out and fought a regiment's worth. They battled their own way; then helped those to the right and to the left. It was real Marine stuff. The accomplishment was astonishing. . . .

What has it done to me? What does it mean to me? I know that I have not become cruel or callous. I am sure that I am hardened. If a man cannot produce, I'll push him into the most degrading, menial task I can find. A man that shrinks from duty is worse than a man lost. He should be thrown out of the entire outfit. He's not fit to live with the men with whom he is not willing to die. Death is easy. It happens often.

The toughest part is going on, existing as an animal. Wet, cold and hungry many times, a man can look forward only to the next day when the sun, flies and mosquitoes descend to devour him.

Few men fear bullets. They are swift, silent and certain. Shelling and bombing are more often the cursed bugaboos. But because we retain some mechanics of reasoning, we can predict something of the artillery shell's course. We listen to the sound of the gun, for its location and calibre. We await the whisk of the shell as it splits the air. We know that it can hit in only one place and can generally isolate that spot. Mortar shells are terrifying. Their high angle of fire hides their coming until too late. The gun only coughs. I'm a mortar man and know their worth. I've had to call for my own to fire close by when I'm observing.

Because my crews are the best in the Corps, the rifle troops trust my presence, and that's a wonderful compliment.

Bombing is something different. You cannot hope to silence the offender by counter-barrage or seizure. You just wait. We all can distinguish plane motors miles away. The "thrum-thrum" of the Mitsubishi 97 was the first our minds recorded. If they are directly overhead and still you can hear no bombs falling, you are safe. You crawl just a little outside of your foxhole and watch the show. The Marine fighters and AA crews are marvelous. No wonder this is fast becoming known to the Nips as "Suicide Island." All the time you hear the bombs shrieking their way down, and you pity the poor souls in that area. The next time it may be your turn. The heavens are burst by the falling bombs. Prayers and curses run intermingled off your lips and the earth retches and writhes. The close ones all but bash your head in. You pray that yours won't be a near miss but will take you in one blast. At first, I was innocent and never quivered. Then a few close by shook me inside out. A few weeks more and I reached the veteran stage. Indifferent but watchful!

Our stomachs have been ravaged with the food we've eaten and the way in which we eat. We've fought the Japs for water and cigarettes. Often we have shot and ripped off a Jap's pack and canteen before he has a chance to fall. I've buried both Japs and Marines. That is probably the most odious task of all. Decomposition begins within four hours in this climate. Some of the sights I've had to see would sicken a good intern. But I have to go back and eat lunch. There may not be another for a while.

But all is quiet again. I'm sitting by. Long ago I wished to go into aviation. I'm convinced now that it is the only way for me to finish out this war. Today, my request for a flight physical goes to the regiment. I pray that I pass. My superiors have commended me on my action to date, and were glad to recommend me in my preference of duty. Have all keep their fingers crossed, and I may make it. It will take time, though. But time to me ended yesterday.

    Love,

                                      Jack

*A*dmiral William Halsey, commander of the Third Fleet in the Pacific, wrote the following letter to Fleet Admiral Chester Nimitz, commander in chief of the United States Pacific Fleet.

SOUTH PACIFIC FORCE
OF THE UNITED STATES PACIFIC FLEET
HEADQUARTERS OF THE COMMANDER

Nov. 29, 1942

Dear Chester,

My sincere gratitude for the many fine signals you have sent me lately. I accept them in all humility for myself, and as representing the splendid body of fighting men who did the actual job. The last one, in regard to my promotion, I have not acted on. I have received many congratulatory messages but no promotion. When, and if this arrives I will answer.

Things have been very quiet in this area lately. It is the first breathing spell we have had. Have used this time to establish ourselves ashore, and while our space is not adequate or all that could be desired, we are well dug in. The house is thoroughly comfortable and modern, for this place, and it has a wonderful outlook over the harbor. Four other members of my staff are with me. The remainder of the staff is living in great discomfort in town. This will be corrected as soon as we can erect some Quonset Huts. This has been ordered.

During the lull we have been piling things into Cactus, as fast as possible. The last of the tankfarm should be unloaded today. This operation has taken about 4 days. When this tankfarm is finally set up, and we can have a small gasoline tanker to scuttle back and forth between Button and Cactus, we should be well off for gas in Cactus. We have also gotten Thanksgiving turkey to them, plus such other good food as possible.

It would appear that Phase I of the present campaign is drawing towards a close. According to the present directive the next phase crosses the foolish 159th meridian. The present answer to that is written on the books. Directives for planning should be underway now. We are looking over the situation and making up our ideas. If MacArthur is to handle this, we should know his plans so we can prepare accordingly. A tempting thought, we have toyed with, is to bypass everything up the line and hit direct at Rabaul. If it can be done, we would save a large number of lives, time and material. I believe with Rabaul in our hands the war in the Pacific is approaching an end. To accomplish this it is necessary to have men and ships, both for the land forces and the sea forces.

My own Naval forces are growing stronger almost day by day. At the moment I have a fairly strong striking force established in Button, and with the addition of the cruisers now approaching will be well fixed. The arrival of the INDIANA counter-balances the loss of the SOUTH DAKOTA. The NORTH CAROLINA is one additional strong battleship. The MARYLAND and COLORADO are just that much gravy for us.

We exercised the NASSAU as a carrier and we are about to do the same thing with the ALTAHAMA. The NASSAU is ready to go now, albeit not too well trained, and the ALTAHAMA should be in a few days. Shall take advantage of every opportunity to give them training and hope it may be sufficient before I have to use them.

I take it that Charley Mason is coming down to command these ships. We shall be more than glad to see him. The addition of the two converted tankers will give me 4 auxiliary carriers. These 4 ships will more than equal the striking power of one large carrier and I am delighted to have them. We shall probably be shy some planes, probably TBF's, to complete the two groups on the NASSAU and ALTAHAMA. I shall make an equal distribution of what I have and use them as is, if the necessity arises. I am having worked up a scheme for getting into it, in case the enemy attempts an all out against New Guinea. We are rather far away but we will get there somehow. Nandi is a particularly disadvantageous place for operating in the New Guinea area. At the moment, because of lack of moorings and nets I do not feel at liberty to move that force down here. A bit later this may be possible. Havannah Harbor in Roses offers the best spot to place these ships. When the SUMNER survey is completed and moorings are established, I hope to use it. This should be soon.

We have only three sub-chasers in this area that are fitted with listening gear. I have had two of them in Button and one on escort duty in Australia. She is returning here shortly. Until further ships are received, I intend to place two of these vessels in the Cactus area and keep one at Button. Button, Fantan Two and White Poppy all should have vessels of this type for patrol work outside the entrance. I shall be most appreciative of any vessel of any type that can be used for this kind of work.

Our destroyer shortage is acute. The possibility of having my force augmented by 2 ships of the NEW MEXICO class appeals greatly. I think we proved in Lee's night action that the day of the battleship is far from a thing of the past. How are all the experts going to comment now? They certainly inflicted terrific damage that night. The use we made of them defied all conventions; narrow waters, submarine menace, and destroyers at night. Despite that, the books, and the learned and ponderous words of the high brows it worked.

I am enclosing herewith a list of hits claimed by the ENTERPRISE group. It sounds fantastic but I am convinced that it is true. As I wrote you in my last letter, the occasion was a dive bombers and torpedo bombers paradise. We have about completed the final sweepup of the 3 days actions. When completed I shall send you a list of the damage we inflicted. I shall send you at the same time, for your comparison, a list of the damage that Southwest Pacific inflicted according to their dispatches. No further comments are necessary.

I had the very disagreeable duty of relieving the commanding officer of the HELENA immediately following his return from the night action. I consider that his conduct in abandoning the JUNEAU to her fate was inexcusable. A court martial was probably indicated, but I considered that it would take up too much valuable time and would bring no profitable results from the morale standpoint. I believe the summary detachment accomplishes the purpose. A full report of this matter was sent by air mail on the last plane.

Aola Bay turned out to be a flop. Terrain not suitable for a landing field, and beaches thin barland—no good for unloading. Are moving to Kolli Point.

We are slowly but surely digging our way out from under the difficulties that beset the establishment of new bases from nothing. I believe we shall have a smooth going concern very shortly. Everyone here is working like a beaver, and we have received a tremendous uplift from the confidence that you have shown in us. In the meantime we are all happy, cheerful and trying to do a little bit better than our best. My best to you always and all your fine staff and my friends in Honolulu. I almost forgot to thank you for the very acceptable Christmas gifts that Cobb brought me on his arrival. The others have gone forward to Fitch and Vandegrift. Many thanks. I shall save it for Christmas day and toast you.

As ever,

BILL HALSEY

★ ★ ★

*P*rivate First Class John Conroy served with the 1st Marine Division. He wrote the following letter from Mare Island Naval Hospital.

Dec. 24, 1942

Dear Mother and Dad:
Received two letters from you today and am just sending this quick note. Phone connections down here are very difficult so I could not call you. I received your gift of $25 just in time to accept a Red Cross weekend (four days) with a San Francisco family. Had a nice cozy time, turkey and all.

Marines landing at Guadalcanal

A Marine on Guadalcanal takes time out in his dugout to answer a letter he has just received from home.

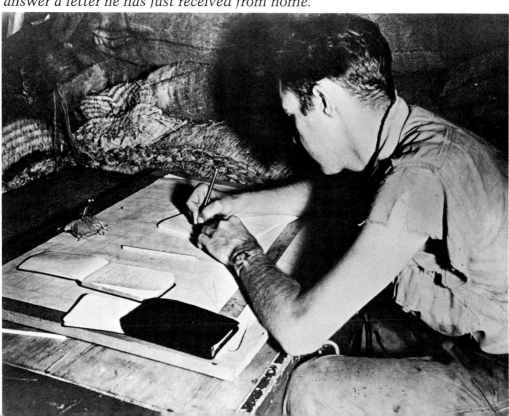

You keep asking so I'll tell you. I have been shell-shocked and bomb-shocked. My memory is very dim regarding my civilian days. They feel that sudden shock in action now would affect my sanity. All the boys back here have received the same diagnosis. Injury to my back helps to make further combat service for me impossible. It's so very difficult for me to explain, to say the things I want to, my thoughts are so disconnected.

Of course I'm not insane. But I've been living the life of a savage and haven't quite got used to a world of laws and new responsibilities. So many of my platoon were wiped out, my old Parris Island buddies, that it's hard to sleep without seeing them die all over again. Our living conditions on Guadalcanal had been so bad—little food or hope—fighting and dying each day—four hours sleep out of 72—the medicos here optimistically say I'll pay for it the rest of my life. My bayonet and shrapnel cuts are all healed up, however. Most of us will be fairly well in six months, but none of us will be completely cured for years. My back is in bad condition. I can't stand or walk much. The sudden beat of a drum or any sharp, resonant noise has a nerve-ripping effect on us.

Ah, well, let's not think, but just be happy that we'll all be together soon.

Loads and loads of love,

John

The following letters were written by Lieutenant Robert Lewin* to his family in Greensboro, North Carolina.

---

* Another letter from Lieutenant Lewin appears on page 38.

Dear Mother, Dad, Doris and all:

. . . There is actually so Godawful much to write, and it is so difficult to write it. All about Christmas and the 55 chickens we killed, and the men tight on a slight wine ration, and their laughter in the darkness, and Captain Peterson getting his child's photo for Christmas, and saying that it was all he wanted, and the Colonel trying to create camaraderie, and a letter from Peggy, and wanting to be home, and our Christmas tree (a cork tree with tangerines and Life Savers and toilet paper and the skull of a camel), and reading the reviews of The Skin of Your Teeth, and much, much emotion stifled by men who want to be un-men, and un-men who want to be men, and the glorious powdery dreams dreamed in stillness on the ground by lonely soldiers, and Dave getting no mail, and Cliff and I sympathizing with him, and dreams of fulfillment everywhere, and Howdy absorbed in a book entitled Flash Gordon on the Planet Mongo, and the endlessness of the war is over all. Strange.

Corporal Ryan says after the war his children will have to line up for chow, have physical inspection before getting their allowance, police up the street every morning, and stand guard every night. Eek!

The funniest answer I ever got from an enlisted man:

"Schinn," I said, seeing a mattress covered with yellow things on it, "what are you doing?"

"Drying my noodles," he said.

And he was, too. Made them himself.

And so, he said, let us end another letter, another chapter, another book, another era in the life of a liver of lives, for is not each end the end of everything, and each beginning the beginning of infinity? And each beginning is a song, for in the war of man against man, and good against evil, and much against little, we come to know the blessed and the dear, and good shall triumph, for one good deed can cancel a hundred of evil. Know yourself deeply, believe in your goodness only, and in ten years life shall be perfect.

God Bless you all, and send me alcohol!

Bob

★

Dear Folks and People:

I would rather fight than sit here on my fanny and see that trucks are kept clean after driving through mud. I count my blessings daily, however, and have, without doubt, the moon and stars and sky that holds them all, and in the day perhaps the sunshine. If it rains, I have the rain and the clouds, and the storm about me, and the leaves with their secrets in the forest. I have the camels and the donkeys, and the egrets and the partridge, and the storks and a friend who owns a kerosene lamp. And I have daily a little precious inalienable time to myself, and my holiness and my dreamblankets, and a book of Hemingway and three Shakespeare plays, which I have never opened, but think about all the time. And I have those that like me for my humor and kindness, and those that dislike me for my sharp tongue and my stupidity, and I would not have it any other way, for who is not seeking and searching in his own minute way for his place among the blind of the world? And I have one new thought a week that is worthwhile, so that by the time I come home, I shall be rich and quiet and more impractical and dreaming than ever, and I shall wander interminably in the same small circle that I have always wandered, in testing the bitter perfumes of experience, in giving, lending, loving, losing and failing. Failure is such miraculous strength, and winning such easy glory, and thinking and dreaming and being pushed about are the living things for the soul. And after quiet shall come to the soul, and time will go on, and we shall die, and if all the good we leave the world is one amazing good deed, done in silence and in sacrifice, and a large family of howling children, we have lived a good life. And all the thieves and dirt and disease in the casbah shall be whole and singing again, if we but lean towards thinking a little firmer, and loving a little harder. Whatever pain there is here among the trees and the birds and the silent sky is brought in because of thinking of oneself only, and yet this is the only way to learn how to think of others. Blah! Blah! So, I'm writing a Brand New Testament. I love you all.

Bob

★　　★　　★

Charles Badley served as a captain with an engineer regiment stationed "somewhere in England."

December 30, 1942

Dear Mother, Dad and Gang:

Though I can't tell you exactly where I was, or the mission engaged upon, or the military impediments of the moment, I think even the hardest of censors would let a guy tell you just a bit about Christmas Day as I enjoyed it over here. I must, of course, start with Christmas Eve. 'Twas then that I opened the various Christmas parcels which had been arriving for two weeks or more before Christmas. Piled beneath my cot they began to assume more importance than .30 calibre ammunition to an isolated Infantry company in combat. They soon became the talk of the other officers who (the greedy little brutes) had crawled away to dark corners when their packages had arrived and opened them in places far from the rest of us where there was little danger of mass appropriation. There in the room before me as I entered were all my officers, grouped like a tribunal council, sitting in a semi-circle around my cot on their haunches. I could have charged them with violations of every article of war, and the Constitution to boot, and they wouldn't have budged. Together we opened my Christmas packages. The guard on the post outside was given instructions to admit no one, not even Eisenhower himself if he, too, should attempt to crash my Christmas party; the entrance was strapped shut, the field phone was taken off the hook, the blackouts adjusted, and the session began.

Dad will remember Christmas on Cebu Island, some forty-odd years ago, and can add that part of the tale I can't describe. It's about the way a guy feels when the holidays roll around, and it hits him with a jolt that the home folks and the old gang and the Statue of Liberty are thousands of miles, and a war and a victory away, and the going a bit rough in spots, and there are strangers everywhere—and it's Christmas Eve.

ing party, one that would be shelling the shellac out of us around one o'clock the next morning. The weather was very bad, cloud layers and, to the northwest, where we were going, you could see from the field a heavy weather front. This was our first big attack. We took off around 5:30, rendezvoused with other planes and headed up the alley. The "alley" is a natural channel for shipping from Bougainville and runs between the New Georgia Islands and Santa Isabelle, right down to Savo and Guadalcanal. It was getting dusky when we headed up and we had to go around several squalls.

As we went up, the fighters climbed way above us. Then we got where we couldn't see any of the fighters because of an overcast.

We sighted the ships at about 6:40, 160 miles up, off the western tip of the New Georgias. We could still see an edge of the sun, but down below it was blue gray, and the wakes of the ships showed up more than anything else. They were in three perfect lines, but when they saw us the outside lines fanned out in unison and started to weave. Also to throw up one helluva heavy curtain of AA. They sent up a few feeler bursts and then started to walk it towards us and when they got the range all twelve ships opened up, each one blinking white along its whole length. The sky was filled with the black puffs.

The fighters had made contact above us and, as we were coming up for our approach, I saw two planes go down in flames, hitting the water with a big flare. They were Zeros, but I didn't know it at the time. The fighters did such a good job that not one of us was bothered by a Zero. They knocked down eleven of them and lost one Grumman. Through a non-habit-forming tactic, our approach lasted about ten minutes in full range of the AA. In that time they were bound to get good, although we were bouncing up and down as much as possible. It seemed that you would turn and there would be a puff right where you were. Three were inside my wing so I could hear the hollow furranng they made or maybe it is bullanngg. Just before we pushed over, one hit the belly of my plane, bouncing me up and blowing out the bomb-bay window in my face, so the rest of the flight I was spitting out glass, but no other harm. I was second to dive and glad to get the hell out of there. I could see the leader in his dive ahead of me and the AA and tracer from .50 calibres springing up at us. Surprisingly enough, you pay no attention to it. It is impersonal, not like Zeros on your tail, and there is nothing you can do about it.

I went on down and released quite low, afterward going right down to the water to get out of the cone of the explosion. Then they really started to give us hell as we went out through two lines of ships, getting a cross fire of .50's and AA which they bounced off the water. We were going with all the power we

News from the home front. Marines sort a shipment of mail brought to Segi Point, New Georgia.

could get, shaking the plane up and down and sideways. My gunner screamed something in the phone, but I didn't get it. I saw the leader ahead of us, right on the water, and he was getting through and so were we.

I went over a Zero still burning on the water, the oil spreading out in flames on the surface. A destroyer turned in on me ahead but I was able to get around it. Then I saw the torpedo planes coming in low on their attack, one after another, on a heavy cruiser.

Out of range we circled to wait for the others. It was dark by this time and we turned on our wing lights. We could see several ships in flames. We started back home, a few of us, and almost immediately ran into a heavy front. We tried to go under it and then over it. On top you could see a few stars. But most of the time the wing lights of the plane next to me were blurred by fog.

Then, inappropriately enough, one of my wing tanks cut out before its time, and I had to shift tanks and work the hand fuel pump. In doing so I had to leave the formation and I never found it again. I thought I saw three lights and called up to tell them I would join up in a minute. I started to climb towards them with much power but they came no closer and then I realized that the lights were three stars above the clouds.

I looked at my compass and found that I had made a 180-degree turn and was headed away from home. I felt plenty much alone. I figured out a course and got on it, but the weather got much worse and I had to fly the whole way on instruments.

If you look out and try to see an island you get vertigo. Twice I had to pull myself out of sliding turning dives. For no reason I felt very confident of my navigation and it came out right on the button. I saw what I hoped was a glow on the clouds and let down to 40 feet and there lay the blessed field with the search-lights turned up for us. One guy cracked up on landing. We all agreed the trip back was much worse than the attack.

I cut the engine and felt very tired. Then all was chatter. My gunner got out, a little Cuban, very excited, and said to me "I'm not very much around here, but my family back in Cuba is well off, and if you ever want anything . . . I know we were lost up there and you brought us home" and so on, so somebody gave him a small bottle of medicinal brandy, but it was nice of him. . . .

You can live and do this and still think about other things. You can get scared to death in the morning, come through it, and spend the afternoon reading or playing cards. There is nothing great about it. It is what you have been trained for and have become used to, and in a way it is routine. This is not trying to be smart but to explain it.

Before I came out here I always thought that so-called "physical courage" was one overrated virtue and it sure is. You can have it if you want it. The guys who have proved yellow were mentally yellow in the first place. And for my money the guys who think this is all, the great, and the highest mode of living are also full of bull, because it isn't and there is plenty more.

We have been here for over five weeks, and things that at first seemed strange are now becoming routine. It is impressive how adaptable people are, how they make the best of things without consciously thinking they are doing so. This is amazing and wonderful to me, especially as the assorted smallnesses seem to go on, petty jealousies, irritability, ego blossoms and so on.

And one thing I don't mean to say, by golly, is that war brings out beautiful attributes in people, because it doesn't. But it does show an energy and natural worth that should give a lot of promise if it were later put to better more building-up use.

I think I can put up an argument against the group that accuses our generation of being incurably desiccated, degenerate, nihilistic, unenthusiastic, et al. There is enthusiasm and vigor in these guys that cannot be pooh-poohed even by the most agile tearer-downers nor cheapened by the most blatant builder-uppers.

1943

Ballad of the Bombardier

At night a white-faced nineteen-year-old bombardier
Sits writing.
The wonder of his crew tonight,
Before the flight,
Sits writing.
Behold the stern precision of time and plan:
Regard one sudden man
In a given hour
The hand, the eye, the deliberate brow—
This veteran now
Sits writing a letter home.
"I take my pen in hand, Emily,
To make you understand
What you are to me. I write as far as 'Dear Emily'—
And cannot make it clear
What you are to me.
You are my heart's one cry.
Foolish words that I
Wish to say, and try,
So terribly.
The words are like a wall, Emily.
I cannot write at all
What you are to me.
You are my heart's one cry.
If you were nearby,
You could tell me why,
So easily.

Write me you will be true, Emily.
Write me I am to you
What you are to me."
At night a white-faced nineteen-year-old bombardier
Sits writing.
The wonder of his crew tonight.
Before the flight,
Sits writing.

CORPORAL MARC BLITZSTEIN

★ ★ ★

Corporal Kenneth Connelly* served as chaplain's assistant with the 333rd Regiment, 84th Infantry Division. As an infantryman, he took the combat training with the rest of his company, in addition to his numerous duties as secretary for the chaplains. His letter is extracted from an anthology that the writer privately published after the war.

Texas Hospital Ward, January 1943

Last night I had a good laugh here in the ward. After "lights out" at 9 o'clock it was practically impossible to get to sleep. There was a section of snorers so magnificent in massed symphonic effect that one couldn't refuse to listen. In addition, a Texas lad with a ringing clear voice was expounding his views on life and they were dull. Then, of course, there was the usual hacking and coughing. Finally, in a sweat of desperation, one old fellow stood up in bed with a sheet wrapped around him. He cleared his throat and solemnly announced "I personally SING," whereupon, with absolute murder in his heart, he began to sing "Tis the last rose of summer—". The entire affair made me think that a movie with Monty Woolley as a draftee might have rather rare possibilities.

---

* Other letters from Corporal Connelly appear on pages 238, 270, and 277.

Whatever communistic ideas I may have had are now dead forever. The Army, save for its class system, practices the most thorough communism—the same clothes, the same hospital robes, the same diet, the same tooth-brushes—absolute division of "wealth." However ideal it may be from an ethical stand-point, temperamentally I can't stand it. Individualism is too much a part of me.

One is also inclined to be rudely shocked by "the common man" when meeting him in the barracks. He is no more pre-pared to guide intelligently the destinies of his country—politi-cally, economically, artistically, etc., than a Dodo bird. Whatever intelligence he possesses has been wasted and warped chiefly because of faulty environment. I think it is quite a seri-ous and legitimate question when one asks: "How can we ex-pect an intelligently directed democracy in a nation where the average male adult finds his favorite reading in a comic book, his greatest sense of beauty in hill-billy songs, burlesque and peep-show magazines, and his profoundest philosophy in a bot-

Corporal Kenneth Connelly

tle of liquor?" Of course the people of the United States, contrary to a ridiculous but wide-spread theory, never have directed their leaders. The leaders have directed the people.

You mustn't think I'm a fascist. I still believe in the potentialities of the people. I still believe in the struggle to attain the democratic ideal. I believe more firmly than ever in the necessity for more and more education and sufficient reward for physical labor. But when people talk of the state of American civilization they mean the state of civilization at Columbia University instead. All of which means: America has a long way to go.

★   ★   ★

Lieutenant William Ellison,* a dive-bomber pilot with the Marine Corps, wrote the following letter.

Jan. 7, 1943

Dear Elizabeth:

Everything is quiet here these days and boring in comparison to a few weeks ago. I have read all the trash on the island.

I have been thinking of these guys and trying to see if they are in any way like the novels want them, most particularly the group in Signed with Their Honour by James Aldridge. It probably isn't a fair comparison because those people were English, and they were fighting a losing battle. But still there have been plenty of attacks when it looked like a losing battle and when our planes have been in such tough shape that they would not have been allowed off the ground ordinarily. Anyway, just looking at the flyers as such, all of them with combat hours, and forgetting the set-ups, these guys are not more like those than they are like the World War I pilots.

I'm not saying Aldridge's people weren't the way he says,

---

* Another letter from Lieutenant Ellison appears on page 56.

but these seem a helluva lot more human, less pompous, and cold, more understanding of what the hell is going on, and they don't take themselves so damn seriously. They are not terse and bitter and full of meaningful glances, but they love to jabber about their flights, to exaggerate and make close calls sound funny—even the New Zealanders like to do this. Above all, they have a helluva lot more fun, even without love affairs, but I'll be damned if they like it any better. And there are plenty of chances not to have fun. One guy, who had the whole camp on edge waiting for news of his wife's expected twins, went out on an attack the night before the day they were due, and his plane crashed in Jap territory. Another guy, aged twenty-one, got a letter telling him his wife had been killed in an automobile accident, and two days later he went out, got caught in a storm, and went into the sea.

Another time a fighter pilot went nuts high above the clouds. He picked up his microphone and for fifteen minutes we heard through our headpieces the wildest, most devastating final speech, part raving and part sane—the most tragic thing I have ever heard—and then he came spinning down past us.

But still the people are human. There are pettinesses and absurdities; people get yellow and people get conceited, but yet they don't get pompous or self-righteous. They admit they are scared, everybody is scared at times, but they talk about it openly and laugh at it. They are as serious about wanting to live as anybody and are not frivolous nincompoops with cheesy to-morrow-we-die philosophies.

Everyone intends to do just as much as he can to get himself home, and everyone has an equal chance. I can't see anyone setting down and prattling about "You know, I have a rendez-vous with death"; or "If I should die, I want you to think only this of me." Of course, those men were poets, much more sensitive and melancholic, but even a poet out here would not write like that. There is too much of another feeling out here for that —of guys who want to get home and raise damn good hell with their wives, or get back a job, or work on a farm (a lot of this), or buy an old airplane—much of it absurd, possibly, but not just bluster.

A writer might try to squeeze a whole lot of tragedy, high-flown courage, longing and self-conscious significance out of this group, and he might find it wasn't the way he wanted it, and fling up his hands, saying, "You're all just a bunch of dumb, unfeeling bastards." But he would be wrong, and he wouldn't have seen what there is.

I cannot write any more. Something just happened. One of the guys in our tent brought in a whole case of Jacob Ruppert beer, pried from the Army. You don't know what this means. I have had two bottles of beer since I've been out on this island, and this is a whole damn case.

★   ★   ★

*W*illiam *Vana served as a private first class with the 128th Regiment, 32nd Infantry Division, attached to the 22nd Portable Surgical Hospital. His unit was en route to Australia from New Guinea when the transport ship* Alacrity *was sunk on November 16, 1942.*

PFC Bill Vana 20600193
Portable Hosp.
c/o Station Hosp.
U.S. Army
c/o P.M. San Francisco, Calif.

Jan. 1943

Dear Mom:

Just a few lines to let you know that I'm O.K. and feeling fine, so please don't worry. The Red Cross brought us patients some books and papers to read today, and among the papers was a copy of the Chic. Trib. and in it a story about my Co. so I guess I can tell you a little of what happened now.

We were the first outfit of our kind to move up to the front and set up and the boys are kind of proud of the fact. We sure were scared when them planes dived and started bombing and

67

machine gunning us. I was afraid to jump off as I didn't know how to swim. So I grabbed a machine gun C mounted on the deck and started shooting at the planes. I ran out of ammunition and already the boat was on fire, so I done the only thing left for me to do. I took off all of my clothes and over the side I went and then is when I really got scared and between prayers I yelled for help. All though there was no one to help me I still yelled for help (and did I yell). Well about 75 yards from shore I saw 2 Aussies push out in a row boat and I yelled at them to come over to me. They reached me just as I went limp and I still say if it wasn't for them 2 Aussies I'd be a dead duck today. Well they rowed around and picked up guys, till the boat was loaded then rowed into shore. I had got my breath by that time. So I ran into our officers and they had already started giving first aid to the wounded, a couple other guys and me found some litters so started up and down the beach looking for wounded, picking one Aussie up down the beach a way we started back (by this time it was dark but the boat on fire lit up the sky like day) some ammunition started to explode so we layed low and

Private First Class William Vana

watched the boat burn and I'm telling you a sight I'll never forget. The whole boat was on fire except the back beam and flying on the top of that was an American flag and with the flames all over and to see that flag flying sure was a sight and it never burned until a half hour or so later and I'll never forget that sight. Well the next night we evacuated the wounded to the rear and then the next day we moved up to the front line. We worked day and night and never heard a whimper out of any of the wounded brought back to us. They sure were a great bunch of guys. We only had one can of bully beef a day to split amongst 3 men and you never heard a squeak out of anyone.

We were always under fire, but work went on just the same. Scared, hell yes we were scared all the time, but that didn't stop our working. When the planes would bomb and strafe us we would lay low and pray none of the bullets or bombs had our name on them. After they left back to work. All of the boys in the Co. are from Chic. except 3 or 4 and we while sitting in our

Base Censor's Department in Queensland, Australia

slit trenches used to talk about Chic. or Camp Hornet (they were either from the 33MPs or the 108 Med. Regt.) and we grew to be just like brothers. Sure are a swell bunch of guys. We sure miss the unfortunate ones. But they will always remain in our memories. . . .

Hope you get this. There is lots more to tell, but that will have to wait until we come home.

Give my love to all,
God Bless All,
Your Son,

Bill

★ ★ ★

*C*urtis Allen Spach went to Guadalcanal with *the first wave of Marines on August 7, 1942. He was attached to L Company, 3rd Battalion, 5th Regiment, 1st Marine Division. On December 9 the exhausted 1st Division was relieved and sent to Melbourne, Australia. From Melbourne Spach wrote home to relate his experiences on the island, having been at the front lines for 110 days without relief.*

Corporal Curtis Allen Spach

[February]

Dear Dad,

I think you will find this letter quite different than the others which you've received from me. My health is well as could be expected as most of us boys in the original outfit that left the States together about ███CENSORED███ of us are still here. The other are replacements. The missing have either been killed, wounded or from other various sources mainly malaria fever.

On May 16 '42 we left New River N.C., and went to the docks at Norfolk. On the 20th at midnight we hit the high seas with 7,000 marines aboard the U.S.S. Wakefield. We went down through the Panama Canal and past Cuba. On the 29th we crossed the international date line, latitude 0^0, 0^1, 0^{11} longitude 85^0, 45^1, 30^{11}. Was continually harassed by submarines as we had no convoy whatsoever.

We landed in New Zealand 28 days later and they were wonderful to us as we were the first Americans to arrive there. We lived aboard ship at the dock for about a month loading equipment on incoming ships getting ready for *"The Day."* After working day and night we left and went to one of the Fiji Islands for four days. I was aboard the U.S.S. Fuller picked up in New Zealand. In our convoy were about 100 ships including 3 aircraft carriers and the battleship, North Carolina. We also had air protection from Flying Fortresses coming from Australia. On August 6 we had our last dinner aboard ship and they gave us all we wanted with ice cream and a pack of cigarettes. Just like a man doomed for the electric chair he got any kind of food for this last meal. That was our last for a while. Each one of us received a letter from our commanding officer, the last sentence reading Good Luck, God Bless You and to hell with the Japs. On the morning of the 7th I went over the side with the first wave of troops as Rifle Grenadier, just another chicken in the infantry. With naval bombardment and supreme control of the air we hit the beach at 9.47. All hell broke loose. Two days later our ships left taking our aircraft with them, never to have any sea and air protection for the next two ███CENSORED███ . In the meantime the Japanese navy and air force took the advantage and gave us hell from sea and air. I won't say what the ground troops had to offer us yet. I can say we never once retreated but kept rushing forward taking the airport first thing.

Left to do or die we fought hard with one purpose in mind to do, kill every slant eyed bastard within range of rifle fire or the bayonet which was the only thing left to stop their charge. We were on the front lines *110 days* before we could drop back for a shave, wash up. Don't many people know it but we were the first allied troops to be on the lines that long, either in this war or the last. We have had to face artillery both naval and field, mortar bombings sometimes three or four times a day, also at night, flame throwers, hand grenades, tanks, booby traps, land mines, everything I guess except gas. The most common headache caused by machine gun fire, snipers, rifle fire, and facing sabers, bayonet fighting, the last most feared by all. A war in five offensive drives and also in defense of our own lines. I've had buddies shot down on both sides of me, my closest calls being a shot put through the top of my helmet by a sniper. Once I had to swim a river when we were trapped by the enemy.

With no supplies coming in we had to eat coconuts, captured rice, crab meat, fish heads. We also smoked their dopey cigarettes. We also captured a warehouse full of good Saba Beer, made in Tokyo. Didn't shave or have hair cut for nearly four months, looked rather funny too. Wore Jap clothing such as underwear, socks, shoes. Had plenty of thrills watching our boys in the air planes dog fighting after they sent us some planes to go on the newly finished field that they had built. We found field pieces and pictures of American girls and mothers on Japs that we killed. They were taken off the Marines at Wake Island. They used explosive and dum dum bullets in their long rifles so we cut the ends of ours off with bayonets so that when they were hit the bullet would spread making a hell of a hole in them. You had to beat them at their own tricks. What few of the old fellows here are scarred by various wounds and 90% have malaria. I've been down with it several times but I dose heavy with quinine till I feel drunk. It gets you so that you feel as if your eyes are popping out and very weak and lousy. We want to come home for a while before seeing action again which is in the very near future, but they won't do it even though the doctors want

Mail clerks emptying packages from sacks just arrived in Australia

us to. We were continually bombed and strafed but took it pretty good. The average age of the boys was 21 and were around 18 to 20. When we were finally relieved by the army who were all larger and older they were surprised to find us kids who had done such a good job. My best buddie at the time was caught in the face by a full blast of machine gun fire and when the hole we were laying in became swamped by flies gathering about him and being already dead, I had to roll him out of the small hole on top of the open ground and the dirty SOBs kept shooting him full of holes. Well anyway God spared my life and I am thankful for it. I know that your and dear Mama's prayers helped bring me safely through the long months of it. I hope that you will forgive me of my misdoings as it had to take this war to bring me to my senses. Only then did I realize how much you both had done for me and Dear God, maybe I can come through the next to see you and my friends again. . . .

God bless the whole world and I'm looking forward to the days when Italy and Germany are licked so that the whole might of the allied nations can be thrown in to crush Japan and the swines that are her sons, fighting to rule the white race. I heard an English speaking Nip say that if he didn't die fighting, that is if he didn't win or if he was captured and later came to Japan, he would be put in prison for 17 years and that all his property would be taken over by the government. That's his point of view. Where ever we go us boys will do our best always till the end when we don't have the strength to press a trigger.

Please understand that I didn't write this so as to worry you anymore than I already have but I wanted you to know I am doing my best for your Uncle Sam. Maybe some day I will be able to sleep in that thing called a bed and eat from a table. Just simple everyday things, but they mean a lot when you have to live in jungles and lay in filthy stinking surroundings day after day. If you let the folks over there see this, cut out the names of the ships and certain countries which I mentioned, for they shouldn't be discussed. Wishing you all health and happiness, will say goodby for now. Give Mother and the kids my love.

Love always,
Your son,

Allen

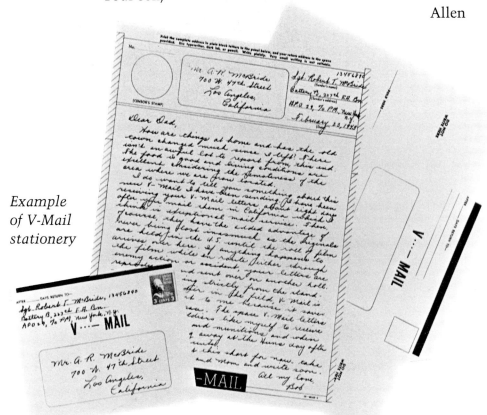

Example of V-Mail stationery

★ ★ ★

*M*ajor General Terry de la Mesa Allen commanded the 1st Infantry Division during the North African,
Tunisian, and Sicilian campaigns. He was relieved of his post
in July 1943 and took command of the 104th Infantry Division
in October of that year, where he remained until the end of the
war. This letter to Major General Allen's wife was written by
his orderly, Corporal Joseph Pennisi.

North Africa, March 18, 1943

Mrs. Allen:

I have received many letters from you, I could not answer them
all, waited for your husband to come back as he was at the front
at the time. I had not seen him for a couple of weeks. I knew he
was well and very busy, and when he did return he was in the
best of condition and looked good. We got him a room in a hotel
with a nice warm soft bed, a fireplace and a bath, which he really

*Major General
Terry de la Mesa Allen*

did enjoy. He is well taken care of so do not worry about that. Well he finally made up his mind to write you and Sonny. This letter is a few days later. He has left again for the front, I'm behind watching his baggage and washing his clothes, always have clean ones ready for him in return. I do my best for him so don't worry. Before he left he asked me to write you, to keep your shirt on and wait until we clean up Africa, maybe he may send for you, as now it is still dangerous.

The things you have read in the newspapers from Ernie Pyle don't believe it. We have yet to see a show, or go to a dance, or any other entertainment like you think. Maybe *corps* or the other bunch of soldiers have the opportunity to see those shows. Not the Fighting First. We are always busy, and on the field, how can we go to Oran to see those actresses when we are about 500 miles away. Remember this Mrs. Allen, it's going to be the 1st Division that is going to win this war.

I asked your husband how come other officers go back to U.S. why don't he? You know what he answered, "Pennisi, I would love to but it can't be done." He wants to stay with the First Division, and if the men can't go back, neither will he. Someday we will all go back. I know you are anxious to see him and help him but just now you must have patience and wait a little while longer. I feel like seeing Angie too, so do the rest of the boys.

We have received all your letters, telegrams, and packages, also cigarette case from Sonny, leather billfold with your picture and everything you sent, including your private letter to Gen. Allen. We were very glad to hear Sonny has passed in school and is feeling well. Also glad to hear your voice on the *Victrola Disc*, on your birthday and did your husband get a kick out of it, he sure loved it very much, also when he heard Sonny's voice.

I have nothing else to say just now hoping this letter finds you all well and happy. Give my regards to Mrs. Robinson, Sonny and Angie. I will close with love and kisses from Gen. Allen, and until we hear from you again.

I remain
Sincerely

Joseph B. Pennisi

★ ★ ★

Theodore Roosevelt, Jr.,* commanded the 26th Regiment, 1st Infantry Division, during World War I. In April 1941 he foresaw the inevitability of America's entering World War II and reported for military service. He was given command of his old regiment and in December was promoted to brigadier general and made deputy commander of the division. He led the division at the invasion of Oran on November 8, 1942, and throughout the Tunisian campaign. Brigadier General Roosevelt wrote this letter to his wife after the Battle of El Guettar.

North Africa, Mar. 25, 1943

Dearest Bunny:

Since I wrote of our attack on the unnamed city much has happened.

First we were ordered to attack again. We moved out for this show as usual under cover of darkness. We had only one road and two combat teams plus supporting arms to be brought down. That meant a truck movement covering twenty miles of road space. After we had done our best to give our directive to the unit commanders and laid on a schedule of movement for units timetable I went forward in my jeep. All went reasonably well. At the time I did not think so for I got furiously angry with countless idiocies that delayed the column.

By dawn the show was on—machine guns spluttered, artillery rumbled. We caught the Italians unprepared. On the north we came down on them from the mountains—a devilish climb. On the south we swept around their right flank. By then the original objectives were taken and crowds of prisoners were being marched to the rear. Our men don't take to all this "bitter hate" business—and all the Sherwoods, MacLeishes, Sarnoffs

---

* Other letters from Brigadier General Roosevelt appear on pages 100, 129 and 152.

77

Machine-gun crew on the alert in El Guettar, March 23, 1943

Brigadier General Teddy Roosevelt, Jr.

etc. with their swivel chairs, daintily fed bellies and soft safe beds can't change their natures. Our men will fight like the devil, but when the battle's over, it's over. They treat war like a football game—when the game's over let's all get drunk together. They gave the prisoners candy and cigarettes and roared with laughter.

Next day we pushed still further to new positions. Among our troubles were the dive bombers. They came down on us constantly. Once I was caught in a valley by a raid. A bomb hit within twelve paces of where I was lying. My helmet was struck by a fragment and knocked galley-west, but I was unhurt though a couple of men were killed. By the way, don't wear your helmet strap hooked. If I had my head would have gone rolling off inside the helmet.

The following day the enemy counter attack came. During the night, which was clear with the bright moon of Africa lighting the arid country, the German tanks came into our position. We got vague rumors of them from our reconnaissance units, and soon I began to hear bursts of enemy m.g.s. I went forward to an O.P. on the front of our main line positions. At dawn the battlefield lay at my feet on a circular plain about seven miles in diameter. I could see it all.

The first move was a swing of German tanks to our right flank—24 in all. We took them under artillery fire. On they came until they had nearly turned our position—the shells bursting around them. Then the going got too tough for them. They hesitated, milled around and withdrew, leaving two destroyed tanks nearly in our lines to mark the high tide of their advance. Meanwhile their artillery had been shelling us and their dive bombers were busy.

Whenever a flight of these appeared they were greeted by a fury of anti-aircraft and small arms. Incidentally, I did not see one shot down, though how they lived through that flood of lead is more than I can tell. From then on the day was a series of assaults, each repelled in turn. Once they brought forward their enormous Mark X tanks. The plain became a smoky, dusty dream, or rather nightmare. It was dotted with destroyed tanks and vehicles, some of them ours for they got in on some of our artillery and our Tank Destroyers made a costly and stupid sally.

Sometimes vehicles would hit mines and blow up. Once an enemy vehicle towing a 37 m.m. gun ran down the road practically into our lines. It was hit by mortar-fire and burst into flames. A couple of men got out and started to run. The m.g.s got them.

The final assault came at five. It was preceded by four dive bombing attacks and artillery. It was composed of tanks and infantry. Just in front of me was a German unit of 400 men. We took them under fire and they went to ground behind some sand dunes. The artillery went after them with time-shells and air-bursts. In no time they were up running to the rear, khaki figures reeling and falling with black bursts over their heads. That was the last of the day. Nightfall brought us rest. We'd thrown back a Panzer division with heavy loss. I never expect to see anything like this again—a battle fought at my feet while I commanded by telephone as I saw the developments before my eyes. Incidentally, I was two days without sleep, washing or even brushing my teeth.

Now we're at it again. We're all weary, but I guess the enemy is wearier than we are. In this war no units in the line get relief. We just go on and on. I believe that the very fierceness of this fighting means that later resistance will be softened.

I got a letter from Q. He sounds well and cheerful. He says he'll be fit for service towards the end of April. I hope he does not get back until the battle of Africa is finished. No letters from you any more. They've all stopped. Nothing since Q's wound more than a month ago. I guess they'll all come in a batch.

Much, much love.

Ted.

---

*A*llen Mott enlisted in the Marine Corps the day after Pearl Harbor. After basic training he attained the rank of corporal and was stationed "somewhere in the South Pacific."

A crude post office set up by the Marines on Bougainville in the South Pacific

South Pacific
April 1, 1943

Darling Addie:

Even though I mailed a nice long letter to you this morning, I am starting another this very evening. You should hear the story about forty marines and myself being on an island where we couldn't get anything to eat, as we left our food rations back in camp expecting to get back from our scouting trip by supper time. We couldn't make it on time for reasons, and Mott's belly was dreaming of a delicious steak smothered in onions. Finally that thought broke out into clear, ringing words. The boys looked startled. I'm sure at the time the raiders would have settled for a vitamin pill and a glass of water. But good old Mott's mind just didn't dream of steaks because he likes to dream, oh, no, not Mott. He knew something. I spoke to the captain in charge and asked him if he would like a nice thick juicy steak for supper. If the boys looked startled when I said it the first time, then there are no words for the look that crept over the captain's face at that moment. His eyes just got glassy. I couldn't tell whether he was picturing a vision of such a meal or if he was getting up nerve to have me shot for demoralizing the Marine Corps. But being a captain, he controlled himself, clamped his teeth together, shot out his finger and poked me in the chest and growled, "Mott, you started something you are going to be sorry for. You are now detailed to bring back those steaks, and brother don't even try to show your face around here if you don't bring them back, or I may mistake you for a Jap! On your way, little boy, on your way."

A grin broke out on Mott's puss like a ray of sunshine and said "Sir, would you give me a detail of five men?" That really added fuel to the fire, but still controlling himself, barked a "Yes" and Mott and his little band trudged off. Ha. Ha. Ha. This really was Mott's best assignment yet. Yes, it was his meat.

Time passes on, ten, fifteen minutes, and suddenly a shot rings out and another, and silence plays her symphony throughout the coconut groves.

A little while passes and finally in the distance the captain spies a little fellow walking nonchalantly toward him, where the boys were already making camp for the night. He gets up and walks towards this little fellow, who by the way is Mott in the flesh.

"Well," he roars, "where in the hell are my men? Don't tell me you turned cannibal and ate them. What in the hell were you shooting at?"

Mott, with a knowing look in his innocent eyes, says, "They will be along shortly, sir, but I suggest you build your fires before the sun goes down so we can cook those steaks, sir."

The captain's eyes popped, his breath came and went with loud gasps. He turned mechanically, issued orders for wood to be brought and fires made like he was in a dream. He kept watching me with a look which could not be defined and when the five marines returned just a little later staggering under the weight of 200 lbs. of nice fresh steak, he sat down and just stared!

What a night! Boy! What a night and what a supper! Steaks for all, all they could eat, cram, push into their tummies that had had no meat for weeks. Two inches thick and broiled over a charcoal fire, they were. I can almost taste them now.

Yes, I know, my darling, you are wondering where in hell did I get those steaks. This is the payoff. The reason I started to think about steak was just a simple matter of being like Whimpy, Pop-Eye's pal. I happened to see a few wild cows grazing a half a mile back. From there on it was just a matter of getting the captain interested enough to let me go back and shoot one. Of course it was not as simple as going over and shooting one in the head, as wild cows, believe it or not, behave just like the opposite of the ones you have seen. They can detect you like a deer does when you are hundreds of yards away and they start moving and moving fast. But cows don't know about the rifle range at La Jolla, so a cow hit the dust with a slug in her leg. A minute later she was steak on the hoof. I never saw food disappear so like magic.

So this is the story of a bunch of marines who ate steak for supper, breakfast and dinner on the following day. The captain is still wearing that satisfied look of a man well filled inside, and I don't mean with vitamin pills. The excitement around the fire that night is another story in itself. How one of the boys confessed he was a former butcher, and how we sharpened our knives for him, and what a swell job he did, would mean another chapter. But it can be said here that there are forty marines who will never forget a little marine who shot a cow, once upon a time . . .

Your marine steak hunter,

Abby

★ ★ ★

*P*rivate First Class Robert Baum served as an aerial radio gunner with the Marine Corps.

[Southwest Pacific]
[April]
. . . A guy gets in some serious thinking out here. We globe trotters and globe fighters are nonetheless dreamers, too. Trust in God. Trust in Him to bring this barbarism to a finale. Its so foolish, and worst of all so futile. Feel sorry for the demagogues

An Army private receiving the news from home by V-Mail

and the blood of those with whom they are drenched, for surely their souls (the demagogues) shall know no rest and they shall burn in eternity. I'm just writing about these things that at the moment occupy my mind and puzzle me no end. Sometimes when I happen to be walking along alone, say for instance at night, I stop and say, "Well Bob, you are in a heck of a fix. What are you doing here? Do you remember how you laughed at the idea of ever bearing arms, and with of all outfits, the Marines?" Its the fellows that have gone before us who make us willingly bear our burdens. Dear God, spare our lives, for we are young and love life so much. This is just a short incident in a fellow's life, I tell myself, and soon it will be behind me and I will have forgotten it, and settle down among you all again.

Here's the way I think of it. If I can think of you all safe and sound at home, getting all you can out of life, why its more than worth it, if only one of us has to give up a little part of his lifetime for a while to have it that way for always. More than worth it. I never thought I'd find myself way down here in the Southwest Pacific, but here I am, and it isn't as bad as its cracked up to be. I have a roof over my head. Luxuries are scarce, but as I write this, the chow is good and sufficient. You people back home have such a vital job. We need a lot down here, and tho' we get along with what we have, all additional equipment makes us feel so much more secure. I doubt that there is a more exciting job being one, but I like it. I'm surprised at myself in a way, because I do not get all flustered and excited in the middle of an engagement. This is one game I'm going to beat. I know. When I played baseball I never wanted to sit on the bench, always wanted to play the whole game. And here too, I'm going out every time, and while I'm playing this game, I'm going to play hard, and to win. Remember to trust in God. I'm coming back. God bless you. Remember me in your prayers, especially in the next few weeks. We have some messy action ahead of us.

★

This was Private First Class Baum's last letter. Shortly afterward he was reported missing while on active duty, and he never returned.

★   ★   ★

Lieutenant Martin Canavan wrote the following letter to his infant daughter, who was born while he was away on active service with the 3rd Regiment, 3rd Marine Division, in the Solomon Islands.

1 May 1943
Southwest Pacific

My dearest daughter:
Though you are now quite young, I am going to write you, saying a few things I may never be able to tell you in person. Your Mother and I love each other dearly. Out of that love you came into being. In the short time I knew your Mother before we were married I had numerous occasions to observe her qualities of courage, force of character and sweetness of nature. Since our marriage I've had ample time and opportunity to prove that I

Lieutenant Martin Canavan

was not wrong in my choice. Try to pattern yourself after her. You could not have a better model.

Be ambitious. Hard work is not a natural tendency. We have to be forced by one means or another to do what we should. Set a goal and strive with all your youth and vigor to attain it. When love comes to you, the real thing, surrender yourself to it. Don't sell yourself cheaply. Be sure of what you are doing and let your mind control your heart. When you are sure, don't let *anything* stand in your way. Your Mother and I had difficulties, but we surmounted them and they now seem insignificant.

At this writing I am half way around the world from you. That may seem far away from you now, but someday you will learn that you can leave your heart with those you love. It leaves one with a warm feeling. In my mind and heart I am with you both, your Mother and you. I have never seen you my dear, but in my mind's eye I can see your image. Undoubtedly I am influenced by my memories of your Mother. I have closely followed your progress by means of pictures, but I have given you a personality which I recognize as that of my own dear wife.

I haven't given this letter much thought, just writing as my heart dictated. To be honest with you, it was your Mother who suggested I write. So you see, she has thought of our feelings for each other already, far apart as we may be. Your Mother and my Wife is a wonderful woman. Be like her.

Consideration of others is one of the outstanding features of your Mother's character. Do you know of anything that makes for better harmony of life? I'm sure that our family life would be one of joy and tranquillity if we were all together. I have been deprived of one of life's greatest joys. That of holding my new-born child in my arms. One thing a man can't share with his wife is the birth of their child. The next best thing he can do is

A cartoon by Bill Mauldin

"My son. Five days old. Good-lookin' kid, ain't he?"

to hold the object of their mutual love against his breast and thrill to his soul at the miracle to which they have been a party.

Should I return I will do everything in my power to guide your steps toward a good, useful life. In the event that I fail to return I'll know that my wife is doing what both of us would have done. My trust in her is complete. So it must be with you.

No matter what our path of life may be like, remember me as sincere in my love. My ideals have always been of the highest and may they continue to be. War does peculiar things to men and women, and I may be changed. Forgive me if I do, and realize that I am the same man who was so humbly grateful to share the life of so noble a woman as your Mother. The same man, God willing, who will take up that life again, to live with the love of his wife and daughter.

Your loving father.

★   ★   ★

*O*n May 11, 1943, Caleb Milne* and a small group of American Field Service men volunteered to help the Free French Forces who were fighting against the main German force in the mountains above Enfidaville, Tunisia. Before leaving for the mission, he wrote to his mother and left the letter with a friend with the condition that it be sent in the event of his death.

[May]

I wish there was something I could say or do to make the next few days less unhappy and lonely for you. Perhaps the love and devotion of my heart that is filling this letter will reach out and be able to fill these pages so strongly that a measure of peace and closeness betwixt us will fill the empty feeling. Not for me, but for you. For it is the one who must bear the au revoir alone, that the sad tears fill up in my eyes. I am not in the least un-

---

* Another letter from Caleb Milne appears on page 32.

sat in the harbor for two weeks while signals were being exchanged. The one man, though, who has everyone's confidence is Halsey, he rates at the very top.

My love to every one.

Jack

P.S. Mother: Got to church Easter. They had it in a native hut and aside from having a condition read "Enemy aircraft in the vicinity" it went on as well as St. Pat's.

★ ★ ★

After viewing the Battle of Dunkirk at the Telenews Theater in San Francisco in June 1940, George Leghorn gave his boss two weeks' notice, walked out on his classes at San Francisco State College, and headed for Canada, where he joined the Royal Canadian Field Artillery. He eventually transferred to the United States Army in September 1942, in which he served as a staff sergeant, 151st Field Artillery, 34th Infantry Division. The division participated in the Tunisian, Sicilian, and Italian campaigns. Sergeant Leghorn wrote this letter to his former boss.

May 17, 1943

Dear Major Bowie:

It has been some time since last I wrote to you and this for two reasons: the first that during a campaign one has little time to write and what letters were written were sent to wife and folks, the second being the fact that one hates to write a letter in which practically everything of excitement and interest must be left out. Now that the Tunisian campaign is over, the censorship restrictions have been considerably lifted and one is free to put in details that would not formerly have been permitted.

First off, we sailed from England, passed through the Straits of Gibraltar and landed at Oran. The ocean voyage was uneventful and particularly delightful to me in that I didn't become seasick. There was some excitement between Gibraltar and Oran, however, though it in no way affected my ship.

Near Oran, we camped out in the open for some time, during which the only eventful thing was a terrific rainstorm that filled our mess kits with water before we could eat our stew. A new definition for the Weather Bureau as regards heavy rain. I did get into Oran once and was quite taken by the city. The French, Arab atmosphere created by sidewalk cafes, myriad urchin beggars, veiled women and coquettish smiles from unveiled ones pleased me mightily. The cognac was extremely good too, which reminds me that I have had but one drink of cognac since then. It was given me by a French police who said that he had barrels of it. So he did. It was distilled wine which the French have been running their trucks on in the absence of petrol. Even in coffee it is fiery and potent as raw alcohol though better flavored. Answered was my repeated question as to why the atmosphere smelled of wine every time a French truck passed us. I could almost get drunk by inhalation. Tlemcen, a beautiful and ancient city situated back of Oran in the second Atlas range was our next stop and we were fortunate in having a good deal of liberty and time in this ruin-cloaked city. There was here a crumbling bastion like fortress of the Turks which was over ten feet thick. It gave one a real thrill to ramble along its walls and climb its castellated turrets. Whew, time out—the 1st Sergeant just came over and asked me what in hell I was doing writing letters when such a commotion was going on. It seems my immediate vicinity is filtered with doors, bolts, and whatnots of the ammo truck which just blew up. The last tremendous wallop was caused by the gas tank, the others by landmines—so much for that.

Up till then we had been more or less (mainly less as regards comfort) on a Cookes tour. From Tlemcen we went straight to Tunisia and the battlegrounds. During dark of the morning we started and not until dark of night did our days journey end, and this for many days. The latter part of our journey was made at night only as Jerry had air superiority at that time and the roads were everlastingly dotted with shambles of burned and blown up material. We had air watchers at all times and any aircraft seen caused an immediate halt and a dash as far away from the truck or convoy as we could go. This action by all but the machine gunners who naturally remained at their posts. Such precautions while ignominious saved a great many lives. Many of those lives lost were due to indifference and lack of alertness on the part of airwatchers. The quick and the dead, it seems, applies to all ranks at all times. As I said in a previous letter, our insurance was of two types; a deep well constructed foxhole and the $10,000 variety. I had both, but relied chiefly on the first one. Had one real heartbreak down here. We got in an area where the soil was nearly solid bedrock and another similarly inclined fellow and myself blasted a hole five feet deep with ample capacity for two of us; said blasting being done with pick and shovel. We had no sooner finished our masterpiece and made

Sergeant George Leghorn

appropriate proud comments upon it to everyone we could get to admire it when we were moved some 300 yards away. It was two crestfallen lads who dug another far less pretentious foxhole to the rhythm of unceasing foul language.

In this area, also, we had one memorable occurrence and that, too, was the weather. The nights were extremely cold and as a result, we made our beds by interlapping our blankets inside a canvas bag made of wrapped together shelter-half. It formed a much cosier nest this way but had decided disadvantages as I learned later. My particular bed roll was under the trailer which offered some small protection in case it rained. At the same time I had the triangular end of my shelter-half tied to the limbs of an adjacent pine tree (bush rather) to prevent pine needles and dirt from getting into my blankets. One day we had, of all things in Africa, a snowstorm which began early in the morning and lasted all day. (We soon started to emphasize the NORTH in North Africa). Our only shelter under such conditions was our beds, but good poker players never say die. As low clouds and swirling snow prevented enemy aircraft from spotting us, we built a roaring fire and played poker all day in the lee of a pine tree. We were continually getting wet and dry at the same time. Plastic cards are a boon under such conditions as a cardboard set would have lasted but a few minutes. I garnered for myself some 500 francs at that time worth 750 but now valued at $10.00.

With darkness approaching (about 6:00 pm) we had to extinguish the fire which left no other alternative but to seek our beds for lack of other shelter. I shed my shoes and jacket and jumped into bed with all of my clothes on as did everybody else due to the penetrating cold. I really got penetrated that time as I found myself sitting in four inches of ice cold slush water. The damned stuff had been draining off the trailer and into my blankets all day filling the bag full as it could not seep out. A rude shock and near calamity as my blankets were soaking wet, every one of them. I put on some half-dry clothes, borrowed a combat suit from a fellow a whole half foot taller than I, crawled into it, put on a great coat and spent the night most uncomfortably in the cab of a truck. Life in the army can sure get miserable at times.

Under cover of darkness, we moved on to Pichon which was our first battle; in the exposure of daylight, we got to hell out of there a few days later as Rommel had broken through to Gafsa and threatened to cut us off by a rear attack through Sbiba and the Kasserine Pass. It was a critical moment in the campaign as any break through the above mentioned passes would have put Rommel's forces in the rear of the British 1st Army. As you know, Rommel was stopped by bloody fighting in the Kasserine Pass and Artillery and tank action at Sbiba. Was doing bath survey and metro work at Sbiba which afforded one an interesting variety. One is particularly fortunate to be in a Headquarters unit as it has much less of the perils of the infantry, etc. and gives one a perspective view of the action. One has the excitement and fascination of battle with only a small share of its attendant dangers. For all of that, it leaves one a battle-seasoned soldier. There is a world of difference in one's attitude before he has been in action and after. One tends to magnify the unknown whereas, after one has been in combat he gives dangers their proper respect but in no way lets them bother him. In England I had been bombed on a number of occasions and innumerable were the scenes of bomb damage to people and material that were witnessed. When one experiences bombing and knows its limitations, he has little fear of it. Bombing, as I have experienced it, comes with a crash and is over; shelling on the other hand is quite different and gives rise to much mental discomfort as I shall tell next.

Our next battle after Sbiba was at Fondouk Pass where the Americans broke through to threaten Rommel's flank at Kairouan. This threat, in spite of being a bit late greatly helped the 8th Army's rapid advance into Tunisia. We took up position in a cactus patch of some square miles in area. That evening, as the advance detail (of which I was a member) was dining on gasoline-flavored stew and gawdawful tea we heard a long low whistling sound quite familiar since Sbiba though by far more threatening. It was funny afterwards to think back upon it. As one man, up went multiple eyebrows—Allah Kazam, everybody prostrated himself on the dirt with emphasis on trying to tuck their rumps a little closer to terra firma. The shell landed across the road and down the way a bit, showering dirt on the men nearby. Everybody got up with a sheepish look on their faces and tried to assume nonchalant miens. Guess we had nothing to feel guilty about as I noticed a colonel from the vastly hardened British 8th Army did exactly as we had done and made no pretense of apology. There were no more shells that evening and I went to bed a tired soldier from a hard day's work. Had neglected to dig a foxhole due to many other duties entailed by an advance party. There were, however, numerous excellent foxholes some ten feet in length, and six feet deep with a covering of cactus logs and sand which were evidently constructed by the Germans. Ordinarily, one would never think of using these foxholes or so much as fool around them, as Jerry is well aware of the American soldiers' propensity to borrow the efforts of others and accordingly oftentimes puts mines in the bottom of his foxholes. One jumps in and comes back out again in small pieces. That night I made an exception. About ten pm, the shells started landing in our cactus patch. Shelling is definitely worse (I think) than bombing as one hasn't the slightest idea how long it will last. When the whistling sound draws close it provokes a tight giddy feeling in the stomach in spite of one's best efforts to counteract it. This seems to be a general reaction and not possessed by me alone. This night the first one came over and burst. Remembering the one shell of the evening, I didn't bother to get out of bed and seek cover but began to get tense when the second and third came over and burst. By the time the fifth came over the two of us who were unprotected got up, took our whole bed roll into the German foxhole and spent the night there. I went in first and not without temerity. It was a case of neglect on my part reducing me to two bad choices. I took the quiet one. The shelling continued for quite a while and caused me much distress as I had had a fluid motion of the bowels for some days. The first lull and I was out like a shot and none too soon. When things begin to happen everything happens. Don't mind adding that our discomfort was further heightened by the insanitary condition of the trench bottom and the odors from two unclean sweating bodies. My last bath had been at Sbiba over two weeks before as had Conkles, the companion of the night.

Baths are rare due to the shortage of water and usually consist of sponging off. Fondouk was our liveliest spot as far as H.Q. Btry was concerned. Fortunately the cactus patch was an extensive one as Jerry would unrelentingly bombard some sections of it the whole day. Also Me109's and bombers would come over and bomb the uncamouflaged vehicles and tanks. Used to dash out and shoot at the planes with a rifle but came to the conclusion that I wasn't hitting them. Got ahold of some tracer ammunition so I could estimate the correct lead more closely only to have Jerry quit coming over. . . .

Here at Fondouk, Djebel (mountain) Troza loomed on our left and another lower range on our right. The right hand range was occupied by Jerry and gave them excellent observation. They had been unable to take it so far and we suffered accordingly from well directed artillery fire so I wasn't surprised when one night the first sergeant came around and told me I was in charge of a commando up the mountain. The word commando has significance with me and evidently the first sergeant was misinformed to the extent that he thought it was a storming party. It's amazing how cool and collected a fellow can be when situations demand it. I calmly checked my poker winnings (some $200) and went forth to whatever fate held in store. It's a grand feeling, this. I take my destiny and calmly so, but this time it wasn't necessary. We were merely stationed between our forces and the mountain range to prevent attack at night. I suffered no more than damp blankets from the early morning dew (meteorologically speaking). . . .

There has been much down here of interest and excitement. Of the numerous battlefields on the globe today, this would be my choice and I feel grateful for it. Simply expressed it could be said thusly "Mine was a sunlit battlefield and green the flowery hills around."

Though this letter is being written to you, I have to admit my lack of ambition precludes writing another one. I wonder if you would be so kind as to send it to my folks that they might read it.

Sincerely,

George Leghorn

★   ★   ★

*A*t *the time of writing, Brigadier General Theodore Roosevelt Jr.* was with his old outfit, the 26th Infantry Regiment, 1st Infantry Division, in Tunisia.*

May 20th, '43

Dearest Bunny,

Do you know what this is—a wedding anniversary letter. I think it should arrive on the right date. Do you remember that hot June day thirty-three years ago?—the church jammed—Father with a lovely waistcoat with small blue spots—the Rough Riders—the ushers in cutaways—the crowds in the street— your long white veil and tight little bodice—the reception at Aunt Harriet's—Uncle Ed—your mother with one of her extraordinary hats that stood straight up.

And do you remember what the world was then—little and cozy—a different order of things, wars considered on the basis of a Dick [Richard Harding] Davis novel, a sort of "As it was in the beginning" atmosphere over life. We've come a long way down a strange road since then. Nothing has happened as we imagined it would except our children. We never thought we'd roam the world. We never thought our occupations and interests would cover such a range. We never thought that our thirty-third anniversary would find us deep in our second war, with me again at the front. Well, darling, we've lived up to the most important part of the ceremony, "In sickness and in health, for richer for poorer, until death do you part."

Much, much love.

Ted.

---

* Other letters from Brigadier General Roosevelt appear on pages 77, 129, and 152.

★ ★ ★

*H*arold *Gottlieb served as a staff sergeant with the 32nd Bombardment Squadron, 301st Bombardment Group, assigned to a B-17 bomber crew as gunner. He arrived in Britain in July 1942, where the crew became operational and flew on missions over France. In November the squadron was sent to Oran to provide air support after the invasion of North Africa. They subsequently operated from Tunis at the end of the campaign, and Italy became their prime target until December 1943, when the Italians surrendered to the Allies.*

May 23, 1943
North Africa

Dear Florence:

Hi sis! I haven't heard from you in some time but thought I'd write again anyway so here goes . . .

Now that the African Campaign is over, the mail censorship has relaxed somewhat so I feel that I can relate a story. In fact I hardly know where to begin, so I'll start and try to remember everything in sequence. . . .

We left England in Nov. and came here to Africa arriving about two weeks after the initial invasion. It was a nice day when we got there but that night it rained and the airdrome was a big mudhole. That wasn't so bad except that we had no place to live, so we slept in the airplane. Pretty gruesome. No mattress. Next morning we went looking for breakfast, and found out that "there ain't any." Apparently someone had remembered to send everything you need to fight a war, except food. To shorten the proverbial long story we traded my Arab buddy "Mohammed" a mattress cover for thirty-five eggs and fried them in some lard that someone had manged to scavenge. After breakfast we had to "gas up" the ship and load the bombs and that was really a job because we only had the ships crew there and no ground crew. After filling the tanks out of five gallon cans, you know you've put out some work. By night fall we finally managed to get everything loaded and had just enough energy left to drag the body to bed. Honestly, I was so damned "crapped out" I fell asleep as soon as my head hit the pillow. Mattress or no mattress. However no peace for the wicked. We got up about four in the morning and after eating a vile breakfast of lamb stew, crackers and sugarless tea we went out to the ship and at dawn we took off for a raid on Bizerta. With *no* fighter escort. Well sis, when we got to the target we found out that we were really in the "big league" down here. Honestly, those "Dutchmen" threw up the heaviest anti-aircraft barrage I've *ever* seen! How the hell they could come so close and miss I'll never know. The "flak" as we call anti-aircraft, looks like puffs of harmless black smoke, but every puff throws shrapnel in all directions and if a piece hits you, well, you may as well cash in your chips. The stuff is deadly and worse than being hit by a bullet, because it has jagged edges. However it missed. Praise the Lord!

Another "flak worry" was the fact that if some of it hit an engine and stopped it, you had to proceed on three engines and as that slowed you down you couldn't keep up with the forma-

*Staff Sergeant
Harold Gottlieb*

tion and would have to drop back. That's what the enemy fighters look for, a straggler, and when they find one, it is also too bad. They will be on you like a duck on a June bug, and they don't *all* miss. However thank God, that didn't happen either but it kept you in a state of mental anxiety over the target area. Getting back to the raid, we laid our "eggs" right down the alley and then proceeded to "get the hell out!" However it's not over yet. About that time "Goering's Luftwaffe" would come diving out of the sun and attempt to give you the "business." Most of the time they were unsuccessful and usually got "got" themselves.

You know when the shooting is going on you're so busy that you haven't time to get scared. Also the action is so fast that both sides do a lot of missing. Finally the fighters usually run out of bullets or get low on gas and decide to call it a day then you're in the clear. The whole affair from the time you hit the target area till you finally beat off the fighter attacks is usually thirty or forty minutes long, but it seems like an eternity. I'd kid you not sis, it really felt good to feel old "Ma Earth" under your feet again.

From there on the deal was quite the same. Gas up, bomb up, clean guns, do any maintenance work needed then get ready to go again. We usually went every other day because it took the day between to get things ready again. What do you think of that routine? Work, fly and fight? No shave, no bath, very little food, no beds, no liquor, no women, no fun, no nothing! Doesn't sound good does it? The upshot of the whole thing was the fact that the whole business went on for a couple of months. It really got discouraging sometimes but we usually managed to laugh it off with the aid of a few jugs of "vino" which we picked up now and then. That helped temporarily but you couldn't stay "vino'ed" up forever!

From the place we were at first we moved out to another base in the Sahara Desert and that didn't turn out so good. The wind blew there constantly and the sand was constantly in your eyes, teeth, hair, food etc. Aside from that, the "Dutchmen" divebombed the hell out of us there. Roughly about twenty-six times . . .

Whenever the "Jerrys" came over the only deal was to dive into a foxhole and start praying if you knew how. I sure saw a lot of atheists get converted quick. You know it was funny after it was all over, but at the time it was anything but.

Well, to get on with the story we went on another raid to a place called La Goulette and that was without a doubt the roughest "go" I ever went through. We got to the target O.K., dropped our bombs, got through the flak, and just as I was beginning to have a big sigh of relief I heard our waist gunner call over the phone, "Gottlieb! down below, get him!" This guy sounded pretty excited as I figured that whoever it was must be getting pretty damn close so I wheeled around and started looking for business but there wasn't a fighter in sight. In the meantime this guy is shouting "Get him! Get him!" I kept on hunting and then I saw him. You see, the fighter had a camouflage paint job on it and as it was partially back-grounded against the earth it seemed to blend right in. You've got to give those Germans credit. They're a smart bunch of bastards. Anyway, I managed to spot him when he broke over the horizon and I got a quick glimpse of two black crosses on the wings and a Nazi swastika on the tail that looked big as a house. He was really throwing lead at us too. Why he missed us I'll never know. He seemed to be perfectly lined up. Well, as you know, two can play at that game and as soon as I got my guns on him I pressed the triggers and fairly started throwing a few hunks of steel myself. I knew I was connecting because I saw a few pieces of something breaking off his wings. However he still kept coming until he got within 200 yards then suddenly did a quick snap-roll and plunged straight down. I kept on plugging at him but I couldn't watch him all the way because some of his "buddies" were still wheeling around. However another, one of the fellows in the ship saw him hit the water so I got credited with one enemy aircraft destroyed. Funny thing, after it was all over I found myself shaking so hard that it was an effort to keep my knees from knocking together. Nervous reaction I guess . . .

As you can see now I've seen a bit of this war but there's a lot of guys that have seen a lot more. A hell of a lot more. Perhaps you can see now why all this conflict in the U.S. politics, strikes etc. irritates everybody over here. It just makes you feel that you're not getting the backing you've got coming. Well dear sis, 'au revoir' (good-by in French) for now and give my best to everyone.

Love,

Harold.

★ ★ ★

John Babbitt served as a corporal with A Battery, 26th Field Artillery Battalion, 9th Infantry Division. He participated in eight campaigns, beginning with North Africa and covering Tunisia, Sicily, Normandy, northern France, Ardennes-Alsace, Rhineland, and the final thrust into central Germany, where the division remained until the end of the war in Europe.

June 9, 1943
Somewhere in North Africa

Dear Mother and Dad:

Sure welcomed your two letters today, May 14th and May 20th, news from you all is good news, makes me feel good. Yes this African Campaign is over, May 13th it was officially finished. From the time I left the states I have travelled well over three thousand miles. When I first hit **CENSORED** Nov. 8, it was midnight we hit the nets and got into the small ramp boats and formed into waves and made for the shore, the sea was rough and on hitting the beach the boat broached sideways and swamped. Getting onto the beach was tough. We were heavily packed, **CENSORED** Pack and all our necessary equipment. We assembled and started on foot our forced march. Our mission was an important airport which we had to reach by daylight. We did and took over.

It looked like Florida, palm trees and all. Heavy shelling, naval fire was underway. I stayed at the airport four days, in which Jerry bombed us nightly. I had nothing, not even a jacket, nights were cold. I slept in a beautiful building on the floor, no sleep as Jerry dropped flares and bombs. I saw my first of many German planes hit in the air and burnt into flames, quite a sight. Was a rough week, food was scarce, was hungry and tired. We got several German bombers at the field.

From then on we were at the front. We went many nights without sleep, many days not much to eat or drink, we moved at night. Dug in and started firing at daybreak many times. We actually moved up under the very nose of Jerry, into position while they shelled us. If it wasn't for a small foxhole I dug with my helmet and hands, I wouldn't be here now. I was actually turned over by the concussion of one bomb dropped on us which got a few men. I'm lucky so far. We began to notice the decline of enemy planes, although they dive bombed us and strafed us. I have one piece of lead that landed at my feet as one souvenir. We made our own roads, went through mine fields, only a few trucks got blown up. Our greatest fear was booby traps, bouncing babies we called them, which Jerry left in brush and when they went off, broken bones was about all you would get. They were made of cement with pieces of steel mixed in. Painful.

Along our way I saw hundreds of wrecked tanks, vehicles we had demolished. Also countless graves freshly and hastily dug. It was all mountainous, hills and valleys. The Germans had elaborate fortifications and machine gun nests, we nothing, but we kept pushing on. Went weeks without a bath, then when I did get one it was from a canteen of water in my helmet that did the job.

We kept on and finally the big day came, they gave up by thousands, into Bizerta we went. They even drove their own trucks loaded with men into surrender. It was a long time before their dead were buried. I saw some rather gruesome sights, which I won't mention.

On the way back I saw huge prison camps containing thousands of Germans and Italians, they were separated because they fight each other. Equipment of all kinds laying around. We had to police our area, never saw so much.

One of our missions was a hill or Gebel (Mt.) which the British five times before had tried to take and failed with heavy losses. We took it.

Someday you will realize why I'm happier to be an enlisted man than an officer.

Enemy planes by the dozens were still left at the airfields, many wrecked. I could go on, but I'll tell you more when I get home next year.

I wish some of the boys that I know would get a taste of this. It's no fun, but makes one proud. I am in a good outfit, hope I never leave it.

It is getting dark and I can hardly see to write. Days are getting hotter and hotter, nights are relief. My tent is home, have to crawl into it, but it's sure been a lot of protection for months now. Food isn't bad, but am always hungry.

So till my next letter I'll close. Mac is with me okay, tomorrow we both are going on pass. The French are swell. I received one-half pound package, did you send another? You can send a five pound package now. Hope you do. Need more blades, face powder and candy. A watch, ahem. Let anyone read this letter. Hope you can read it. Show it to Lois.

    Love,

                            Johnny

Corporal John Babbitt

"I got a pitiful letter from your wife, Soldier. You better give her an allotment after I pay you back that loan."

A cartoon by Bill Mauldin

★ ★ ★

Ray Salisbury served as a sergeant with the Ninth Air Force.

Somewhere in North Africa
July 6, 1943

Dear Sis:

Patriotism in its true sense is difficult to define. According to Webster it is the feeling of undying faith that one bears for a cause. It is the willingness of a person to die in defense of an ideal. In my case, and many others, I AM NOT WILLING TO DIE. Dead, I would be of no further use to the Government. They realized that a long time ago—which is no doubt why they spend millions of dollars training soldiers to do a job skilfully. I can really appreciate the careful planning and foresight that went into my military education. Teamwork, initiative, willingness, cooperativeness, timing, skill and courage are the only requisites a soldier requires. Of course, sometimes the timing is faulty, or some member of a chain doesn't cooperate and casualties inevitably result. But on the whole, this war is being run like clock work with the pleasing results you read about in the newspaper. But behind all these successes, major or minor the underlying factor is an individual's bravery and guts. One person can provide the spark that causes an Army to do unheard of things. That's the true spirit of Americanism. That's why we as a Nation will never be beaten! We can complain to ourselves, grouse about conditions and yell about anything or everything but when something comes up that needs everyone's cooperation the Americans are there to do it. Then they go back to their complaining . . . Just to witness the ingenuity of soldiers who aren't provided with the comforts of home, to see them make crystals for their watches out of a turret canopy—to watch them repair their shoes with nails made from carpet tacks. There are countless other things they do. They do not complain because they are without facilities—they make their own. . . . Here is where you get down to bed rock. Here is where you discover that you have pools of energy that have never been tapped—and because you live so closely with other men, YOU have to be a regular guy. I wouldn't miss the experience I have encountered for any amount of money. There's something new every day. . . . .

Yours,

Ray.

A fighter pilot with the Ninth Air Force enjoying
Christmas in April when he received gifts from his wife

★　　★　　★

At the time of writing, John M. Bennett was serving as a major assigned to combat duty with the 100th Bombardment Group, Eighth Air Force, and was a commanding officer of the 349th Bombardment Squadron. The group flew the B-17 (Flying Fortress) and while under Bennett's command received a presidential citation for their performance.

Dear Father:

There is an old saying which goes somewhat like this, "Cowards die many deaths, but a brave man dies but one." If this saying be true, then I am not only a coward myself, but I am fighting this war with a lot of other cowards. A story in the 8th Air Force tells about a group commander who read an over-zealous advertisement in a magazine which asked the question, "Who's afraid of the new Focke-Wulf?" This group commander cut out the advertisement, signed his name to it and pinned it on the bulletin board. After all of the pilots in the group had confessed their fear by signing, the page was mailed back to the U.S. advertiser. We are all afraid and only liars or fools fail to admit it. There are a variety of possible deaths which face a member of a bomber crew and each man is free to choose his own pet fear. A tire could blow out or an engine could fail on take-off. The oxygen system or electric heating system might fail at high altitude. There is the fear of explosion or midair collision while flying formation. In addition to these there is the ever present possibility of being shot down by enemy fighters or anti-aircraft fire. In dealing with the enemy, there is a certain feeling of helplessness about the bomber business which I find to be very distasteful. Imagine, for a minute, that you are required to carry two five-gallon cans of gasoline down a dark alley. These cans weigh over 30 pounds each so your hands are full and you can't run very fast. As you pass a certain corner in this alley, you know that a number of thugs are waiting to club you as you pass. However, there is a policeman patrolling this beat (your fighter escort) and if he happens to be at the dangerous corner at the time you arrive, then everything will be O.K., unless, of course, there are more thugs than the policeman can handle. Some of the thugs don't attack with clubs, but stand back (out of sight) and throw firecrackers at your cans of gasoline.

The bomber pilot can't fight back, but must just sit there and take it. I believe this explains why there is such a difference between the bomber and fighter boys. The men in this latter group can match their skill against the enemy. He carries a club of his own with which to fight back. I do not find the light-hearted devil-may-care spirit on the bomber station which has been so often described in stories about pilots in the last war. Our men go about their grim business with sober determination.

Major John M. Bennett. The medal is the Silver Star awarded to Bennett for leading the March 8, 1943, Berlin attack after the lead wing had been disrupted by fighter attacks.

When we are alerted for a mission, the bar closes early and everyone goes to bed. To be sure, at our monthly parties if there is no mission the next day, the boys get pretty drunk. I do not discourage this as I feel it gives them a much needed chance to blow off some steam.

When a new crew arrives on the station I try to have a talk with the men during the first 24 hours after arrival. One of the points stressed is that we are all afraid. I tell them that the worst part of a mission is just before the take-off. If they can "sweat it out" through this period, they will get through the rest all right. The flight surgeons are particularly helpful in spotting men who are showing signs of anxiety. If a crew goes through a particularly rough mission and is badly shot up, we try to send it to the "flak house" (rest home) for a week. In fact all crews are sent to the "flak house" for a rest at some time during their combat tour. Although I never find time to get to one of these rest homes myself, I am told that they are well run and very successful.

Winston Churchill's personal physician, Lord Moran, wrote a book about courage in combat. I like his definition of courage: "a moral quality . . . not a chance gift of nature like an aptitude for games. It is a cold choice between two alternatives, the fixed resolve not to quit; an act of renunciation which must be made not once but many times by the power of the will . . . Some men were able to see more clearly that there was no decent alternative to sticking it out to see this not in a hot moment of impulse but steadily through many months of trial. They understood on what terms life was worthwhile."

As leader of a group I am constantly inspired by the soldiers under me. Their heroic acts are always a challenge. I frequently ask myself what the men expect of me. Living up to what I think they expect and deserve is a driving force which is ever present. Another point which I always remember is that I asked to be sent to England and the 8th Air Force. My good friend Colonel "Chuck" Clark had warned me against it before I left Washington. Chuck had told me that this was the toughest of all theatres. Since I requested combat duty with the 8th Air Force, I am determined to see it through.

Although the losses in the 100th Bomb Group are high, they are by no means the highest in the 8th Air Force. The Century Bombers losses are nearly always spectacular. We might run along for four months with very low losses and then one day we might lose half of the group. This news spreads about the air force and men get the idea that we always have heavy losses. What the 100th lacks in luck it makes up in courage. The Men of the Century have fighting hearts.

Love,

John.

★ ★ ★

Captain Curtis C. Davis, who served as a combat–intelligence officer with the 324th Fighter Group, Ninth Air Force, based on Cape Bon, Tunisia, wrote the following letter. Subsequently, he served in the Mediterranean and European theaters as an interrogater of Luftwaffe flight personnel.*

10 August, 43

Dear Mom:

Your V-mail letter of July 16 just arrived, the latest I have received from you. In all, I should say I have had some 6 or 8 letters—probably all you have mailed to date. It takes about 20 days for your letters to find me now, chiefly because you are still mailing them to my *former* APO (3744). The correct one, the one I shall have so long as I remain with this outfit, is APO 485. Tho our mail ordinarily arrives twice weekly by plane—on Wednesday and Saturday—it has been out of kilter for the past two weeks . . . no mail at all. The men are becoming quite dispirited over it, as they always do when (a) mail is slow in arriving, (b) when food is not good. These two factors are the chief builders of the much-discussed 'morale' of the Army. I have written you to mail me some Air Mail envelopes like these,

---

* Other letters from Captain Davis appear on page 118.

since that is the best and fastest type of mail: well, from now on, do indeed write me *via* Air Mail, but forget about mailing me the envelopes. I can buy them here quite handily. Besides, any sort of package apparently requires at least 2 months to arrive! The town of Tunis is jammed with soldiers, chiefly American, but is far more lively than Tripoli. Although its port facilities have been precisely and thoroughly pulverized by Allied bombing, the rest of the city is untouched, with the result that the civilian population has largely returned, a few shops are open, and bars and eateries flourish. Wine, in enormous quantities at little cost, is the chief article of consumption by the soldiers. It is not very good, but it is potable; and there is no liquor. Three theatres are open, for the soldiers. Bob Hope appeared at one of them in person the day we left. All American Officers stay at a hotel sponsored by the Army, free of charge; meals there, the best in town, cost 40 c. French money exclusively is used, and we are paid in French francs (one franc: 2 c). Speaking of money, beginning with September, I have increased my allotment to $130 monthly. Since I receive 10% extra pay for overseas service, this means that I now earn $165 instead of $150, base pay. And $30 a month out here in the wilderness is much more than I need. My only expenses are paying the natives to do my laundry—an affair that takes place every ten days or so and usually costs me $2. Then about once a week Post Exchange supplies are flown in; and my share of permitted candy, toilet supplies, or what-not, usually sets me back $1 or so. So that, out here, I can spend about $15 a month if I try real hard. Of course, if I am reassigned to Interrogation and quartered near a large city, I shall need more money and may reduce my allotment again, but even then I believe I can manage quite well on $35 a month. On the way to the beach, we pass occasional dumps where are collected piles of Axis rubbish or ruined material; and most anywhere in the fields you pass a wrecked car or truck or, from time to time, see the slender snouts of the famous German 88-millimeter anti-aircraft guns sticking their forlorn noses into the sky. On our own field we are using a German Messerschmitt fighter-plane for occasional training flights. It was captured intact and has been repainted in our colors. I sat in its cockpit and went all over it with one of our Crew Chiefs (head mechanic). There is also in operation here, appropriately repainted, the equally celebrated German transport plane, the Junkers 52. This was the job that carried the German troops to Crete in their air-borne invasion of that island. Considerably inferior to American and British transport planes, the Junkers is a dead duck if it is caught by any of our fighters unescorted; and the pilots consider it little sport to go after a group of Junkers since it is too easy to shoot them down.

Give my love to Aunt Imma, and also to Maggie. But keep most of it for yourself.

Lots of love to you,

Carroll

John F. Kennedy's letter home was written shortly after his boat, the PT-109, of which he was in command, was sunk by the Japanese while on patrol off the Solomon Islands in August 1943.

Dear Mother & Dad:

Something has happened to Squadron Air Mail—none has come in for the last two weeks. Some chowder-head sent it to the wrong island. As a matter of fact, the papers you have been sending out have kept me up to date. For an old paper, the New York Daily News is by far the most interesting . . .

In regard to things here—they have been doing some alterations on my boat and have been living on a repair ship. Never before realized how badly we have been doing on our end although I always had my suspicions. First time I've seen an egg since I left the states.

---

* Another letter from Kennedy appears on page 90.

As I told you, Lennie Thom, who used to ride with me, has now got a boat of his own and the fellow who was going to ride with me has just come down with ulcers. (He's going to the States and will call you and give you all the news. Al Hamn). We certainly would have made a red-hot combination. Got most of my old crew except for a couple who are being sent home, and am extremely glad of that. On the bright side of an otherwise completely black time was the way that everyone stood up to it. Previous to that I had become somewhat cynical about the American as a fighting man. I had seen too much bellyaching and laying off. But with the chips down—that all faded away. I can now believe—which I never would have before—the stories of Bataan and Wake. For an American it's got to be awfully easy or awfully tough. When it's in the middle, then there's trouble. It was a terrible thing though, losing those two men. One had ridden with me for as long as I had been out here. He had been somewhat shocked by a bomb that had landed near the boat about two weeks before. He never really got over it; he always seemed to have the feeling that something was going to happen to him. He never said anything about being put ashore—he didn't want to go—but the next time we came down the line I was going to let him work on the base force. When a fellow gets the feeling that he's in for it, the only thing to do is to let him get off the boat because strangely enough, they always seem to be the ones that do get it. I don't know whether it's just coincidence or what. He had a wife and three kids. The other fellow had just come aboard. He was only a kid himself.

It certainly brought home how real the war is—and when I read the papers from home and how superficial is most of the talking and thinking about it. When I read that we will fight the Japs for years if necessary and will sacrifice hundreds of thousands if we must—I always like to check from where he is talking—it's seldom out here. People get so used to talking about billions of dollars and millions of soldiers that thousands of dead sounds like drops in the bucket. But if those thousands want to live as much as the ten I saw—they should measure their words with great, great care. Perhaps all of that won't be necessary—and it can all be done by bombing. We have a new

Commodore here—Mike Moran—former Captain of the Boise —and a big harp if there ever was one. He's fresh out from six months in the States and full of smoke and vinegar and statements like—it's a privilege to be here and we would be ashamed to be back in the States—and we'll stay here ten years if necessary. That all went over like a lead balloon. However, the doc told us yesterday that Iron Mike was complaining of headaches and diarrhea—so we look for a different tune to be thrummed on that harp of his before many months.

Love,

Jack

*C*aptain Curtis C. Davis* wrote the following letters from Cape Bon, Tunisia, and Italy.

26 Oct. 43
Tuesday, 12:30 pm

Dear Dad:

. . . In other amusement lines, we 4 officers had a collective date the other night. It was with 4 nurses from a near-by hospital, and it was my first contact with American women since leaving our ARC girls in Cairo. As a rule I consider nurses, generally, an uninteresting and certainly un-pretty group of women; but over here their Dun & Bradstreet rating is A-1 with the men. We drafted these kids from one of the numerous hospitals in this vicinity; and the bunch of us took off in one of our Squadron command-cars for the little village of Ferryville, about which I wrote in my last, for supper. There is a French Officers Club there which possesses a presentable dining room, a lounge, a bar, and Allied Officers may attend. In fact, we not only attend, but as is the gentle way of Americans, take over the joint. We

---

* Another letter from Captain Davis appears on page 114.

118

carried with us two bottles of Tunisian whiskey (a combination of carbon tetrachloride and fuel oil) and high hopes of finding more. Though I stuck chiefly to wine, the North African vino as the soldiers call it is nearly as lethal as its whiskey, with the result that I got good and sick. Not drunk, dammit, but sick. But this was toward the end of a pleasant evening; and we all had fun. Ferryville is little touched by war, the French Officers Club has a friendly atmosphere (particularly when seen thru the bottom of a drinking glass). There were officers of all branches about us, and merriment was unstinted. From a para-trooper I heard secret details of the landings on Sicily, and from everyone more rumors than you could blow a bugle at. All of which will make for sprightly narration after the war, but which the Base Censor would most certainly excise.

This was the first date my 3 fellow officers had had for months, so you may imagine what it meant to them. Luckily for me, I can speak French, and on my earlier trips into Tunis to take the Jerries to the POW camp, I had managed to scrape off an acquaintance here and there with a couple of kids in Tunis. I have also had a little luck this way in Ferryville, since I have had to drive over there frequently on squadron business of one sort or another. I early made it a rule never to bother with American girls over here if I could get out of it, for several reasons. For one thing, they are too besieged with offers to get a date at all. Again they speak English, while I enjoy talking in a foreign language. And lastly, I have the rest of my life to listen to American women. Tunis will remain in my memory as a very pleasant little town wherein I knew Marcelle and Lucienne, through whom I learned more about North Africa and its people than I ever should by going out with a nurse or WAC. (Yes, the WACs are in Algiers in force; and a recent ruling by the Commanding General of that area has permitted non-commissioned WACs to date officers, much to the annoyance of the nurses. All of whom are already commissioned.)

The boys of our sq. are amusing themselves these days mostly with poker. Games last often from 9 am until 11 pm and antes often go as high as $10. All of which of course is strictly forbidden by Army Regulations, but of course we do nothing about it. And more of these boys than you would suspect from that last sentence are sending home substantial money orders every day or so. Moreover, they are a lot happier when operating, rather than idle, as now awaiting activity. They write this home daily, and I believe them. I intended to write home myself yesterday aft. but one of our Corporals was writing an article for the Saturday Evening Post (God save the Mark) and wanted my help. Though this chap is over average in intelligence (he was principal of an Elementary School in Cal) his article "What Soldiers are Thinking" was so bad in every way it took me a couple of hours to tighten it up a bit for him. After 4 months of reading the mail of enlisted men I wonder that our secondary schools system is worth one quarter of the money the taxpayers put out for it. Of the 300 odd men in my sq. I have about 5 who write reasonably mature letters, perhaps 15 in all who write presentable letters, i.e., letters which according to the grammar book are correct and intelligible. Naturally, it is almost useless to look for such intangibles as Style or Individuality, or any epistolary sense. I have made a compilation of the cleverer or more amusing or unusually articulate sentences which I have found in the boys' mail over a period of a couple of months; and I intend to work it up into an article on some topic as "What the Soldier Writes *About*" or something like that. Since I find to my surprise that one of my class mates, Harry Shevelson, is one of the editors of Coronet, I think I'll mail the article to him, if ever I accomplish it.

As a Company Officer, most of whose time is taken up with considerations about his men's comfort, and not his own, I've learned large amounts about human personality, the bittersweet flavor of self-denial, the satisfaction that comes from squeaking something thru for the men, in one manner or another. Certainly, it takes your mind off yourself, and if you are a self-centered sort, does wonders against that failing. Naturally as a very Junior Officer, I don't have overly much constant contact with the boys, but I have a modicum; and during this move I have had even more. Here, for the first time, I am learning Camp life as it is lived by most of the Ground Forces all of the time; and I am coming into a much more detailed association with them than ever before. This is a very beneficial experience for me. The rich pattern that is human personality has become far more apparent to my eyes than ever before. More than ever I have come to realize the almost pitiful dependence of the unled mass upon the leaders; and I see with clarity the utter necessity for wise and constant guidance which people need in order to survive and progress. For our Squadron with its ills and aspirations is but a State in little; and you would be perhaps dismayed to learn, if my experience be relevant, how easily a State may be totally misled if its guidance be not thoughtful and alert. To live in the Army as an Officer over a period of months, in the field, is graduate course in the civics of Democracy.

All my love to you, plus several big hugs,

Carroll.

★

10 Nov 43
Wednesday
Somewhere in Italy

Dearest Mom:

. . . Paid a flying last visit to Tunis a couple days before we left Africa. It has blossomed forth most much. Many more small stores are opened, all the air-raid trenches in the main drag have been filled in, the streets swept up; and more crowds than ever throng the sidewalk. I went back to say good-by to my French acquaintance there, a local girl I've been going out with whenever I got to town; and also to see what, if anything, had been done about my transfer to Interrogation. It's still *en route*, 'thru channels'; and I am still praying, but fervently. And so, completely and finally, we watched the shores of North Africa drop away, one evening. It is unlikely that I shall ever see them again. To me, it was rather an awesome emotion to realize that one can, so neatly and so inevitably, snip away a vivid part of one's life. All the activities, the acquaintances, every familiar hangout and locale—everything that spelt Tunisia to us is gone with the abrupt finality of a change-of-scene in some movie melodrama. Now we are in an entirely different milieu, faced with a wholly novel set of surroundings; and I, for one, realize once more the almost shocking narrowness of man's life, the small meadow wherein he dwells, and tills his field, quite conscious of his individual importance—the lack of which he cannot well understand unless he can travel, as I do not, swiftly from one meadow to another. At the same time, I also understand now how small are distances in Europe, and how petite, after the War, will all global distances become. The transport plane will render the citizen of Cairo at home in New Zealand, and the native of Tunis will know well the streets of Baltimore, Maryland. I can state this so patly, because I myself have seen all these far quarters of the globe within 8 months. The more I travel, furthermore, the more I begin sadly to understand that Romance is a matter of the mind. These exotic names of such bright plumage go up in the soot of chimneys and the curbstone noises when actually you visit them. Though I shall never admit that there is nothing new under the sun, I must concede that the brave rovings of the young child's mind will take him into countries that do not appear in our geography. Everywhere he will learn, when he travels, that humanity is something of a piece; and in that sad discovery there will be an inevitable disillusionment. When Keats wrote of "the light that never was, on land or sea" and when Emerson described the far gleams of "The Fore-Runners" they both perhaps well knew that only in our mind's eye can we hope to see the Magic Mountain. For I found—now that I am away from them—that the green hills of Baltimore County beckon to me with all the lure I once felt for the Nile; and the blue horizons of the Great Smokies are ateem with as many a fairy as ever did the Carpathians contain. Which reflections prove all the more forcibly, to my secret pleasure, that being a romantic novelist (as is my ideal) is a matter, after all, of inborn hankering, not of outside stimuli. Which pleases me mightily, since I am of a hopelessly romantic cast of mind and have no desire to change . . .

So this letter wishes you the merriest of Christmasses, with the knowledge that we shall be together in spirit and heart, no matter where I am. And with the knowledge too, that the Allies and all who fight for them are 'over the hump' by now and on the down grade to a swift and ever increasing march to victory.

That is indeed enough to make this one a Merry Christmas.
Certainly, as I attend Mass Christmas Day in one of the large
cathedrals of some Italian city, I shall feel that the very fact I
am doing so—in company with Italian and American soldiers—
is in itself a blessed portent.

All my love, & many a kiss and hug,

Carroll

(Love to Maggie)

★

Friday, 19 Nov 43, 7 pm
Somewhere in Italy

Dearest Mother:

... Italy suits us all delightfully. We have set up a Squadron
barber-tent, in which two local barbers strut their stuff every
morning, at 5 c. a shave and 10 c. a haircut (at which prices they
are most pleased to work). Our own tent has a firm floor-board-
ing, plus a stove, on which we can boil water for our prepared
hot chocolate, or fry french-fried potatoes (bought from the natives). As we have only three of us tenting in it now—Dorger,
the Doc; Myers, the Armament Officer; and I—we have plenty
of room, with all our baggage under our eyes. We are well set up
for the winter. And these nights are cold, no mistake. We burn
close to a fruit-box of coal in our stove from 4 pm to 9 pm, when
we usually turn in. The only really bad thing about the cold
nights is that possibly, just possibly, you might have to get up,
out, into them and jump half clothed into a slit-trench if Jerry
came over. We haven't, however, had a raid since I wrote you
last: the German fighter-plane power in Italy is low indeed compared to ours. Local labor—which digs a slit-trench for a pack of
Raleighs—has made of them deep and capacious hide-outs
really deserving the name of air-raid shelter. Some are not so
well dug that the boys are joking, "Any trench deeper than 6
feet is not a trench: it's an AWOL". I have drawn from Supply a
pair of Winter Flying-Boots, intended for the pilots at high alti-
tudes, but obtainable by Ground 0s, too. These are thickly
fleece-lined affairs that zip up, over the ankles, and encase the

foot snugly in a rubberized covering that resists below-zero Ts. So, in any emergency at night, all you have to do is slip right into these, throw on your trench-coat and steel helmet; and you are all set . . .

It is most certainly not I who dislikes Donald Kirkley. He is the only movie 'critic worthy the title writing for a Baltimore' paper. And I thought his critique of *For Whom* hit it right on the nose. That picture would seem to exemplify the sickening Hollywood equivocation on matters of high moment if ever a dollar be involved therein—an equivocation shown with equal blatancy in the nauseating panegyric of Russia, *Mission to Moscow*. It is a deplorable trait in certain strata of Americans that they cannot keep their values, especially the ideological ones, clearly distinguished. To see *For Whom* on the screen, I am told, you would not know which side we were against. The side we are against, the Fascist, Franco, regime, the so-called 'Loyalists' who received the support of the Church of Rome, are our mortal enemies and, at this very moment, hold Vatican City within their palm. And yet the Holy Father can continue to issue bulls about the necessity for peace at any cost, and ask the Allies not to demand an unconditional surrender. With such talk no enemy of Fascism can hold a moment's thought. This is a war for keeps; and we will not rest satisfied until starvation and butchery have been visited upon German soil. There can be no parleying with the Devil. There is no such thing as a conditional victory; for then neither side is the conqueror, and the issue is still undecided. It is an all-or-nothing question and I for one trust that many a head will fall.

This matter-of-fact, hard-headed view of the war, together with an eye-witness' knowledge of some of the things it can *do* to people in these lands, results in an outlook that the American back home resents having forced upon him. He likes to think that we are sweeping on to a splendid finis, and that the going will not be hard. Which is the opposite of the truth. But which is the crap that we hear coming over the American short-wave stations every day. Which is perhaps why many an American soldier, certainly including myself, habitually listens to the British Broadcasting System. BBC tells you just what happened, including what we lost; and it does not lard all its programs with highschool adulations of the bravery of American soldiers. We don't need to be told these things. We are proud to know that they *are* true. The danger lies in the fact that such mouthings tend to make you think the Germans are *not* brave and able. Jerry is not only capable but clever. Some of the best dance-music on the air waves comes from *Deutscher Ubersee-Sender, Berlin,* to which we listen often. At least once, after a half-hour of good fox-trot and rumbas, a dulcet woman's voice, in perfect English, announced: "This dance-music, of the past half-hour, has been broadcast for your listening pleasure. It comes to you with the compliments of Your Enemy." That is smart propaganda. . . .

It is so good to have your letters, and to see your familiar handwriting once more. Now that I am off at a distance, and can look back, so to speak, I begin to understand more completely how much I love you and how much my life is centered about our sharing of it together. It has required half a world's circumference to show me that all the world, to me, lies in you and Dad. I have not always acted, in the past, as though I believed this, though I really did, because the nature of my work kept me from you for an enormous amount of time. As it did so, it threw me more and more onto myself, so that I came to be more and more a solitary goer. I used to prize such jaunty independence, but now I see that it was closer to isolation. Self-dependence is admirable, but to be selfishly self-contained is a paltry and circumscribed ideal. Life among hundreds of men, and work as an overseer of many of them, teaches me that existence for oneself alone is a *mean* thing. It is *not* enough. We are fighting a war to prove the fact.

All my love plus some kisses

Carroll

★ ★ ★

Lieutenant Colonel Russell Lloyd, 6th Regiment, 2nd Marine Division, wrote this letter to his wife from Tarawa. On November 21, 1943, the 2nd Marine Division invaded the Tarawa Atoll in the Gilbert Islands. One of the bitterest attacks in Marine Corps history, it lasted for two days, killing one thousand Marines and wounding two thousand.

29 Nov. 1943

Dear Mary:

Here goes just a note to tell you that I still love you and am still in one piece. I cannot go into any of the details but I'm on Tarawa in the midst of the worst destruction I have ever seen. You have seen pictures of city dumps and people living in holes or pieces of tin made into tent shaped huts. Well that is us and the dirt, dust and smoke is awful, however we are getting it

Lieutenant Colonel Russell Lloyd

Marines at Tarawa take a reinforced concrete pillbox used by the Japanese.

cleaned up. The other islands of the atoll are very nice. Warm, cool and comfortable.

Marion Wolbern said he would send you a note so I presume you have heard by this time that I'm in one piece. Saw Justin Henry IV yesterday when he was ashore here sightseeing.

The Battalion sure did a damn good job and I'm proud of them. Bill carried the ball and played a bang up game. His outfit was hit the hardest of any of this regiment.

Darling, I have been debating with myself on what to write or whether I should write it at all. However I have decided to tell you so that you can be on hand when the news comes thru. Please do not mention this to anyone if the news is not already out. Herb was killed the first day. He did not suffer and never knew what hit him. He died instantaneously like a man leading his troops. His last words were: "Come on, they can't stop us." I have had a headstone made for his grave which has the following on it:

When the one great scorer
Comes to write against your name
He will not write if you won or lost
But how you played the game
As Man, Father, Friend, Marine
Well done.

Please dear, take it easy and do not let it get you down. Betty will need your strength. I'll write her later. In envelope No. 2 is a letter to her written by Herb on 19 Nov. Read it and if you deem advisable give it to Betty. You will know best.

Again dear, take it easy and be as thankful as I am to still be with you.

All my love,

Bill

Aftermath of casualties and destruction following the savage battle for Tarawa

★ ★ ★

*F*ollowing the Tunisian campaign, Brigadier General Theodore Roosevelt, Jr.,* participated in the invasion of Italy. While there, he served as liaison officer with the French Expeditionary Corps and was representative in Corsica and Sardinia for Dwight D. Eisenhower.

December. 28, '43
[Italy]

Dearest Bunny:

I'm snatching a moment to write. I think it will be like that in the near future.

Yesterday some Americans gave me some coffee. They were members of a mortar company living in scooped out hollows in a muddy hillside where the rain stood in dirty pools. Their clothes were sodden, mud-stained and torn. God alone knows when they had last had a bath. When I came up to them they had just finished firing a concentration. I too was nothing to write home about, cold, weary and wet. It was the sergeant who recognized me under my disguise of mud and said "The General had better have a cup of coffee." It was made in a canteen cup over a tiny front-line stove. We sat in the rain and dripped, for there was not enough shelter for us and the stove at the same time.

The soldiers and I talked. We talked of the two things that form practically all a soldier's conversation—details of battle and home. We spoke of the battle first and then we settled down to Marysville, California, and the trout streams nearby—to a town in the peninsula of Michigan and whether the trout streams there were better. The sergeant from South Carolina said that trout were all very well, but how about quail in the scrub-lines and duck on a marsh. Then we turned to things to

---

* Other letters from Brigadier General Roosevelt appear on pages 77, 100, and 152.

eat, steak, ham and corn—clam chowder suggested by a New Englander.

Can you wonder I'll always remember that sergeant and think of him as the man who gave me coffee?

I've been up in the snow and it's cold. Where I've been the snow is wet and the wind sweeping down from the mountains cuts like a knife. It's not bad for me for I don't stay there all the time, but it takes something to be a G.I. dough there.

I'm sure I wrote you that some months ago I was made, with proper ceremony, a corporal of a company in one of the French regiments. I went up with this company the other day. During an attack it distinguished itself. The Lt. who commands it has been wounded severely in the war and now is unbelievably gaunt, with eyes burning deep in their sockets. He seems fey. The chief of the section (squad) of which I'm a corporal has been

Soldiers check the mail lists of Christmas packages.

desperately wounded. He's a big half-breed. I gave him my four-leaf clover to bring him luck. He talked to me with the nervous clarity of the man just hit before shock takes effect. They gave me the insignia of the 85th German Infantry, the troops they attacked . . .

Ted.

* * *

*L*ieutenant General James Doolittle wrote the following letter to his son, a cadet at West Point. At the time General Doolittle was commander of the Northwest African Strategic Air Force.

31 December 1943

Dear Son:

I am sincerely sorry that the results of your exhibition show egotism and indifference have finally overtaken you. I cannot sympathize with you as I feel no sympathy for you. Sympathy is reserved for those whose sorrow results from no fault of their own. I can, however, offer you some encouragement. You have the courage, character, determination and intelligence to solve your problem if you will. The first thing to do is to impartially analyze the cause of your difficulty. Next decide to correct it and then exert every effort mental, physical and moral to the accomplishment of your objective. You will have to exercise care in your self-analysis as there is a strong tendency to give one's self best of it. You will have to want to succeed in your undertaking more than you ever wanted anything in your life before and you will have to try harder than you have ever tried before. It is always much harder to correct a bad mistake than to make it. The Lord, in his infinite wisdom, has probably arranged it that way so we won't make so many. Honest regret is salutary. Remorse is strong medicine and should be taken in small doses if at all. Self-pity is a sign of weakness and must not be indulged.

Son, you have been penalized about one year in the game of life for stupidity. It is now up to you to strive sufficiently to make up that loss during what is left of the "game". I know you can do it and, fortunately, when you do you will be a better and a stronger man through having had the experience.

As ever.

Lieutenant General James Doolittle

1944

Mail Call

The letters always just evade the hand
One skates like a stone into a beam, falls like a bird
Surely the past from which the letters rise
Is waiting in the future, past the graves?
The soldiers are all haunted by their lives.

Their claims upon their kind are paid in paper
That establishes a presence, like a smell.
In letters and in dreams they see the world.
They are waiting: and the years contract
To an empty hand, to one unuttered sound—

The soldier simply wishes for his name.

RANDALL JARRELL

Lieutenant Will Stevens wrote the following letter on the eve of his departure for overseas duty in Europe.

[January]

Dear Mom:

You are sitting in the rocker beside me as I am writing this letter. You will remember me as I am at this minute and on many lonely evenings you will wish I were here again.

You will cry because I cannot be with you. You will recall most of the things we have done together in the last few days. You will wonder why we cannot be together. You will question the sense of the entire war and nothing you decide will be of any great consideration.

Remember this, Mom, when you think back on this night. Remember me as your little boy, if you want to—you will do that anyway—but remember it is for your security, in your rocker by the heater, remember that it is for the pleasure of sitting at home and writing letters, remember that it is for the folks uptown, and for the millions of girls like [*name deleted*] that this going-away business is done.

It's not for you and not for me—it's really for us that I must go, and it's for our own happiness that this war must be pushed to a complete victory.

Remember, Mom, that I am where I want to be because I feel that I may help in my small way. Don't worry about me, because worry will not help.

This war is bigger than any of us and it is going to take something big to end it. Many men will never know if we win or lose, but if anything does happen, I'll try to be good enough so I can meet you somewhere else and maybe we can have a cake together up where things are not rationed.

★

Lieutenant Stevens was killed in action on June 25, 1944.

★ ★ ★

*B*eaumont Newhall served as a major with the Joint Target Group Headquarters, Army Air Forces, attached to the Fifteenth Air Force. His wartime job was extracting from aerial photographs as much information as possible about the activities of the enemy. He wrote this letter to his wife in New York City.

Major Beaumont Newhall

San Severo, Italy
2 Jan. 44

Dearest,

... And now Churchill says that 1944, April I think he mentioned, will see the climax of the war in Europe. Let us hope that his prediction—coming as it does from one who should know as well as any person can—is true, and that the climax will be the end as well. For we all want to get this business over and return. The most frequent toast on New Year's Eve was: "Here's to next New Year's Eve! May we be together again, but in the States, and with our wives!"

It was, for us, a quiet New Year's, although there was merriment and festive drinking available, we preferred to refrain from gayety.

Our boys (i.e. enlisted men) gave us officers a party, as a return for the Christmas (dinner) we gave them, and there was wine and turkey and, best of all, real ice cream and cookies—made by local chefs with materials supplied by us.

Two episodes on New Year's Day warmed my heart. The first was the purchase of charcoal stoves. The Major (Pollock, our commanding officer) had asked me to get hold of eight stoves for the billets, and I found several days ago a shop where they could be had. But there were none ready made, and I was asked to return on Saturday, after the holiday. So I went there on foot, hardly expecting that any would be ready. The proprietor of the shop was just closing up for lunch. I told him, in my faltering Italian, that I had come for the stoves. I couldn't understand his answer, but I gathered that he wanted me to follow him, for he waved his hand vigorously at me—which, confusingly enough, is the come hither gesture of these people. We walked around the block, up an alley way, to a green door. He knocks. The door swung open, and we climbed up a very steep flight of stairs to a large room which was divided into a living space and a work space by a curtained partition. There he had a dozen or more braziers. I made a date with him for two o'clock, when I would return in the jeep (which I called "little auto"—automobilino). Hank Berry, a fellow officer, and I drove the jeep over after lunch. No sooner had we entered the room than chairs were placed for us around the flat, circular foot warmer—a brazier at least two feet in diameter, heaped with glowing coals, and with a wooden ledge on which to prop your heels, while the soles of your shoes fast became fairly toasted by the fire. There was the brazier maker, pater familias, his wife, and four boys around the table. Glasses were filled, refilled, and then filled again, almonds were shelled for us, and they prayed that we might eat some, saying, as they passed the plate, "Prego, prego" (I pray, please, that you take some.) Mama brought out some candy, made of cocoa and almonds, and we were given oranges. I did my best to carry on a conversation with these good people —it was tough going. I felt embarrassed and tongue-tied—but, with their willing help it was at least sustained, and we all had some good laughs. "I spoke only Italy. It is most kindness of you to gaving wine with us, it am much good." I suppose that's how I sounded if our places were reversed. The old man encouraged me: "Excuse me, sir. You speak all right. By and by you'll speak well. Now it is by the book. You asked if I had 'stufe' (stoves)— I knew what you meant, of course. But these I make are 'fornacelle' not 'stufe'."

They were so hospitable, so obliging, so anxious to please— sharing their food in the most friendly fashion. True, the refreshments were local products and not dear. But the mean living quarters, cold, damp, cheerless except for their laughter and the glowing coals and the amber wine. Two sons, lieutenants— both prisoners of war. We had to make more than one determined effort before we could leave—a glass for the road was insisted upon, and they couldn't let us carry even one of the stoves down those steep stone steps into the jeep.

The second episode occurred just as we were finishing dinner —a pick-up meal of turkey scraps, canned corn, coffee, cheese and pineapples. The kitchen help, Italian kids in their teens, put on an impromptu song fest. A little fellow, in rags and tatters, standing not more than 4' 6", sang like a bird, filling the room with a voice that hardly seemed to belong to him, and with an assurance and stage presence of a mature professional. The others joined in the chorus. Then there was "O Sole Mio" and "Santa Lucia" and local songs of strange rhythm and tempo, not a little oriental. It went on, one following the other. Songs so funny that the singers had to laugh, solo songs accompanied by the others in imitation of the instruments of an orchestra. Done with spontaneity, naively; sung to us as a thank you for the jobs they have and for the food which we have given them. It was a moment which to me was more religious than formal church service of a week ago, and I longed for you, for you would have been gripped by the loveliness and unexpected beauty.

    Love,

                                                B

A drawing on V-Mail stationery
by Sergeant William Josvai to his mother

★ ★ ★

Geddes Mumford served as a private first class with the 363rd Infantry Regiment, 91st Infantry Division. In 1947 his father, Lewis Mumford (author of Technics and Civilization, The Culture of Cities, *and many other books), wrote* Green Memories, *a biography of his son, from which this letter is extracted. Private First Class Mumford wrote this letter from training camp.*

Private First Class Geddes Mumford

[February]

Dear Mother and Dad:

The fat-headed calf has finally gotten to writing the long miss-ing letter. Life here at Adair has been one heck of a mixup. Inspections, new equipment, firing new weapons, packing equip. in waterproof boxes, getting lectures on silence and se-curity and what all else you could think of. We even have the new ten-inch bayonet which looks more like an oversize knife; also trench knives which have eight blades, leather washer han-dles, and which personally I don't like. Anyhow, this looks to me like the real thing. Those knives and short bayonets aren't for training. I however wish you (especially you, Mother) would stop worrying about it all. My training as a soldier is plentifully sufficient for me. It might have stood some city bred lad a little short, but I'm sure I know at least as much if not more than most riflemen here. My only deficiencies lie in the technical, complexities of message center. As far as worrying about my getting killed, this is foolish. I have no intention of doing any-thing but returning. Most men get killed in battle because they forget to take cover or make some such tactical mistake. I'll make no mistake like that. I don't know if you remember the passage in Captain Ingersoll's book about the Rangers. They lost more men in training than they did in combat. You would do better to be happy that you, I, and all of us are alive than to be worried about the day when one of us is dead. To me death is a thing to be left alone. It comes when it is least expected and there are no ifs and buts about it. Once it has happened nothing could have stopped it. I know I'm not very clear but I hope you get a little of what my feelings are.

★

Geddes Mumford was killed in action between Septem-ber 12 and 15, 1944, in Italy when his company was spearheading the attack on the Gothic Line near Monti-celli.

141

★　　★　　★

*James McMahon served as a staff sergeant
with the 93rd Bombardment Group, Eighth Air Force. While in
the 93rd, he flew on missions with the 329th and 409th Bombardment Squadrons. He was wounded on his second mission
to Berlin on June 21, 1944, when his plane was hit several times
by direct bursts of flak. The plane made a forced landing in
Sweden, where McMahon stayed until December, at which
time he returned to Britain and was then sent back to the
United States. A good friend and fellow crew member delivered
the following letter to his parents in St. Albans, New York.*

March 10, 1944

My Dear Parents:

This letter will introduce my best buddy Bill Nelson. I was on
Captain DeMont's crew with him. I will now give you some
information that I *don't* want you to pass on to anyone but . . .

10.18.43. My first raid was a diversion over the North Sea.
We had no fighter escort and got lost and ended up over Holland
(Friesian Islands). I saw my first enemy fighters, four ME-109s,
and they shot down a B-24. It went into a dive and no one got
out. The next raid was Wilhelmshaven on Nov. 3rd (1943). The
sky was overcast, but we bombed anyway and did a good job. I
only saw one other B-24 go down. My next raid was Bremen on
November 13th. About 10 minutes from the target I noticed our
waist gunner was unconscious and appeared to be dying (which
he was). Immediately Captain DeMont dropped down to 5,000
feet and headed for home. The waist gunner (Erderly) was dying
from lack of oxygen and frostbite (57 below). On the way home
he came to and when we landed he went into the hospital. That
day Freddie's ship and two others from our squadron went
down. One of the waist gunners on his crew is safe but we
believe all others are dead. It was over the North Sea they went
down and you can't live more than 10 minutes in that water.

Well, my next raid was Kjeller, Norway, November 18th. It
was cold as hell and Bill will go more into detail for you. No

flack but coming out we were about 50 miles from land and the Jerry fighters jumped us. There was about 25 or 30 (maybe more) twin engine jobs. JU88s, ME 210s, etc. . . . Well, Bill got the first one, and then things popped. Our tail gunner Ray Russell got the next one and then (I was on the right waist gun) one popped up out of a cloud and tried to draw a bead on us. I shot his left engine off and killed the pilot and it went down in flames, its wing falling off. Bill in the meantime is having a party for himself. I looks over to see how he's going and he is firing so long at one of the bastards that his bullets are coming out red hot. He kills the pilot of this one and shoots the left wing off, and down goes number four in flames. In the meantime 12 B-24s get shot down, but then the fighters leave us and we pat each other on the back. Boy what a day. Man did we have fun. Well on my next raid, Kiel Dec. 13th, I was engineer riding the top turret. The flack was bad, but again the cloud cover was with us and we didn't get any holes. On the way home the two inboard engines almost conked out from lack of gas and I had to put all systems on cross-feed (very dangerous). The reason I did this, the transfer system was FUBAR. The next day the crew chief told me that in 5 more min. we would have crashed. I resolved then that I would never be an engineer (1st). That is why I am not a T/Sgt. The responsibility is too great.

Dec. 31st. St. Angeley. Again I went to Kiel. This time as a waist gunner. My ship was in the low element flying in "Coffin Corner". The weather was perfect over the target and we didn't even see any flack till we opened our bomb bay doors. Then all hell broke loose. The sky turned black with flack. Our control cables were shot out on the left hand side, and our 4 engine was also shot out. The top turret got about 20 holes in it, and also the nose turret. The bombardier was hit in the throat (he recovered). All at once I was knocked down as something hit me in the back. A piece of flack was sticking out of my jacket. I was so scared by now that I could hardly stand up and I couldn't see as the sweat was running into my eyes. The temperature was 45° below too. Well, we went into a crazy spin and I was halfway out of the window when he pulled it out and we headed for home. We almost didn't make it. The fighters stayed a way out and didn't attack us. After this raid my nerves were so shot I could hardly write. We were under artillery (flack) fire for 12 minutes that time. It is the most terrible experience you can have. It is just like going "over the top" into an artillery barrage. I saw 2 ships blow up this day, and one go down by fighters. It makes a guy so damned mad and you can't do anything about it.

1.7.44. Well I figured I'd better go on another raid damn quick or I'd never fly again so, 2 days later I went to Ludwigs-haven. It was wonderful going in, and we had plenty of fighter protection. Coming out after getting our 4 engine shot out and plenty holes in the ship, we figured we'd go to Switzerland. We decided we'd better stay with the formation (which we now lost) two groups of 24s. Well we headed for home (without our fighters) and ended up at Paris. It is a very pretty city. Well then

Sergeant James McMahon

all hell broke loose. About 150 of the Goering Sqdn. (Abbyville Kids, sometimes called the yellow noses) hit us with everything they had. I got some pretty good shots at them and am pretty sure I hit a few of them. Well, our right wing man pulls out and blows up. Then our other wing man pulls out and goes down in a spin and blows up on the ground. All around us they were blowing up, going down in a dive and in spins. After an hour of constant attack the fighters leave us and later I find out that we lost two and the other group lost 10. All because of a damned lousey navigator. I hope he goes to hell. This raid was the 7th of January. They picked on our ship because we had one engine shot out. Our bombardier and the other waist gunner got one FW-190 apiece. This raid cured my case of nerves and put me back in the groove.

2.20.44. Well my next raid was Gotha. It's a wonderful trip. I was in the nose turret and I didn't even see a burst of flack. This raid is a milk run. Too bad they can't all be like that. Well now comes the next one. This one will slay you.

BERLIN! on the 6th March. I was in the tail turret and we were high element and "coffin corner". The sky was perfect, no clouds, which meant the fighters were going to come up and the flack would be accurate. On this raid I should have been as nervous as hell, but I thought of Thom, Henn, Fred, and all the fellows I had seen go down. I figured if I came back, O.K., but if I went down it would be for Thom. Gee I felt glad. Well, all the way in to the target the flack was bad, and the Jerry fighters sure played hell. Our fighters sure gave them hell too. Well I didn't get any more shots at fighters till the target. I saw one FW-190 shoot down one of our planes which went into a dive and went straight down. Then all hell broke loose. The flack was terrible and the fighters everywhere. The group right behind us was catching hell with fighters (FW-190s) and I got in about 10 squirts at them. We kept flying through the flack and made two runs on the target which took about 20 minutes. All this time I can see Berlin, and man there are 24's and 17's all over the place. I see our bombs hit smack on the target and my heart bleeds for those damned Krauts down there. Well after that for 100 miles I can see the fires and smoke. It looks like all Berlin is on fire.

Boy do I feel good. I'm laughing like hell for some reason. I guess it is because I am still there. Well after I get back to base (after squirting those Jerry fighters all the way home) I go to sleep and dream of Thom. All the time over the target I was thinking about him and Dad and Mom and Sis and . . . Everything was going through my mind at once. I sure feel good, 'cause we knocked the hell out of them. We didn't even get a scratch on the plane either. And that sure is something for the books. By the time you get this letter, I will probably have 5 or 6 more raids in, but I will explain them to you myself. I want you to promise that you will not tell about anything in this letter. Except maybe that I've been to Berlin. I am sure proud of my record. 9 times over the target and 7 times deep into Germany.

I want you to know that if anything ever happens to me that I think I have the most wonderful and courageous parents in the world, and the most beautiful and wonderful sister on this earth. I am proud of you all and my brother Thom . . . God Bless you all and keep you safe. I'll come back. I can't say I know I will, but I have as good a chance as anyone. Give my pal Bill the best you've got, 'cause he's the best the E.T.O. has. Let Joe take him down to Eddie's and give him plenty Scotch. He was raised on the stuff. God bless you. I hope this letter gives you an idea of what Bill and I have been through. So long. Hope I see you soon.

Your loving son,

Jimmie

*T*hree days prior to writing, Lieutenant Colonel Jacob Bealke* arrived in Britain with the 3rd Battalion, 358th Infantry Regiment, 90th Infantry Division, to prepare for the Normandy landings.

---

* Another letter from Lieutenant Colonel Bealke appears on page 166.

April 12, 1944
Somewhere in England

Beloved Lady,

Have not as yet received a letter from you since arriving here. Hope you didn't stop writing when my letters stopped coming, in the belief that you had to wait for a new address. If you did, it will be a long, long time before I get a letter, and I'm very anxious to hear from you and find out how you and the kiddies are getting along. Hope your letters have not become lost. Hope I get one tomorrow . . .

The British people seem very queer to us, and I suppose we seem just as queer to them. The dark blouses and pink trousers of the American officer have been a source of great wonder to them. They can't understand why we don't wear coat and pants that match. Being too polite to ask, they conjecture among themselves about it and arrive at some curious answers. One of them, overheard and reported by Capt. Burns, was that the American officers were too poor to buy trousers that matched their coats.

So many things have happened to me, I have come so far, travelled across an ocean, and been so busy in the past months that your lovely little house at 108 Elm St. seems to belong to another world which I visited a long long time ago. The whole U.S. now seems to be a highly desirable dream which is way out of reach. There are so many of the . . . ordinary everyday things of the American way of life that I miss a great deal. Funny papers, magazines, cokes, just any one of the million and one things that we accept as the usual thing are gone, and I have suddenly realized that I don't know when I'll see them again.

That wonderful, wonderful week that we spent in Trenton and New York seems like a dream too. I wish I could have that dream again. It has got so it is hard for me to realize that it was actually me who took you to theaters, and held you close and kissed you. Only the most terrible form of torture could for Schicklegruber repay me for what he has done to us and what he has done to us is only a drop in the bucket of the total suffering he has caused. I love you, my dear girl, and I want to come home to you in the very worst way. I love you.

Bill

★ ★ ★

First *Lieutenant Teddy Shaw served with the*
748th Bombardment Squadron, 457th Bombardment Group,
Eighth Air Force. He wrote this letter to a young neighbor back
home in Jacksonville, Florida.

May 5, 1944

Dear Jack,
Glad to hear you are working hard at your school studies. That
is the spirit if you want to fly after you graduate. It must be
drawing near vacation time so you are probably getting ready for
your final exams. Get in there and pitch and I'm sure that the
results will be good. Your desire to fly makes your studies the
most important factor of your school work but don't forget that
knowing how to work is not good enough, you will have to learn

First Lieutenant Teddy Shaw

how to relax also. When you are in the classroom forget everything but your studies and when you are playing forget your studies and just have a good time. Sports are not only a good way to rest after a hard day at school but they help develop a healthy body so necessary to a pilot. They make you think and act faster and the one who can find the other's weak spot and hit him there is always the victor. So you see that it takes a strong mind and body as well as a strong ship. Over there we play for keeps and when it is a game in which you win and live or lose and die you want to be well trained in every way. You do not realize it but you have already started to learn to fly. You started when you learned that flying is the one thing you wanted to do most. Even now as you learn more and more in school, you are getting closer and closer to the day when you will be sitting up there above the clouds in your own ship looking down at the guys who are earthbound. Some of your friends may say you don't have a chance or that school is a waste of time, they may laugh at you and tease you but always remember that they are either lazy or jealous of you, and it may seem to you that sometimes you'll never get those wings, but you will someday have the last laugh. We are picked men in the Air Force. The best the Army has, no matter what anyone says. We know it is true and we're proud of it. Don't sell those Navy pilots short, either—they're good, not only as men but as fliers. If they were not they would not be where they are today.

The Army and Navy don't have time to wait on you. You either make it or you don't and if you're not good enough you lose those wings. Yes, even after you get them you can lose them. You may not believe it but I am still going to school. It cost the Army over thirty thousand dollars to give me my training to get my wings and they are spending quite a bit every day after that on my further training. I have an airplane worth over three hundred thousand dollars and the lives of nine men besides my own whose lives no amount of money can buy. All these are trusted to me and everything depends on our combined skill to do our job and get back safely. So you see I cannot sleep or daydream during classes. My mind must be clear at all times. My crew trusts me with their lives and obey commands without question. The time it would take to explain an order might mean life or death for everyone. I, in turn, trust my life to them and carefully consider even the smallest of their suggestions. I am their hope of returning after the war is over and they are mine. We are a team—we think, act, and talk as one. We are fighting for the right to live an American life and I think that I have the best crew ever assembled. They come from all over the country; east, west, north and south. But all of them are just the

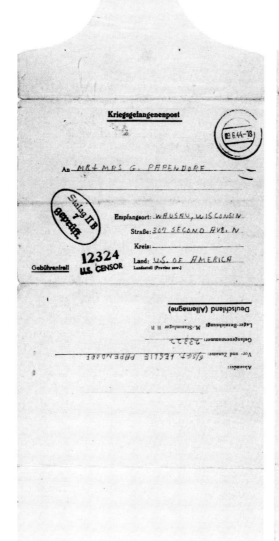

average American. My ball turret gunner is only nineteen, not much older than you. We call him Junior, but he is a man of experience. Even though we kid him a lot, we all are glad to have him with us. He can write his name with his twin 50 calibre machine guns and when he puts his sights on a target, it's just too bad for that target. Let me know how you are getting along and let's have more letters. Take it slow, and may you have smooth landings.

Your pal,

Teddy.

★

Lieutenant Shaw was killed in action in a raid over Weimar, Germany, on August 11, 1944.

*The 100 millionth V-Mail letter to come out
of the European Theater of Operations
was a short note by General Dwight D. Eisenhower.*

Example of letter form provided by the Germans for prisoners of war

★　　★　　★

After transferring to Britain in April 1944, Brigadier General Theodore Roosevelt, Jr.,* was named deputy commander of the 4th Infantry Division. Although he was suffering from pneumonia, he managed to lead a wave of assault troops onto Utah Beach at Normandy on D-Day, June 6, 1944, becoming the first infantry general to land.

June 5th

We are under way. The time is short now. What the future holds for our enemies or us as individuals, no man knows. All afternoon the ships have been steaming east and then south. The sea is covered with them—convoys of many types, going at different speeds, one passing another, all timed to arrive at their rendezvous. And we're only a part. There are other convoys crossing at other places. The Great Armada that sailed these waters was but a group of ships compared to this gigantic effort. Every quarter hour brings its alarums and excursions—unidentified planes approaching or unidentified ships.

All are tense—and all are pretending to be casual. Bravado helps. We had some proclamations read over the loud speaker, pompous declarations about "liberty" and "rescuing the oppressed." Afterwards I spoke a few sentences of plain soldier talk to buck up the men. God has been good to me—far better than I deserve. Whatever may come we must remember this. Take very good care of yourself. Remember that should anything happen to me you are all the children and grandchildren have which they respect as an authority which has only their interests at heart. Never worry for fear what you may do is not what I would have done. It will be better than what I would have done.

Darling, we've been very happy together—and Q.'s marriage

---

* Other letters from Brigadier General Roosevelt appear on pages 77, 100, and 129.

has shown us that the children understand the things we felt were important.

Much, much love. I pray we may be together again.

Ted

★

June 11–44

Dearest Bunny,

Well, here I am writing you from an orchard in France in the long twilight of a June day. Our planes are droning overhead, a battery of artillery is firing just the other side of the hedge and the ripple of machine-guns punctuates the silences between the salvos of the artillery.

To go back several eons to the time I last wrote—five days ago. At 1:30 a.m. I was standing in the dark with the shadowy shapes that formed the boat load with which I was going. At the signal we climbed into our craft which was still on the davits. The ropes whined through the pulleys, we landed on the water and cast off. It was rough and spray burst over us, soaking us to the skin and leaving us shivering with cold. In the darkness the boats circled in their rendezvous stations, cockswain calling to cockswain to gather the different waves and sort them out. Then began our long run to the beach—the transport area was some fourteen miles off the coast.

For some three hours we jockeyed and pushed toward shore and then the naval bombardment began. In the dusk flashes came from the big ships as the great guns were fired. Gradually it became brighter and I could make out on all sides the craft of the flotilla—most were our small landing launches with the assault troops. There were also destroyers on our flanks, rocket ships with racks for their rockets and many smaller craft— L.C.S.S.—land craft support ships with m.g.s to run close to the shore and fire.

Now we began to make out the low line of the shore—revealed by the flash of the explosions as the naval shells landed —and now German shells began landing among us, sending up towers of spray.

Suddenly we heard the drone of planes, and silhouetted against the colored clouds of dawn formations of planes swept by and passed toward shore. Flight after flight dropped its bombs on the German emplacements. There'd be a ripple of thunder, blazes of light, clouds of dust, and the planes would pass us again on their way home. One fell by me, flaming like a meteor. We passed a capsized craft, some men clinging to it, others bobbing in the waves. The little boats were now going full speed, slapping the waves with their blunt prows. As we peered over the gunwale the shore seemed nearer, but veiled as it was in the smoke and dust of the bombardment it was hard to make it out. Suddenly the beach appeared before us—a long stretch of sand studded with wire and obstacles. Then with a crunch we grounded, the ramp was lowered and we jumped into water waist-deep & started for the shore. We splashed and floundered through some hundred yards of water while German salvos fell. Men dropped, some silent, some screaming. Up the four hundred yards of beach we ran—Grandfather puffed a bit—then we reached the seawall. The Company C.O. with whom I was, Lees, a great tower of a man, led his troops splendidly. He with his men started into the dunes to attack the German strong points.

The moment I arrived at the beach I knew something was wrong, for there was a house by the seawall where none should have been were we in the right place. It was imperative that I should find out where we were in order to set the maneuver. I scrambled up on the dunes and was lucky in finding a windmill which I recognized. We'd been put ashore a mile too far to the south. That meant I had to hot-foot it from left to right and back again setting the various C.O.s straight and changing task. Fortunately it meant little change in plans. Stevie of course was with me, devoted and competent as always, his tommy gun ready to defend us if it became necessary. We set up a tiny C.P. with my radio behind the wall of a house. The radio never worked for nearly three hours. Most of our work was done on foot.

As the succeeding waves landed I pushed them inland if they halted and redirected them when they started wrong. Shells con-

Assault troops of the 8th Regiment, 4th Infantry Division, move onto the continent of Europe, June 6, 1944.

tinually burst around us but all I got was a slight scratch on one hand. The day gradually wore on. More and more landed. Our ships shifted their bombardments to the flanks.

Then Gen. Barton arrived and we set up our C.P. in earnest. By this time the immediate beach was cleared of Germans and the soldiers began to push their way inland over a flooded area about two miles broad. This had been inundated by the Germans by damming the streams. Through it the hedges stood out and occasional houses. Our paratroops had been landed on the land side and had put out most of the German defenses there or we never could have got across.

I must have walked twenty miles up and down that beach and over the causeways. Towards afternoon I went inland myself. Everything was in wild confusion still. It always is on a landing. Soldiers were everywhere. Occasionally groups of prisoners would pass, dishevelled, dirty, unshaven. There was the continuous rattle of rifle and m.g. I managed to see the three regimental C.O.s. All were well set and confident. My sole food was a cake of D Ration chocolate but I did not feel hungry.

By this time the Rough Rider was ashore and Stevie and I

were set. When night fell and we got back to the Division C.P. I was delighted to find Show with the quarter-ton trailer. That meant our bedding-rolls. I was still soaking wet & shivering with cold. I did my old trick—took off shoes and socks and went to bed in my wet clothes. At the end of the three hours sleep I was dry.

Next day we were battling forward. Incidents have come & gone like flashes of landscape seen from a train. We took towns and strong points. We took hundreds of prisoners. We have had alarums and excursions. Counter-attacks have driven us back.

Much Love,

Ted

★

Still seriously ill, General Roosevelt continued to lead his troops on the Normandy battlefield. This strenuous exertion proved to be fatal, and he died of a heart attack at a field camp near Meantis on July 12, 1944.

★ ★ ★

*P*rivate First Class Thomas Raulston served *with the 506th Parachute Infantry, 101st Airborne Division, during the Normandy landings. The outfit parachuted into France around midnight of June 5, 1944. Raulston was wounded on June 13 and evacuated to a hospital in Britain.*

[June]

Dear Dad and Annie:

I am fine and dandy. The Red Cross and some British outfits are doing wonders for all the fellows but I want only one of two things—the old outfit or home. They need all the old men back in G Co. It would be nice to be home but after seeing everyone and a date or two, I'd want to come back. How the guys at home can lift their heads is beyond me. Of course there are a lot of things in combat that a man doesn't like, but several times I felt the same as when a debate got hot or before a football game. All in all my experience has been worth all the trouble and fears. Our outfit was the very first to hit France 6 hours before the beaches were stormed. The flight over was strange, the plane was dark except when someone lit a cigarette, then you could take a quick glance at white drawn faces. There was very little talking at first but when a guy did say something, it was very far from the jump. I don't think the boys were frightened, in fact they could and did talk over the prospect of doing the job ahead. You know me and how lazy I can be, it got the best of me and I slept a bit. The door was being removed when I woke up. The red light was on by then but in the confusion of standing up and hooking on it wasn't so noticeable. Standing there with the plane bucking things became real. The red light gave everything a sullen glow. The men didn't look like men but rather huge machines, small men look huge with their equipment on, a steel pulled low, chin straps high and the red glow on all skin, can change a man, we weren't flesh and bone at that moment but hard, cold things of precision. Then there was the door, a black exit in our little world, all of a sudden the night became alive with red, yellow and white flashes and streaks of light; among

Members of the 82nd Airborne Division are given V-Mail blanks to write their last letter home before taking off from Britain to participate in the Normandy invasion.

these tracers, one could notice the burst of explosive ack-ack. I prayed then most of the guys did; it wasn't much of a prayer but a very sincere one. Over and over I said "give me guts".

We might have been there for 5 seconds or 5 minutes before the green light came on and our officer screamed "let's go!" Our stick had 8 leg packs (will describe a leg pack—it is of heavy canvas about the size of toe-sack, it fits on the front of the leg and rests on the foot with two quick release straps on it. After the chute opens you pull the release and let the pack down by a 30 foot rope, the top of the rope is tied to a harness strap. One falls much faster but when the pack hits the ground and its weight quits pulling, you almost stop and thus your landing is much easier. My pack had a 20 pound battery, 24 pounds of rockets, a 20 or 30 pound field bag, my shovel and a few bits of personal equipment). These leg packs make the stick much slower and for 6 or 7 seconds the door kept grasping the men before me and throwing them down. When number 4 hit the door, or about that time, we hit a thick spat of ack-ack and the plane did a fine Irish jig. The floor was jumping and we could hear a drum-drum on the plane, like when birds crawl on a tin roof. Just as I hit the door the plane rocked in such a way as to throw me from the door. I had to drop the static line and leg pack rope and grab the door. In pulling myself out I went down head first and the opening shock was as easy as being hit by a truck. A quick check proved that I had no leg pack, whether the darn thing was shot off, blown off by the prop or just couldn't take the opening shock, I'll never know. We jumped too high and the trip down took a thousand years. My straps were twisted (proof of bad body position) and I couldn't slip or turn. The sky was still full of those streaks of death. It would have been beautiful if we had been in the mood for an early 4th of July. A river began to take shape below and then before I could do anything I made my first river landing. Hit right on the edge and my chute pulled me well up on dry land. You can guess how sweet that ground felt . . .

Give my regards to all.

love,

Tom

★ ★ ★

William Preston served as a corporal with the 743rd Tank Battalion, 1st Infantry Division. The following letters to his family in Southampton, New York, are extracted from an anthology that Corporal Preston's father privately published in 1950.

France
June 21, 1944

Dear Dad:

This being fifteen days after the fateful June 6th, I am free to discuss what happened to me of a military nature on "D" Day. Here goes.

You remember from my last letter I said we were the assault wave which was the first to touch down on the beach. Then followed a day I shall never forget.

As has already been mentioned in the papers the landings wcrc made at low tide. There were three rows of obstacles to get through. These were above the low water mark, but under water at high tide. Therefore we had to get through them before high tide. This we were able to do with the engineers' help, and our own guns.

Corporal William Preston

In front of us were cliffs, and to the right there were two exits from our beach through the cliffs to higher ground. Both of these were mined and defended heavily. In the cliffs were a whole series of underground fortifications, mostly inter-connecting machine gun nests. These played hell with our infantry and engineers as they came through the obstacles. Some never got through, some fell and were claimed by a rising tide, but others slowly worked their way past the high water mark to the base of the cliffs. It took real guts for these boys to advance. Ernie Pyle in his column said it was a miracle a foothold was ever established. Perhaps he's right. I know at times I thought we had had it. There were some 88's in open emplacements which could have ruined us, but shortly after they started to fire a shot from a destroyer put the one near us out of action.

I cannot say enough for the Navy, for the way they brought us in, for the fire power they brought to bear on the beach, for the coordination between us. Whenever any of us fired a burst

U.S. troops with the local belles in St. Marne du Mont, Utah Beach, June 7, 1944

of tracer at a target, the destroyers, standing in so close they were almost ashore, fired a shot immediately after us each time hitting what we were firing at on the nose the first shot. It was amazing and plenty encouraging to have those big shells pour in there. It might have been a different story without the Navy boys. Meanwhile we were sweating it out on the beach unable to move off of it because the engineers could not clear the way out. All this time not a single German plane in the sky. Nor did we see many of ours, I guess they were further inland. I expected a counter attack all the time we sat there like ducks unable to move forward or backward. We knew something wasn't going right. We were never supposed to be on the beach so long, yet I never considered the fact that we could fail, that we wouldn't soon get off that terrible strip of sand. Time flew by, before I realized it the tide had risen, fallen, and risen again. Night was approaching.

The infantry said they were thankful we were there, the feeling is mutual. Without them we would still be on the beach.

The Germans adopted old Japanese custom. There were snipers everywhere. The country is very wooded, the foliage extremely thick. The result, perfect concealment for snipers. They also hid out in buildings as well as tying themselves in the trees and took an inevitable toll before they were sought out and destroyed.

Some of the women civilians tried their hand at the same trick. Apparently having acquired a slight Nazi veneer from their associates of four years. They would wave and flash the "V" sign, then take a shot at your back. They didn't last long. I spoke to some French people who live on the coast; they said the hun had been at his station for three days before we landed. During which time they were confined to their homes. This may, or may not be true. Whether they were expecting us momentarily is anyone's guess. There was certainly plenty of opposition. Farther in a woman told me the boche was terrified and sick of the war in that town, that the soldiers had broken their rifles and run away before we entered the town, that one of the officers had taken a walk to never show up again, that others changed into civilian clothes to disappear. That garrison's age was from 20 to 27, most of the soldiers being forced into service from Poland, Russia and there were even Mongols (very few). Definitely not the fanatical young Nazis we'll probably meet later on.

"D" Day evening we bivouacked about a mile in, still not feeling quite secure, as there were not visible an over abundance of troops. There was no counter attack, no bombing, no artillery fire that night on our positions. Others had seen to that I guess, a few Nazi planes came over but focused their attention on the shipping. Anti aircraft barrage was magnificent to watch.

So ended "D" Day. I shall never forget that beach, it was some way to start combat, but I am satisfied we did a good job.

I need catsup and mayonnaise, if it is possible to get and send them, for we get our own meals with vegetables added from French gardens, and these brighten it up no end. Those small boxes from Altman's have begun to arrive, they really hit the spot, please order another set after this runs out.

Also would you send me the Life magazine with the story of the Invasion in it and subsequent issues, if they have good stories and pictures of the show. My love to all, please write soon.

Much love

Bill.

★

France
July 1, 1944

Dearest Phyll:

That was a truly wonderful letter, yours of the 11th and the 12th one which I read and reread. One really lives for letters from home out here. It's hard to express but mail gives me just that much greater desire to come back from each succeeding skirmish with the enemy, and it is never ending because you are always expecting more. Before you go you think to yourself you must come back this time because there are two or three letters you still haven't received. So you come back, receive and answer them and the whole thing goes on again.

You know I heard so much about the changes war makes in people, that they return so different after combat. "D" Day then

*An Army private writing a letter in a foxhole a half mile from
the Normandy beachhead*

should certainly have changed me, because I saw as much then
to make me cynical, bitter, irreligious as I may ever see at one
time, and yet today I find that I am just about the same person I
was before it all, with the same philosophy, the same hopes,
sadder that what happened did have to happen, but wiser because of it. To me now, dead men, especially enemy dead bring
no emotion whatsoever. I was a bit shaken at first, but I soon
became hardened to seeing the worst of casualties with no feeling because in the beginning I had a curiosity which made me
see everything, so now I am not affected. When I see an American soldier I get angry and sad that here he should have died so
unnatural a death. I wonder about him, what were his plans
never to be fulfilled, what fate brought him to that spot at that
moment, who was waiting for him at home? Yet there is not too
much time for such idle reflection.

Horrible as this was, has been, I think we both have benefited in some small way from it. I don't think there is much we won't be able to adjust to in the future. I think we've learned how important it is to be open minded, to ban silly prejudices which contribute so greatly to warping your viewpoint on life, how important not to criticize until you know the whole story, which makes criticism difficult because it is so seldom we ever do know the whole story. I believe we've learned to appreciate things we might well before have taken for granted; that the present is important to a degree that we should not miss one chance to make it a happy present yet not to a degree that we live for it AND IT ALONE. We have found things out that I for one might only have learned after long years, and therefore, life cannot but be richer and fuller for our whole family.

The "Battle of the Hedgerows" continues as near to jungle fighting as anything I can think of. The small open fields surrounded by thick bushes and trees on all sides are only traps for the unwary, and as there are hundreds of these small meadows, so there are hundreds of traps to be sprung before the enemy is beaten. It makes advancing agonizingly slow, nor do I ever feel more like a goldfish in his bowl than when we advance across these fields from hedgerow to hedgerow. There is absolutely nothing in the books which covers this type of fighting. Every advantage of terrain lies with the enemy.

Sorry this letter isn't up to par. I think this rainy weather did it. My best to Tal. Love to the family,

Much love,

Bill

★ ★ ★

Corporal H. W. Crayton wrote the following letter to the parents of Raymond Hoback. Sergeant Hoback served with A Company, 116th Infantry Regiment, 29th Infantry Division.

Cpl. H. W. Crayton
6657549 A.S.N.
453 A. & C.
A.P.O. 230
c/o P.M. N.Y.C. NY

July 9, 1944
Somewhere in France

Dear Mr and Mrs Hoback:

I really don't know how to start this letter to you folks, but will attempt to do something in words of writing. I will try to explain in the letter what this is all about. While walking along the beach D-Day plus 1 I came upon this Bible and as most any person would do I picked it up from the sand to keep it from being destroyed. I knew that most all bibles have names and addresses within the cover so I made it my business to thumb through the pages until I came upon the name above. Knowing that you no doubt would want the book returned I am sending it knowing that most Bibles are a book to be cherished. I would have sent it sooner but have been quite busy and thought it best if a short period of time elapsed before returning it.

You have by now received a letter from your son saying he is well. I sincerely hope so. I imagine what has happened is that your son dropped the book without any notice. Most everybody who landed on the beach D-Day lost something. I for one as others did lost most of my personal belongings, so you see how easy it was to have dropped the book and not known about it. Everything was in such a turmoil that we didn't have a chance until a day or so later to try and locate our belongings.

Since I have arrived here in France I have had occasions to see a little of the country and find it quite like parts of the U.S.A. It is a very beautiful country, more so in peace time. War does change everything as it has the country. One would hardly think there was a war going on today. Everything is peaceful and quiet. The birds have begun their daily practice, all the flowers and trees are in bloom, especially the poppies and tulips which are very beautiful at this time of year.

Time goes by so quickly as it has today. I must close hoping to hear that you received the Bible in good shape.

Yours very truly,

Cpl. H. W. Crayton

★

Raymond Hoback was killed in action on June 6th, 1944, at Omaha Beach along with his brother Bedford, who was serving in the same outfit.

★　　★　　★

*A*t the time of writing, Lieutenant Colonel Jacob Bealke's* regiment, the 358th Infantry, 90th Infantry Division, had linked with Patton's Third Army and was driving west to capture the Brittany Peninsula and open the ports in the region.

France
August 4, 1944

Dearest Butch:

Here it is another line to let you know that I'm still around and about. The going has been good lately, as you have seen in the papers. We have covered a lot of ground. The reaction of the French people where we are now is much different from the people where we were first. The first place it didn't seem to make much difference to them whether the Germans were still around or not. Here the people hate the Boche—they are so glad to see us they are almost a nuisance. Every Frenchman seems to feel it his duty to shake hands with every American soldier he sees, and since they can't remember too well, sometimes they shake hands with the same soldier more than once. Especially when they dig up some of the wine they had buried and hidden

---

* Another letter from Lieutenant Colonel Bealke appears on page 146.

from the Germans. As we marched along the road the people threw flowers to the men, and some of them handed eggs to the men as they walked past. Eggs are highly prized items—they really add a lot to our K rations diet. They can be fried with butter in a mess kit when there is time for such, or they can be boiled in a canteen cup and eaten at odd moments between bullets and all that sort of thing. . . .

I wish I could be with you. Those pictures sort of look like the promised land. I hope I can get there soon. I love you, Butch mine, sure do hope this war ends soon. I want to come home.

Your

Bill

A private receives news announcing the birth of his son.

Two French children receive gum from a paratrooper.

★ ★ ★

*M*ajor General Andrew Bruce* commanded
the 77th Infantry Division from May 1943. He wrote this special letter of condolence to the widow of Colonel Douglas
McNair, who served as chief of staff to the general. His father,
General Lesley McNair, had died several weeks earlier. At the
time of writing, the 77th Division was on duty in Guam.

APO 77, C/O POSTMASTER
SAN FRANCISCO, CALIF.

14 August 1944

Dear Freda:

I am writing the same letter to Mrs. McNair and to you. First
let me say that when I heard over the radio of General McNair
being killed in action I stopped all communications to Douglas
and after I heard it verified later at the 7 o'clock p.m. broadcast,
I called him into my tent and told him of the radio news. He
told me many things . . . how he loved his father; how worried
he was of the effect on Mrs. McNair; and he repeated over and
over again to me, "Don't let them send me back, I want to
fight." Fortunately, as we were fast friends, I was able to get him
to let down, and give way to his grief for awhile instead of
keeping it bottled up. After an hour or two, he decided to go to
bed and his last statement to me that night was, "Don't let them
send me home, I want to do my bit out here." Let me say here
that while his grief was intense, his one object was to keep going
in order that he might help defeat the enemy.

I watched for the next two or three days to see if I could help.
I gave him all of the work that I could find for him to do and
kept him very busy. About August 5th the work lightened a bit
in the rear areas where I had kept him most of the time. He
went forward to see the regiments on the afternoon of the 5th

---

* Another letter from Major General Bruce appears on page 257.

and when he returned after dark, about 7:30 pm, I spoke a bit sharply to him to the effect I was worried as to where he was and that I wanted to be kept in touch with his movements by radio. To be perfectly honest, I was mentally hovering all of the time like a father and when I was worried I spoke sharply to him like a father would.

On August 6th, he asked me where I wanted my new CP and I gave him a general area but said that I didn't want the forward reconnaissance detail consisting of himself, the headquarters commandant, the signal officer, etc., to go until I was sure that the road from Finegayan to Liguan was safe. I told him that I thought he ought to take two light tanks with him. He demurred and I said "Alright, but you must stop at Finegayan and let me know what the Marines think before proceeding further." At 12:40 pm I received a message, "Marines think Liguan area not clear." I answered "I am sending you two light tanks to Finegayan. Wait for them there." About 1:20 pm, he sent me another message, "May we leave guide and proceed. Time's awasting." Finally I received a message from him, "Tanks have arrived, on way". My next message from him was, "We are with (a certain battalion, using code name). Will join regimental commander when road clears. Country thick." This was at 4 pm, August 6th. At 4:45 pm, I received a message from Major Mc-Kithan, "(*Code name for Col. McNair*) has just been killed by enemy sniper. I am returning to CP with remains."

It is needless for me to say that I was stunned. My alter ego was gone. I could not comprehend it. I was in the midst of planning for the next day's action, which was the biggest action we had on the island, and I had to finish the plans in order that the troops would be informed in time. I would not let myself think of him at the moment. About the time all of the orders were issued they brought him back to the CP. Funeral services were conducted by the Chaplain (Major) Horace M. Taylor on August 7th and he was interred in Joint Army and Navy Cemetery No. 5. I must tell you the truth, as much as I wanted to I could not leave the combat zone to be present at the services but I assure you I was there in spirit.

I refused to talk to anyone about him and this is the first

time, in my letter to you, that I have done so. I do not want to dwell on my loss because it is so small compared to yours. But let me say that night when I looked across to his tent, dug in the ground, with the words "Chief of Staff," and saw it empty, I thought my heart would break. I knew that no one could ever replace him either professionally or in my heart. He was so calm, so square, absolutely devoid of any favoritism towards any faction, unselfish, so devoted to the cause of his country, and so morally unafraid of doing the right thing that it is hard to give an adequate description of what he meant to me. I have questioned Major Cutting and Sergeant Alfred Cauley and this is what I understand happened after he had passed safely over the road I was concerned about. He came to a small clearing near a road, where over 4,000 troops had passed. While they were going over this clearing with a view of locating different elements of the Command Post, the sergeant observed someone in a grass

Major General Andrew Bruce

hut, which was about 50 yards to their right. The three went around to the left of the building when Colonel McNair said, "Follow me." Colonel McNair and Sergeant Cauley went around to the entrance while Major Cutting covered the flank and rear. Colonel McNair approached nearest to the door opening and fired four or five shots. Colonel McNair then said, "They are in the corner, fire on them." So the sergeant fired 8 rounds, reloaded and fired 8 more. A grenade was thrown and the sergeant yelled. "Down, Chief, grenade." The grenade proved to be a dud but some Japanese fire came in and when the sergeant got up he saw that Colonel McNair was in the prone position and had been killed instantly by a shot in the throat. It afterward proved, when they were destroyed, that there were three Japanese in the shack. I am recommending him for some medals. I know they will not replace him but at least they will be a proud memory for his daughter. His effects and other details have been handled according to Army regulations and will eventually reach their proper place.

If there is anything that I can do, please do not hesitate to call on me.

A. D. Bruce
Maj. Gen., U.S.A.

★ ★ ★

*A*t the time of writing, Richard Kennard* was a first lieutenant in K Company, 3rd Battalion, 5th Regiment, 1st Marine Division. Acting as a forward observer, he saw active service during the Peleliu and Okinawa campaigns. His letter is chosen from a collection of more than two hundred that he wrote to his parents. All are highly significant because of their uncensored nature. As an officer, Kennard managed to escape the restrictions imposed by censorship and sent letters home exactly as written.

---

* Another letter from First Lieutenant Kennard appears on page 190.

September 25, 1944
On the island of Peleliu

Dear Mother and Dad:

This is D-Day plus ten and my first opportunity to write and
say that I am alive and well. You want the details, so here goes:
On D-Day this island was blasted by the most terrific amount
of naval gunfire and air bombardment that was ever given to any
piece of enemy territory. It was a wonderful show as seen from
the landing boat I was in a thousand yards off shore. The island
is surrounded by a wide coral reef, over which the LTVs (am-
phibian tractors) transported us after we changed into them
from the transport ship's Higgins boats.

I landed with the battalion executive officer at H plus 120, a
half hour late. So many amphibs were knocked out on their first
run into the beach that succeeding waves were late coming in. I
saw no dead Japs on the beach—only dead and wounded Marines. The Nips had taken off to their caves and pillboxes in this
island fortress. The smoke of battle was so thick I could hardly
see ahead of me. I spent the morning and afternoon of that first
day with the company commander of an assault company advancing south down the island. While in a mangrove swamp I
received a radio message from my colonel to move across the
island and get into position to register the artillery on a certain
spot. This meant leaving the unit to which I was attached. Our
team struggled along and suddenly got pinned down by sniper
fire. We were exhausted, and as I felt that I had myself and FO
team out in front of the lines of the adjacent attacking battalion,
I decided to move back to where we first hit the beach. We got
there at 6:00 pm and fell into a large crater utterly exhausted.
All night long there was firing of small arms, and the beach was
under constant shell-fire from the enemy's mortars. The Japs
kept themselves and their weapons hidden in the coral caves in
the hills, where no kind of gunfire can get them out. How I lived
through that night is beyond me, when so many men were hit
by shrapnel from the mortars.

D-Day plus one I got out of the crater where we had spent
the night and started to go back to my unit when my radio man
was hit by flying shrapnel. He was evacuated. The infantry had

172

First Marine Division at Peleliu on October 7, 1944. Tanks and infantry assault Japanese positions on a Peleliu ridge.

First Lieutenant Richard Kennard

been forced back during the night, so I tried to get up the beach in the other direction to our CP. It took me two hours to go four hundred yards, the enemy mortar barrage up and down the beach was so terrific. I was always able to seek a deep trench in the sand, and fortunately no shells landed on us, though many were killed and wounded not more than ten feet away from where I was lying. At the battery position, which I finally reached at noon, we took off our packs and rested. I took my men down to the beach two hundred yards away from the battery to see my CO, and while there, the Japs laid down a heavy mortar barrage on H Battery. Two guns were knocked out, many boys wounded and killed (I can't mention figures). The 105 ammo blew up and everything was destroyed there. My pack burned up completely, with the New Testament Marilyn gave me and all the pictures of her that I was carrying.

Because G Battery lost two of its guns when the DUKWs* sank on the way into the beach, it combined with the two remaining guns left from H Battery. D+2 and D+3 I spent in the southern part of the island with the men not needed on the guns as a reserve for the infantry outfit. We set up beach defenses and killed quite a few Japs who tried to counterattack our line at night.

On D+4 I went to an OP with a new FO team up in the coral hills. There for two days and nights it was a perfect hell. The temperature was 134 degrees, no shade at all, and the Nips were continually shelling us on the top of the ridge I was on, or shooting their machine guns. I was under sniper fire continually, and let me tell you, it is an awful feeling to have those bullets whiz past your head. I still don't understand how I could have gone through all this without being hit, when I was deliberately shot at so often. Many boys near me were hit by sniper fire or shrapnel from the Jap mortars, which could never be located. During the night I had to observe and direct fire three

---

* DUKWs were four-wheel amphibious vehicles, able to propel themselves through the water and then travel at truck speeds on flat ground or roadways.

different times, and once while doing so, a Jap sneaked up the ridge and was about to crawl into our CP. I woke up two men near me and we opened up on him. He sure looked good stone dead the next morning. I hate to think what would have happened had that Jap had a chance to throw some grenades in on us. Of course, I never slept while on OP, for it was too dangerous. After two days of hell on "Suicide Ridge" or "Bloody Nose", as the hills here are called, I came down to the southern part of the island and had a good night's sleep and a day of rest.

Then I was sent up to the hills again with another FO team four days ago. I forgot to say that while leaving the OP where I had spent two days, a Jap sniper shot one of my men in the knee. While carrying him out on the stretcher and almost to safety, he fired again. The bullets went right through my legs and hit one of my other men in the ankle. I got them into a medical jeep safely and sent them off to the beach. All casualties are evacuated to the hospital ships off shore.

Today I came down from the awful coral hills after three days and dangerous nights up there as the FO. There were more

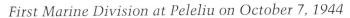

First Marine Division at Peleliu on October 7, 1944

wounded and killed when the Japs shelled the ridge this morning. None of us were hit this time, thank God. I have my fingers crossed every minute up there in the front lines, and pray each night that I won't get hit. For the present, I have been relieved by another officer and FO team. In a few days, I suppose, they'll send me up there again, but I hope most of the mopping-up process will be over with by then. I'm lucky to be alive and uninjured now, after going through what I have tried to describe to you. We have the airport and all south of the hills. It just seems impossible to get the Japs out of those coral caves, though, and I don't know how the problem is going to be solved . . .

War is terrible, just awful, awful, awful. You have no idea how it hurts to see American boys all shot up, wounded, suffering from pain and exhaustion, and those that fall down, never to move again. After this is all over, I shall cherish and respect more than anything else all that which is sweet, tender, and gentle. This has been the toughest fight in Marine Corps history. We have won an excellent, important airfield, and I am proud that I have been able to do my part in taking the objective. The war on this island isn't over yet, however, so I still have my fingers crossed and keep very alert and careful. I am doing my best for you all at home who count upon my safe return, someday soon, I hope. You may take excerpts from this letter, Dad, but I don't want anything printed publicly at all.

> Much love to you all
> (Your son and Lynn's sweetheart)

> > Dick

* * *

Sergeant Thomas Giordano was aboard a transport ship en route to Peleliu Island when he wrote to his son in honor of his fourth birthday. Sergeant Giordano was a member of Island Command attached to the 1st Marine Division.

October 1944
At sea

Dearest Tommy:

Life is full of disappointments as you will later discover, but let's take these disappointments as one of the factors of life and strive to look ahead to the days when we can overcome them. My present great disappointment is in not being with you to celebrate your 4th birthday.

You're certainly growing fast as I know from Mommy's reports; also growing sturdy, strong, and intelligent. Mere words cannot express the pride that swells my heart at the thought of you on this day. As you know, this separation and our present circumstances are not of my own volition, but rather brought about through the inability of mankind to follow the precepts of God. I sincerely hope that what we do out here will insure that in your days ahead some means may be developed to bring

Sergeant Thomas Giordano and his son

all mankind back to the fold. Furthermore, to grant you the opportunity and privilege to romp and play throughout each day with your children, and to beam with pride and satisfaction as you watch them blow the candles on their day of days.

I know that Mommy will endeavor to the best of her ability to make your 4th birthday a memorable one. I feel confident she will succeed. She has been both mother and dad to you for this past year and her efforts are manifested in your sterling character. I know you are co-operating with her and doing your share to make us both proud of you. Please continue to do so, and soon I'll return to take up where I left off following the pattern of not just the father and son relation but the friendliest of pals that will rival Damon and Pythias.

Today all my dreams, thoughts and plans revolve around you, I pray that the Good Lord sees fit in blessing us with the fulfillment of all these dreams and plans.

I love you more than life itself and I know you are possessed in your own little way of this same zealous love towards your Mommy and I. Take care of yourself and be the man of our little family in my absence. Love and honor your Mommy always and some day your rewards will be great. I trust that your birthday meets all your expectations and anticipations and that you and I, with Mommy, will be together to celebrate many many more of your future birthdays. God bless you and keep you well. Farewell until we meet.

Dad.

*K*eith Winston* served as a private first class with the Medical Detachment, 398th Infantry Regiment, 100th Infantry Division. He wrote the following letter to his wife in Havertown, Pennsylvania, en route to France.

---

* Another letter from Private First Class Winston appears on page 251.

At sea
[October]

My dearest Darling:

I received your letter, written after you were convinced I was going over, and your reactions were identical to mine. You know, dear, I never realized that my family would be the only thing on my mind when leaving. I knew it would be uppermost, but surely I felt I'd be thinking of the boat ride—would I be seasick—where in God's world were we headed—would I ever come back. And once on the boat I was sure I'd be constantly worrying abut the crossing hazards—the subs and mines.

But strangely enough none of that seems to bother me—in fact I'm hardly concerned.

The only thing I can think of now is that every day and every mile on this boat takes me farther and farther away from you and our boys.

On the day we were leaving—I don't think any of us realized the significance of it too much. We all seemed to be rather

Private First Class Keith Winston

numbed by the final turn of things. It was weird—not until retreat, when the National Anthem was being played did the actual impact hit me—and I realized I was leaving my homeland, and that this would be the last time I would hear it—for a long time—on native soil. And for the first time I knew well what the Star-Spangled Banner meant to one who was leaving his country. And it hit hard. Another thing that touched me deeply was the warm way the Red Cross handled us as we were ready to march up that gangplank. What a wonderful feeling to know that somebody cared—even strangers—and on hand to say goodbye. Besides the liberal refreshments, each of us was given a large pouch with a number of useful things in it.

It was good that we had discussed the probability of my leaving when I was last home. And the clue that I would give you if I couldn't call you, so I was pretty certain you would 'see through' the bouquet of roses I wired home. I felt so damn helpless, being so close, yet unable to talk with you. But as I think back, maybe I would rather have said goodbye as we did—I shall never forget you as you stood outside the train window. You were so beautiful, so refreshing a sight, and such a pleasant thought to look back at.

There's absolutely nothing to do on ship. We sit on deck when and if we find the room—no comforts whatsoever. If I'm not talking with someone I'm thinking of you and the children, and yearn and yearn and yearn, and as I realize the ship is taking me farther away from you, it becomes unbearable. I've read your letter over a number of times—the one I received on ship—and being the only real 'home touch' I have among my possessions it means so much to me. While I'm thinking of it, mail me copies of those two pictures I like so much of the three of you.

★

Another Day

Oh, dearest, they go so slowly, and I miss and love you more than ever before. Just read your beautiful letter again, and each time I read it, it touches me just as much. I was thinking of Neil and David today. How much I'm proud of Neil's maturity, and what a little gentleman he's becoming, and praying and hoping

I'll get home before David learns too many words. Just as you say, "Thank God I have Neil and David"—and I say the same, as just thinking about them gives me so much pleasure, and pain, perhaps . . .

From what I can see, the small percentage of officers on board have as much room as the combined troops. I have not seen one, solitary chair where an enlisted man can sit down to write a letter. He sits on deck or on his bunk to write. I tell you this since it's about over and you need not worrry—but it has aroused a resentful feeling, not only within me, but in everyone around me. I wonder if things like this come under the heading of military discipline (officers are not to mingle with enlisted men—to instill respect and dignity). If this is so—that thinking is way off base as it has created the exact opposite effect, a complete lack of respect for the officers and the System. I could say much more—but what's the use. I doesn't bring us any closer (in spirit), and to me that is the main purpose of our letters. . . .

On this deck where we're packed like sardines, and this is no idle simile, I have to stand to write you. However, the spirit all around seems to be pretty high—what with the sight of land, a beautiful day, and the calmest of waters. Activity on the deck consists of roving from place to place looking for a place to sit (no chairs, as I've said—just a small empty space on the floor) reading and card and dice games. When and if I lay my hands on a periodical I read it from cover to cover, advertisements and all. Lately, I've gotten a kick watching the dice games, which at times run to pretty high stakes. The gamblers have plenty one day, and nothing the next. I'm thinking of one who just cleaned up $225, but yesterday he dropped $250, and that's how it runs. Don't have the slightest desire to get into a game, but watching them is one means of passing the hours. I've become friendly with one of the boys, Harry, who was in the old rifle outfit with me. He's 29, unmarried, a graduate of Boston U., native of Boston and a very likeable character. He, too, likes to gamble, and whenever he wins he insists I hold some of it, so when he's on a losing streak, he won't lose it all. So far the plan has worked well because each day he can start again with what I've held from the previous day. Watching him, I've realized more than ever what a wonderful wife and family can mean to a man with the difficulties we're now facing. Thinking of you, praying for you, waiting for you and loving you means more than anything in this world to a man. That is something I have and thank God for it. He doesn't have it—and misses it. He's written to about 20 girls, many of which he knows are probably going steady with men, but craving feminine contact, writes them. As he asks me to edit them all, I can get a pretty good idea of what he's thinking (between the lines). So you see, with all our heartache, we have something we should derive a great deal of happiness from. . . .

I love you,

Keith

*M*anny Krupin, an Army sergeant, wrote the following letter to his family in Los Angeles.

France
October 4, 1944

Dearest Mom and Pop:

For Yom Kippur I was allowed to attend services in a nearby city. This city dates back to 400 B.C. No chaplain being available, a sergeant in the audience conducted the service. He did a fine job. The finishing touch was a short but very realistic talk by a Catholic priest. There were about five hundred or six hundred fellows present. The reception the priest received after his talk would have shaken any and all idiotic prattle that people of different faiths can't cooperate with one another. It was truly a heart-warming event. Upon the close of the services, we left the "Hotel de Ville" (French for City Hall) and started to examine the city and its beauty. At the foot of the steps was huddled a man, woman, a girl of 12 and one of 17. At once it was apparent they were Jewish. Rather shyly the man approached me (probably because I was the first to descend from the Hall) and in Jewish told me, this was the remains of a proud Jewish settlement in this town. For the past month he had hidden in the nearby fields with his family to escape from the Nazis. His plight was a repetition of tales we have heard: children forced to live with soldiers either as mistresses or servants, then killed; parents just wiped off the face of the earth. The Nazis had left this town just seven days previously. This family lived in Paris before the war, were quite well read and well mannered. However, their plight was becoming unbearable so they began traveling, trying to evade the clutches of their pursuers. Each town and village was meeting the same systematic search for "undesirables". Four years of this hounding has had a great effect upon these people. The effect can't be described in words. One has to see it and, rest assured, it becomes engraved on one's mind. My own background had taught me, and I had also seen persecutions of racial minorities, but the thoroughness of this plot surpasses one's wildest imagination. The man asked if anyone was going back to Paris. He wanted to go and see if his home was still intact.

From among the crowd of boys someone shouted: "Let's start a collection to help this family get started." Need I say more? This family though destitute and hungry, refused to take any of the money we offered, protesting we would need it. After several hours of bickering the fellow who led the services convinced the man and he accepted it. However, as he accepted, I witnessed a scene that really tore at one's heart. Both the man and his wife began to cry and I don't believe I'll ever forget that scene.

Manny.

Arnold Gates served as a sergeant and troop clerk for the 27th Cavalry Reconnaissance Troop. He was also a unit combat correspondent, troop historian, and librarian. He wrote the following letters to his family in Cleveland, Ohio, from the island of Espirito Santo in the New Hebrides.

6 October 1944
Somewhere in the Pacific

My dear folks:

This afternoon I received a pleasant and quite flattering letter from Ridg Underwood. In answer to my last note he comments on its contents and adds that he has sent it back to his folks and wife. Now I don't recall what all I said but I'm sure he's exaggerated the significance to whatever it was.

But it must ever be true that accounts of happenings strange to the recipient hold a special fascination way out of proportion to actuality. I can't seem to convince anyone that I would have just as soon foregone things like combat experience. You see, the way of my reasoning follows the basic principle and realization that some men didn't come back even if a kind providence spared me. When I see a man win a good deal of money at cards or in a crap game I always consider those who have lost to make his winnings possible. And carrying that a little further I can see the same rule applied to all things in life. There are certain deep and sure realizations a man can take away from a battlefield. And the first is that life seems quite valueless stacked against the incalculable certainty of missions and tactical necessity.

Sergeant Arnold Gates

As I search back over the rush of rapid impressions I try to pick out the moments of dawning and newer comprehension. Sometimes the days would be sunfilled and calm with soft cloud shadows and easy contours to the hills and long canefields. Then, if I was standing on a ledge or high ridge I might watch men in movement thru a valley and marvel over the drama enacted. You could hardly believe that these men were out on a hunt that was as deadly as the strike of a snake.

With each passing day I would ask myself what the next would hold. Time was doled out carefully and the air about each man was filled with potential destruction. With growing fatigue and shortened tempers many of us, I believe, grew a little indifferent to shot and shell. I remember that after that hot Saturday afternoon we pulled back a few hundred yards and set up our perimeter. I dug a foxhole with two other men and just in front of some barbed wire. The dusk was heavy with the feel of storm and a gloom had come over us all as we thought of the men killed in the fury of that afternoon's action. There was something ominous and oppressive to the scene that none of us could shake off. I was kneeling before the barbed wire, putting oil on my tommy gun when we could hear a shell whistling in rapid flight. Men started to dive for foxholes but I just looked over my shoulder. I could hear the missile thud nearby and only then dragged myself to my hole. That, of course, would have been too late if that had been an exploding shell. Come to think of it a projectile that goes off anywhere near a man produces enough concussion to kill him. But don't get excited over this confession since it doesn't indicate my general movements. Probably the most trying experience of any is to be under enemy mortar fire. Whenever I heard something far off I ducked fast and bolted for my hole! The next is to lay in a foxhole at night and watch ack ack explode overhead, all the while fervently praying that no fragments of steel would drop into your little hole.

But as the days lengthen most of us begin to see the comic to much of that experience and something like a legend weaves itself out of the individual impressions men gathered.

Goodnight. Son,

Arnold.

★

13 October 1944
Somewhere in the Pacific

My dear folks:

Mail has dribbled off to just about nothing so the stimulus to writing every day has lost some of its original luster. But when a topic pops up I can still rattle off a reaction or full opinion. In going over The Reader's Digest for September I came across a rather interesting item by Dorothy Parker. She reflects on the days to come after the war, when men from all the battlefields will return. Then she adds further, that it will be next to impossible for those of a civilian world to understand or come up to the plane of experience we've known. I can't agree with her for the strong and constant urge in all of us is ever toward the day when we can forget the mud and filth and the smell of bloated death. The natural tendency with all men is to forget the unpleasant quickly and almost thoroughly. And the fact that we've known absolute misery will make us the more appreciative of the simple things in normal life. As a matter of fact, many of us fear that the way of things as we left them will be gone when we again set foot on American soil. We are concerned over the prospect of returning to find our folks, our sweethearts, and our friends changed.

In my own concept of things ahead and present I realize full well that man continues to be affected by the passage of time and that this holds true with all. I've changed on the mere strength of three years and you have done so for the very same reason. When I was part of the family and its daily activities we were all changing and growing but no one noticed because it was a slow and even process. Life has always been like some polishing ingredient bringing out the glow and warmth of human character. The fact that the span has been wide and crowded with all the possible levels of emotion and knowing only makes simplicity and serenity that much more inviting! I want to sit in an armchair again and walk across a carpet. Then I'd like to play some of my favorite symphonic records and sip a drink with ice cubes tinkling in the glass and a frost of white coating the chilled container. And at night I can think of noth-

later. Mike's latest is really a killer—Lil wrote him that she was moving, and gave a PO box number for her new address! The poor fellow is batting his brains out trying to figure out what it means and the suggestion that she is living in a box on account of the housing shortage didn't help at all. . . . . . .

Ken

★ ★ ★

*A*t the time of writing, George Patton was commanding general of the Third Army.

HEADQUARTERS

THIRD UNITED STATES ARMY

OFFICE OF THE COMMANDING GENERAL

APO 403

19 October, 1944

My dear Jimmy:

This is to inform you that those low bastards, the Germans, gave me my first bloody nose when they compelled us to abandon our attack on Fort Driant in the Metz area. I have requested

a revenge bombardment from the air to teach those sons-of-bitches that they cannot fool with Americans. I believe that this request will eventually get to you, and I am therefore asking that you see that the Patton-Doolittle combination is not shamed in the eyes of the world, and that you provide large bombs of the nastiest type, and as many as you can spare, to blow up this damn fort so that it becomes nothing but a hole.

 With warm regards, I am as ever,

  Devotedly yours,

        G. S. Patton, Jnr.

Lieut. General J. H. Doolittle
Headquarters Eighth Air Force
APO 634
U.S. Army.

When the battle for Peleliu had ended, First Lieutenant Richard Kennard* wrote home to give his family a retrospective of the 1st Marine Division's work on the island.

        Peleliu Analysis
        G. Btry 3rd. BN
        11th Marines
      C/PO FPO San Francisco
       October 20, 1944

Dear Dad and Mother:

I write to you now on the evening of my twenty-fourth birthday. Being overseas so long now, and having been in the toughest battle the Marines ever had, I know of no better way at present than to celebrate the occasion as I am now. I came aboard this ship yesterday and we are lying off the island of Peleliu waiting for the convoy to make ready to sail.

---

 * Another letter from First Lieutenant Kennard appears on page 171.

The first shipment of mail to reach the 1st Marine Division bivouac area on Peleliu

This is not a Navy ship, so the chow is not very good. They don't have enough food aboard to feed ninety officers good food three times a day, so only field officers and above in rank (majors on up) eat in this lounge, so to speak, where I am writing now. The rest of us have to eat below with the enlisted men, receiving only two meals a day which consist of B rations—no fresh meat, eggs, or real good chow.

Most of us do no complaining, for we all feel lucky to be alive, and for that reason alone, I am very happy. We sleep in deck houses that are satisfactory during the night, for we can keep the doors at each end of the house open, thus having a draft blow through. I find a bare mattress quite comfortable after the coral rock, rain, and heat on the Peleliu ridges.

A few days before my birthday it was decided that Peleliu had cost enough Marine casualties, so the problem of killing the remaining Japs was left to the Army Wildcat division. Where they got that name is beyond me. I shall devote the remainder of this letter to a general discussion of the thirty-five day battle which cost the Marines twelve hundred killed or missing and seven thousand wounded. (Note. I counted 1050 Marine graves at the cemetery here, and two hundred were buried at sea). News columns made the folks back home believe the war here was practically over with by October 5, when Admiral Nimitz published the total casualty list, with it broken down into services (as I read in a Hawaiian newspaper). Until October 14 many, many more Marines were being wounded and killed in their efforts to clean out the Japs. My analysis follows:

GENERAL: The strategists planned this campaign very well but they did not figure on so many caves and tunnels to provide the Japs with a veritable fortress. The Naval bombardment was the heaviest given and most concentrated amount on one spot. Nothing escaped the flying shrapnel of our shells. The island was ringed with warships. (One of them being a battleship which took us three boys aboard while she was in the Hudson River back in 1927 sometime, I believe; maybe later. You have a picture of us standing next to a turret in your photographic album). Before the first wave landed, you couldn't see a bit of the island, it was so covered with smoke and sand.

INTERESTING AND AMUSING INCIDENTS: An Army sergeant was checking over lines his men had just occupied after relieving the Marines. To an agent in a position he asked, "How many hand grenades do you have for tonight, Mac?" The lad replied, "The Marine left eight here in the hole, and I have a caseful of them [25 grenades to a case] right outside my hole here." Replied that Army sergeant, "Hell, that ain't enough. I'll have another case sent up to you before dark." Lieutenant Zimmerman and I got a big laugh out of this conversation when we heard it. You see, a single Marine lies like a cat at night in his position, and only throws a grenade when he hears definite movements which sound suspicious out in front of him. We train our men so that this one man is the only one who throws the grenade, unless it is ordered that all hands have ONE grenade. You see, there is always danger of our own grenade hitting a tree in front of the man's position and then bouncing back into our own lines, causing us casualties. It is our effort to keep firing and grenade throwing to a minimum, so the mental strain on our troops won't be any harder than can be helped. If I have a man who is too "trigger-happy" and throws grenades too often,

I'll jerk him off the line and use him to carry chow in and out of the ridges. The Army boys come up to the line loaded for bear, with a couple of bandoliers of M1 ammo around their shoulders, and they throw grenades all night long. Another incident occurred when Lieutenant MacDonald of my battery was showing the Army platoon leader, who was coming up with troops to relieve him, the front line positions. It was raining very hard. The Army lieutenant said, "Dammit, every time I move into a position it has to be raining." Mac replied, "Yes, the weather is bad up here. When it rains it is miserable, and when not raining the heat is over a hundred degrees. By the way," he said, "where was your last position?" The Army lieutenant answered, "Down in southern Arizona, on maneuvers." Lieutenant MacDonald said no more, only chuckling to himself. (The Army officer did not realize that he was talking to a veteran of Cape Gloucester who had fought through twenty-eight days of straight downpour and mud up to his knees).

CONCLUSION: This was the most costly battle for a single Marine division thus far in the Corps' history. We took this island the only way it could possibly have been done, but a fortress is a fortress, and that is all there is to it. Seemed like this was going to develop into siege warfare in our attempt to get all the Japs out of their caves in the jagged, treacherous coral ridges. It would not have been wise to land more troops than we did, for the island is too small and they would have been shooting at each other. However, I think that had fresh troops been thrown in on D+5, to relieve some of the battalions, matters would have been helped a lot. As it was, casualties forced us to reorganize, thus giving the Japs a chance to catch their breath and get their mortars ready. But our high-priced help would never call in the Army like this, for it would hurt the name of the Marine Corps, I suppose, to let the world know that "doggie" reinforcements had to be called in so early!! I doubt very much if the Army would have come in to help then, anyway. The bunch we Marines got out here for any support or coordinated action are on the whole inexperienced and not the best, by any means. And only the finest Army troops could fight on these islands. The type of warfare we wage against the Imperial

Marines of these Jap-held islands is a do or die job, not fit for the Army, because they are not trained the same way as we are. If we had a couple of Ranger Battalions like Frank's to be held for us in support and thrown in when necessary, it would be fine. His men know they will take chances on dangerous missions. For our Corps, all missions are dangerous and we are always given the toughest battles to clean out the Japs. I hope I never see terrain like this again. It will be a pleasure to fight in China if I ever happen to get there.

One thing I like about the Army who relieved us was that they held us in great respect as real fighters, as this First Marine Division truly is. There was much joking between the two services, but we Marines were too glad to see the Army and all their gear to make any nasty remarks. I don't believe it is right to belittle another branch of the services, nor do I think that the soldiers are cowards. The Army has done well in Europe and we shall now see how well MacArthur is going to make out against the Japs on the Philippines where the Sixth Army landed today, on my birthday.

We are all American boys of the same breeding in general, all fighting for the country we love against the Jap and the Hun. But between the two services there is a difference in training and spirit. Out here, it is our belief, from seeing the Army that has worked with the Marines, that their chain of command is poor and their junior officers of an inferior grade. In this campaign we lost more junior officers (lieutenants through captains), proportionately speaking, than in any other battle. Our platoon leaders and company commanders are more afraid of what their men will think of them, if they don't face the enemy fire and danger along with them, than afraid of getting shot by the Jap. The enlisted man will, therefore, hold much praise for his immediate superior officer and never flinch at an order, no matter how hazardous the job is. The FACT and the Marine Corps "spirit," which I cannot explain (one feels it in his body only, and acts accordingly), is the reason why ours is the greatest fighting organization in the world! Look at what we have taken from the Japs in the Pacific since 1941, when we started with only sixty thousand officers and men . . .

Make sure to make a note at the end of it (and any other things you want to include in other letters I have written is all right with me) that nothing is to be put in public print. I may have stretched censorship regulations a little, but don't believe so. However, I don't want to take any chances.

Dick

★ ★ ★

Combat Infantryman Jack Hogan, 184th Regiment, 7th Infantry Division, wrote this letter after U.S. forces invaded Leyte Island, Philippines, on October 21, 1944.

From Leyte—Philippine Islands
[October]

We had a "battle breakfast" steak and all the trimmings. It brought back memories of Kiska and Kwajalein. I had slept well, treated myself to the last shave for at least several days, adjusted my pack, reread the Signal Operations Instructions and placed them in a waterproof bag with my map. Then I checked my carbine for the last time and slipped a shell into the chamber. All was in readiness. All the last minute details were completed. It was a morning of last times, of last preparations. The long sea voyage was at an end and I was grateful for the prospect of dry land once more. Shortly after the convoy dropped anchor in Leyte Gulf, a Jap bomber flew over and someone shot him down with his bomb bays still full. On deck the Navy was lowering booms, putting landing craft into the water, opening hatches, lowering nets over the side. All was bustle and confusion.

It was a clear day with a smooth sea. I went below, propped myself against the radio I would soon carry ashore and had a "quiet time" just as I have had almost every morning of my life for years. Frank Buchman taught me that "when man listens God speaks; that accurate adequate information can come from the mind of God to the mind of man." Quiet times or sacramental meditation are as old as the Prophets, and have been part of

195

the Christian life since the beginning. Listening to God, finding His plan and conforming our will to His, that has been the chief joy of my life, the source of all creative and satisfying living. I reflected that it was the lack of this fundamental direction in the lives of ordinary men that had plunged the world into chaos. That was why I would soon be running across the beach of Leyte with hell and destruction on every side and the bodies of my comrades who had died because modern man had rejected Divine Authority. What a pity that so few of us know why we were fighting. That for so many the cause was still Hitler or Hirohito or Pearl Harbor.

These thoughts among others flashed through my mind and I wrote them down in a little notebook. "Your armor is absolutely invincible. God has willed His truth to triumph through us. Mother will triumph over fear." More thoughts of my family. Of their ceaseless prayers, of the fight they were waging beside me in spirit for a new world under God.

At H. hour the assault craft streaked for the beach. They looked like a lot of race horses vaulting from the gates. We watched them until they were just a mass of bobbing black specks against the sea. The barrage lifted and soon the message was handed down from the destroyer. We sent it with a prayer of thanksgiving. "First wave landed such and such a time. No casualties. Continuing on missions." The Colonel and his party descended from the destroyer and we headed for the pockmarked blackened beach. Soon our command post was established several hundred yards inland. I was busy with messages. Everyone was trying to piece the picture together to see how things were shaping up. The reports were mostly negative. No man on earth could have lived through that bombardment. The Japs had fled inland.

The rest is history. I remember certain things vividly, mostly the nights. I shall never forget the time my radio was jammed at the very moment the Division Commander was trying to warn us of a large-scale counter attack. For hours we explored every means of getting his message through. I kept pleading monotonously into the transmitter, "I cannot read you." I never got it but somehow the wire section found the break in the telephone line and the problem was solved. The counter attack was a false alarm. And then there was the patrolling my intelligence and reconnaissance platoon did with the native guerrillas. There was the night we slept on a rain drenched hillside, about 50 of us, two hundred yards away from where 230 to 300 Japs were bivouacked. They stole away in the darkness and we never found them.

Through all the days and nights I felt the support of the prayers my family and friends were offering. My own prayer was that I might serve without reproach and always have the victory over fear. God seemed very near in those daily quiet times sandwiched in between a hasty K ration and an urgent message. I thought of the sorrow that was with the passing days casting its shadow over many an American home, of the men who would never return. I realized then more than ever that there was in reality not one war but two; that unless we fought and won the battle against moral anarchy, against fear and hate in men's hearts our victory over Germany and Japan would be a hollow mockery, and an unforgivable waste.

185th Infantry Regimental Combat Team post office in New Britain

And my question is this: Are the nations going to slip back after this war into the suicidal path of apathy, materialism, and moral decay that has produced two wars in 20 years and eaten away the very foundations of Christian civilization and turned the world into a vast slaughter house? Is that what my comrades have died for? Are we going back to an America torn asunder by industrial strife, betrayed by political expediency, disintegrated by divorce and immorality and eventually murdered by racial and class warfare? Or are we going to build a new world? Are we going to restore God to the leadership of our personal and national lives? Is obedience to the moral law going to be again the basis for civilization, the one authority accepted by all men and all nations? Is there going to be reborn in the soul of America the passion for the Christian faith our fathers knew when they hacked a nation out of a wilderness, the faith that guided Washington and Lincoln, that made America great? Will we find again as a free people the sense of responsibility as moral beings, the spirit of sacrifice and inner discipline? Will we root out of our national life the spirit of disunity, moral defeat and subversion and hatred that can destroy America?

★

Jack Hogan was fatally wounded while on patrol in the Gaja Ridge area at Okinawa in May 1945.

★ ★ ★

At the time of writing, Lieutenant Colonel John Woolnough was a captain in the 784th Bombardment Squadron, 466th Bombardment Group, Eighth Air Force. He flew as first pilot on a lead crew for thirty missions to targets in France and Germany.

25 October, 1944

Dear Nancy:
Thanks a million for your nice letters. Yours are the most interesting, loving and newsy letters I get from anyone. I really mean

that, Nance. We've certainly grown close to each other since our separation. It is the same with Charlie [twin brother]. I guess that is what our family needed, wasn't it?

I want to thank you especially for your kindness towards me and above that, your prayers for me and my crew. I am indeed a sinner, but I do believe in God and His power and goodness. I've seen God answer my prayers, and calm my nerves, and give me rest. Always before any mission I pray to God for strength and guidance . . . I've said nothing about this to anyone. Now I feel free to tell it, as I have 29 missions behind me and only one to go. I have faith God will go with me in the last one as He has in the past. Our war (in the air), is a different war. It isn't a bloody, ruthless war. It is almost impersonal. It is a cold calculating war. Except in a few cases, we see nothing. Our gunners tell us they saw a ship blow up or go down in flames. If you don't know anyone in that ship, it has little effect upon you. You just shrug your shoulders and say, "This is war."

If your friends go down, you miss them for a while, and cold as it may seem you grieve little for the men themselves. You do feel badly (for a while) for their wives, children, families and

Lieutenant Colonel John Woolnough (right) *with Major Glenn Miller*

friends. You have to be this way in order to go through it yourself.

You can't imagine how it feels to be flying at 20,000 feet with your oxygen mask on, with the temperature down to 30 degrees below zero. Ahead of you lies the target and flak—hundreds and thousands of black puffs, just like a cloud—all you can do is sit there and sweat, knowing you've got to ride right into it. When it is passed, you wonder how you made it, and sometimes you wonder how many holes are in the ship as you heard the "woof" of it and heard the tiny pellets rattle against the fuselage. After a few seconds you get enough moisture back in your mouth so you can talk again. Then you call the crew and ask if everything is all right. Everything is always all right and you thank God. Then you keep reminding the crew of the danger of fighters, telling them to keep their eyes open, and maybe bawl one out for jabbering over the interphone while we were going over the target—when the bombardier and navigator needed positive touch with each other.

Finally, you start letting down as the enemy coast is in view. By the time you're over the Channel, you are low enough to take your oxygen mask off. Then you grab a smoke, eat a candy bar and relax a little—just a very little, because in this game you can't really relax until you're on the ground. You see, Nancy, we're in the Big League over here.

How did you like the ride? This has been incoherent, forgive me for that. I just wrote what came to my mind. I hope to be home by Christmas, maybe not.

Lovingly,

John

★　★　★

After entering the Army in 1941, Steve Hall was commissioned into the combat engineers and attained the rank of captain. His keen knowledge of the Italian mountain country, fluency in Italian and French, and expert skiing ability made him an ideal candidate for the OSS (Office of Strategic

Services, which developed into the modern-day CIA) opera-
tions in Italy. After joining the OSS, he trained as a paratrooper
and spent months preparing for the mission described in his
letter.

October 31, 1944
Andrich, Cadore, Italy

Your last letters, all written in July and August, arrived in a
bunch—by parachute! The heavy cases of arms and explosives
and supplies came floating down silently through the night; and
among them was a package (with its own chute) which carried
all the news from home.

I was the only one of our team who got the mail, so I read
some of the paragraphs to the others to give them a little taste
of home—all about Father's big tomato in the garden, and the
water shortage this summer, and the busted outboard of Bruce's.
We all got a big laugh out of the clipping which showed the
chart on the wall, "My Draft Status" and had the caption, "They
were certainly breathing down my neck there for a while." We
were definitely in a situation where "they were breathing down
our necks" and could enjoy that one heartily. However, for se-
curity reasons, I had to burn all the mail, much as I hated to,
keeping only the birthday cards, which I have carried with me
ever since. You see, we were some 250 miles behind the front in
Italy and actually right up against the border of Germany itself
—in the Italian Alps where, as you know, I'd always wanted to
fight my tiny part of this war, anyway. The letters appeared out
of the dark over a wide place in the bed of the Tagliamento River
near a village called "Enemonzo," about 10 miles east of Ampezzo and the same distance west of Tolmezzo. At Tolmezzo
there were 11,000 Nazi troops and Mongoloids from Turkestan,
picked up in the German retreat from the Caspian and now
serving as mercenaries. We used the river flats for over twelve
"supply drops", although our flaming signal fires were in full
sight of Tolmezzo, on the nights when we got the signal over
the regular commercial program from London to expect a
planeload. To get to the dropping zone we rode in a huge truck
(captured from the Nazis) which roared down through the wind-

ing gorges of the Tagliamento at terrific speed from Ovasta. We went so fast because it was a race to a certain road fork. We had to make it before the Germans did, if they should ever get it into their thick skulls to investigate what was going on. I believe they knew; but psychology was on our side: they imagined our partisan bands of Italian patriots so strong that any attack by them would be suicidal. Actually we had less than 1000 men in our command.

At Ovasta, a medieval hamlet lodged on a shelf overlooking the river and ringed around by the gigantic spears and flakes of the Carnic Alps, we had our "Base" Headquarters. We had a powerful short-wave set with which to communicate with Army HQ 'way to the south; and a room or two; and a tobacco supply composed of old "butts" and corn silk. I was at "Base" very little, spending my time in long swings—deep into zones crawling with Germans but where unarmed groups of patriots waited for help. So my returns to "Base" were always occasions for mutual celebration: it was good to get back to a bed and hot food after sleeping in hay barns or caves and eating mushrooms and cold corn meal, with an occasional squirrel thrown in. The days went very fast then. At "Base" there were corn on the cob and American radio programs; and Smitty (Major Lloyd C. Smith, State College, Pa) had arranged a deal with a pre-war ice cream freezer so that we had ice cream now and then—all we had to do was climb down 1500 feet to the valley floor and then climb up again.

But I'm getting 'way ahead of things. The peaks are plated with ice now; there are drifts in the passes and snow powderings in the valleys. During August, everything was green and warm —we took our showers in waterfalls, went roaring up and down the village streets singing Yankee songs to the delighted grins of the war-weary people who were fed to the ears with the grim and cruel Nazi soldiers.

You know how long I'd worked on this Alps thing —well, I finally sold it to GHQ. We put together a team of five: Major Smith, who'd won the DSC* getting thirteen stranded nurses

---

* Distinguished Service Cross.

out of Nazi hands in Albania; 1st Lt. Joe Lukitsch of Cleveland, a paratrooper who came over on the boat with me: Sgt. Victor Malaspino from New Jersey, interpreter, who worked for me when I was chief instructor in the Spy School in the mountains outside Algiers; 1st Class Seaman Stan Sbeig from Bridgeport, radioman.

Smitty was to organize and direct partisans in Carnia, and I was to do the same in Cadore, having also the mission of closing the Cortina road. Once inside German-occupied territory, we were entirely on our own, as autonomous as soldiers of fortune in a Chinese war or banana republic revolution. But I guess General Devers and General Alexander had faith in us because they okayed the deal. Of course it wasn't as easy as that; the project had to be drafted as carefully as a case before the Supreme Court; and the preparations were as detailed as an expedition to Everest; maps, sleeping bags, foreign money, climbing gear, radio ciphers, medicine, and just about a thousand damn things—all weighed and triple-checked.

Finally, the night of August 1, we gathered under the wing of a big four-motored Lancaster at Brindisi airport. We had on "strip-tease" suits, against the cold at 10,000 feet, and looked like Eskimos. We sweated rivers—and froze later over Udine.

The ride was painful, for we were cramped in among the containers of our supplies, and the roar of the engines was overwhelming—also, naturally, the prospect of a parachute jump into enemy territory at night, or any other time, is none too comforting.

At Brindisi we did not know just where we'd drop. A couple of places I'd been counting on were ruled out in the last two days because of Nazi troop movements. We climbed up through the small hole in the bottom of the plane and found we were bound for Mount Pala in the foothills of the Alps of Carnia, bad news for me, as it was some 85 miles from the Cortina area. Smitty and I squabbled for the privilege of being "first out" in the jump, but he outranked me. We nearly did not make it, as the pilot could not find the right pattern of ground fires in the right place. Jerry was, aside from shooting at us with flak, apparently lighting a few signals to decoy us. Finally the word came back over the intercom that the right fires had been spotted, but in the wrong place. One of the crew opened the hatch, and after a dying run by the plane, Smitty, Vic, and Stan disappeared through the hole—just like that. Joe Lukitsch and I swung our legs into the hole and looked down. With a full moon the tumbled hills far below looked eerie; the fires looked small and distant—they were, about 2500 feet. Suddenly the green light blazed and the bell rang on the wall of the ship, and I dropped through, Joe right after me. The chute opened with a crack, but I had a bad spin and the shroud lines were twisting rapidly—if they twist enough, the chute collapses. I fought for about 1000 feet before the twists came out.

Then I looked around. With the night breezes Joe sailed past like a shot out of a cannon. Below, there was nothing but hill, woods, and rocks. It looked like a trap. I was sure it was when I landed—between two wicked spikes of limestone, doing a couple of back somersaults down a gully into some saplings. There wasn't a person around, just complete silence. I cut my way out of the chute and got out my automatic. For twenty minutes there wasn't a sound. Then I made for a low, bare hillock nearby, and in a little while the others came up. It was 2 a.m. The fires were phony all right. Smitty had landed near them and had seen a man running away.

About 700 yards away a fire shone on the side of Mount Pala, but we couldn't find the path; which was lucky as the fire came from a house the Germans were burning, we found out later. They were too drunk to pay any attention to the drop.

We hid in a deep swale until dawn, and then I went to a farmhouse to ask questions. By noon we had made contact with some local partisans and later were on our way back into the mountains. We felt that we had been granted a miracle. The whole operation was in full sight of Nazi observation towers in the plain below, and the lack of reception and the hideous rock pile we landed on should have made us all casualties and easy prisoners. Aside from cuts and bruises we were okay. It took the Nazis a week to start chasing us.

On August 12 I started out alone for the Cadore, about 30 miles from Ovasta, crossing Lavardet Pass: made contact with the partisans around San Stefano, and started work. The Cadore was tough, because there were Nazi garrisons in all the towns, and the area was much more populated and desirable to Jerry than desolate Carnia. Cortina alone had 1000 picked troops to guard the 5000 wounded Nazis in the hotels and hospitals there.

The Air Corps would not drop to me in Cadore—mountains too high: although I spent eighteen days at a dropping zone on the Austrian border (the Val Visdende)—watching the Army build its "Alpine Line." Whatever you've heard about that in the papers is direct intelligence I gathered. Finally we rigged a system for back-packing arms and explosives across the ranges from Carnia. I traveled back and forth and round about all over the area, always in uniform, often 500 yards from Nazi garrisons, or walking past their front doors at night, and earned a pair of legs like cast iron.

So, by the end of September, I had been able to get an organization of 400 men on its feet, dispatch reams of important intelligence to GHQ, blow out the standard gauge R.R. from Venice and the electric R.R. through Cortina to Austria, and eleven highway bridges, effectively blocking all routes through the Alps north of Venice. Mr. Nazi was proportionately furious, the more so when we attacked three garrisons, taking around 187 prisoners.

But by the end of September there was snow on the highest peaks and the campaign in Italy had changed to a holding action, designed to keep as many Nazi troops there as possible, so they wouldn't reinforce the other fronts. Our time schedule was badly upset. We got the terrific news, too, that Jerry planned to turn over Carnia to the savages from Turkestan, who would massacre all the Italians and take the farms for themselves— thus giving future Germany an area deep into Italy populated by a solid block of pro-Nazi Mongols.

Smitty worked himself green, getting in arms for the poor Italians and begging to have Tolmezzo bombed—but GHQ wouldn't bomb, for some unknown reason. All things taken together, we felt we had to stay until the front had advanced considerably, so as to help the Army as much as possible in cutting the supply lines.

In spite of the shadow that hung over Carnia, everything was going very well in the upper Piave River valley in Cadore. At the end of September I heard about a large group of Italian patriots—all ex-Alpini soldiers—on the other side of Cortina, over near Selva-di-Cadore. They needed help. So I made up my pack and started out, contouring the peaks just at the line where the bare rock jumps from the steep scrub slopes. It took three days to make the 55 miles and involved 32,000 feet of climbing. But from August 12 till now (three months, or a little less) I'd been living and working at 7000 feet and often going to 9000 feet on reconnaissance, so it wasn't too tough. I lost some time skirting the Marmarole range, and Mount Antelao, as I had to slip through patrols of 300 Nazi Alpenjaeger who were out hunting partisans, and the last day was in a snowstorm and a foot of new snow over the flank of Mount Pelma.

This group was all I'd heard, being all ex-officers and noncoms of the Alpini troops, who knew every trail and crag of all the Dolomites. Their HQ was only four hours by foot from Cortina, just over the range I had skied in 1937–38. I got a message back to "Base" requesting a drop. The plane came, two weeks later, in the middle of a Nazi drive on partisans around Cortina, so we did not get the drop, being unable to light signal fires. We climbed up in the rock of the precipices for five straight days and watched the Nazis hunting for us in the forests below. Each evening they fired cannon and machine guns up into the rock gullies—just in case; and we watched the tracers smack on the rock all around us. We couldn't do anything, having no guns, But they never really saw us, and finally went away.

Then I got crushing news; the 10,000 troops at Tolmezzo had overrun Carnia from the south, while the 5000 Nazis, brought in from Austria, attacked from the north. Smitty and the rest were caught between the two forces, and I haven't heard a whisper about them since—over three weeks. I feel sure he must have got through and escaped toward Yugoslavia, that being one of our exit plans before we started.

But for three weeks now I've been the only Allied officer in the whole Alps—and without a radio. Just waiting for some break and trying to keep up the partisans' courage. Not that the time has been wasted. I managed to get contact with certain people in Bolzano and perfected the plan for blowing out one of the tunnels on the R.R. through the Brenner; sent the explosives off to them disguised as crates of jam last week!

Then, too, I managed to sign up a couple of electrical engineers and we worked out a scheme for crippling the entire telephone and telegraph net in the Alps here—important, because of the Alpine Line fortifications Jerry is working on so feverishly. And of course there's been a wad of intelligence coming in; for example, by a stroke of pure luck, I got a map of the Nazi troop dispositions as planned for the defense of the Brenner—stuff like that; another case, the HQ of the Japanese secret service (Hotel Corona, Cortina).

It has snowed every day for three weeks, and is still at it, so movement is out of the question, as Jerry can track you too easily in the snow. However, recently I made contact with an officer (Capt. Joe Benucci) down in the Venetian plain below Belluno; so things are looking up. He has a radio.

At present I'm in the tiny hamlet of Andrich, part of the community of Vallada, 3 miles west of Cencenighe; whiling away the hours reading Ivanhoe and some 1939 copies of Collier's someone dug up!

The position is really good, as it's plunk in the middle of the Alpine Line the Nazis are building. They're laboring over some beautiful targets for us to blow up when and if we get a drop. But you don't need to worry, we're getting to be old hands at the art of running in under the Nazi's nose and blowing the shoestrings out of his boots before he knows what's happened. If he ever catches up with me, all he'll find is another Yank who parachuted from a crashing plane and who is waiting for the end of the war.

How I'll get out, I don't know, although I wish I could give you some assurance. The possibility of crossing the Swiss frontier is out of the question now because of the snow (it came a whole month early this year). Carnia is solid Nazi, so a dash to Yugoslavia—150 miles—is none too good. So it looks like north or south. North, to fall back with the Nazis when they retreat from Italy and take up this Line; south, to try to filter through and meet the Allies when they advance. Either possibility isn't bad. But the best one is, of course, the end of the war before the Nazis move back here in force. That's what I'm hoping for.

No matter what, it may be some time after the Armistice before I get out to wire you—having to hide and linger around awhile before showing myself. So that's why I'm writing this— the family here will mail it with the Armistice.

The mission (called Mercury Eagle) has already paid for itself and been a success. We got a lot more accomplished than anyone thought possible. If Smitty is okay, then everything is all right; and I have high hopes for the future. Luck has really played a big part, with countless hairbreadth escapes from Mr. Hitler's animals, and universal success in whatever we undertook. It's only regretted that we did not get even more support from Rome, for opportunities were boundless in August and September. It would be a lie for me to say that this has been an adventure or good time for me. True, at times there have been light moments, a few; and at other times the work has been long and exhausting. I've seen more gorgeous scenery than three men will in a lifetime—sunrises and sunsets among the peaks, moonlight glimmering on glaciers, storms swirling around tremendous pillars of rock, cataracts, forest glades, ancient villages. But full enjoyment is not truly there when you are on eternal guard against guns appearing behind every rock and shadow. The "threat" never leaves you, asleep or awake; and I have not yet lain down to sleep without a cocked pistol at my right hand. In a land where you regularly have to hike and climb 11 miles to reach a point only 3 miles away by road, there's usually more to occupy the mind than breathless vistas of beauty. You are usually "breathless" from the close acquaintance with the bare bone and sinews that make up this magnificent scenery.

It has not been sport, but rather a deadly business—an unending struggle to plan each tiny detail for days ahead, when you really don't know what's going to happen in the next fifteen minutes. If you make the slightest error, someone dies; I found that out quickly. It seems as though life and death have been in my hands since this started, for as the only representative of law and order wherever I've gone I have had to sit as judge at trials of criminals and spies; to determine the fate of prisoners taken;

to issue orders for the general good that meant violence to someone along the line before they were consummated. It was the
one feature of this job I did not foresee, and would have avoided
with all my heart. I have saved many, many lives that would
otherwise have been lost—Nazi prisoners, circumstantial cases,
petty cases—for the law of the partisans before I arrived was
death for anything, or anyone, sadly. But for the rest, and for my
mistakes—well, I guess I've forgotten how to smile. Militarily,
I've thought of it as a game of chess, with the whole Alps as a
board, whereon you try to outguess the enemy and move always
into a square where he won't come. The feeling of being hunted
is something that can never leave you; it's very tiring, and requires fierce self-control when you have so much else that requires the best sense and judgement you can exert. This village
of Andrich happens to be a square where Mr. Nazi won't think
of looking for a while.

If there has been any recompense for us, it has come, not
from the scenery, but from the reactions of the people—persecuted, starved and enslaved by the Nazis. We've been able to
bring them medicines; a few of the comforts of life (cigarettes,
coffee, sugar); a little money; but mostly HOPE. There's nothing
anyone will ever be able to say or show that will make me think
there's anything good about a German. The atrocities are true;
I've seen them: and they're universal. Villages burned, children
hanged, men tortured, old people turned out in the snow, civilians shot for sport—I've seen those things with my own eyes.
These hideous acts yield a crop of men whose fury knows no
bounds—they make up the partisan bands I've helped to organize; they're the sword of God, if there ever has been one in
history.

If any of you ever travel to these parts in the future, don't be
afraid to mention my name. It's known from one end of the Alps
to the other (a fame far out of proportion to what I've been able
to do). You'll receive hospitality undreamed of, assuming you're
in the little inns with the real inhabitants.

This job hasn't been world-shaking and may never be recorded even in Army records. But I've told about it so that you
will know that, even if it hasn't been as much as many, many

others have done in this war, at least I've done something. In my last report by radio to Rome I was able to say:

"Have organized 6 battalions and 4 intelligence units. Have blown 14 highway bridges and 3 railroad bridges. Have organized 1600 square miles of Alps, and distributed arms therein. Have led 3 attacks. Have sent over 300 intelligence reports."

★

In January 1945 Captain Hall received orders to blow up the hydroelectric plant at Cortina. He embarked on this solo mission on skis in a heavy snowstorm the night of January 25. A game warden found him the next morning in the forest near Cortina d'Ampezzo—unconscious with both feet frozen. The warden took him home and then quickly notified fascist police in order to claim a reward for capturing an enemy soldier. Hall was taken to Bolzano, where SS officers tried to extract information from him by means of torture. After two weeks of brutality and failure to break him down, they hanged him. Captain Hall was posthumously awarded the Legion of Merit and Croix de Guerre avec Palme.

Mail arrives at the front for the 290th Infantry Regiment, 75th Infantry Division.

Men stop temporarily from cleaning their 81-mm mortar to read their mail, one hundred yards from Japanese positions on New Guinea.

★　★　★

Kermit Stewart,* who entered the Army in 1944, wrote the following letter. In May of that year, as a second lieutenant, he sailed for North Island, New Zealand, to join the 169th Regiment, 43rd Infantry Division. The division was rehabilitating in New Zealand prior to landing at Aitape, New Guinea, on July 14, 1944. Upon arrival at Aitape they assumed defensive positions until October 10, when they were relieved to prepare for the Philippine invasion.

New Guinea
5 Nov. '44

Dear Folks:

Well, you called the wrong shot this time. You will note that I am still sitting, safely and monotonously, here in New Guinea. Don't know how much longer it's going to last, but here I am . . .

---

* Other letters from Lieutenant Stewart appear on pages 220, 236, and 246.

Don't worry about the "literacy" of your letters. Remember that I censor a pile of letters every day, and it's an education about U.S. education to read them. Many are quite good, of course—but the rest!!?! It is also an interesting job (however boring) in that you learn that you are not the only person in the world who has troubles. Staying here, isolated this way, and comparatively inactive, is very depressing to everyone's morale. You can sense it in the letters. Worries about home affairs become magnified, lack of feminine companionship becomes unbearable, petty annoyances assume large proportions, the specter of a coming campaign becomes terrifying. In our small company alone the past 3 weeks two boys have been evacuated as psycho-neurotics. That's a polite name for going batty.

In a neighboring company a chap's wife became pregnant—by his father! He went completely nuts. One boy in our company died recently from natural causes. One of my jobs is to gather up personal belongings of evacuees or casualties and send them on. It's a depressing job to sort out the pitifully few trinkets and the mementoes of a frustrated life—and send them home where they will open old hurts anew. Hope I have very little of that to do. A few nurses have been shipped in recently with a hospital unit. I saw a couple of them from a distance the other day—the first women I've seen in months. There are just enough of them to be a nuisance. We have had to put canvas screens around showers, latrines, etc—and to wear bathing trunks on the beach. Gone is the life uninhibited. That's all for now. I enjoy your letters—Keep writing—

Love to all,

Kermit

1945

Aside

Mail-day, and over the world in a thousand drag-nets
The bundles of letters are dumped on the docks and beaches
And all that is dear to the personal conscious reaches
Around us again like filings around iron magnets,
And war stands aside for an hour and looks at our faces
Of total absorption that seem to have lost their places.

O demobilized for a moment, a world is made human,
Returns to a time that is neither the present or then,
But a garland of clippings and wishes of who-knows-when,
A time of its own creation, a thing of acumen
That keeps us, like movies, alive with a purpose, aside
From the play-acting truth of the newsreel in which we have died.

And aside from the candy and pictures and books we receive
As if we were patients whose speedy recovery were certain
There is proof of the End and the lights and the bow at the curtain
After which we shall smile at each other and get up to leave
Aside from the play in the play there is all that is fact,
These letters, the battle in progress, the place of the act.

And the optimal joy of the conflict, the tears of the ads
May move us or not, and the movies at night in the palms
May recall us or not to the kiss, and on Sunday the psalms
May remind us of Sunday or not, but aside from the lads
Who arrive like our letters still fresh from the kiss and the tear,
There are mouths that are dusty and eyes that are wider than fear.

Say no more of the dead than a prayer, say no more of the land
Where the body is laid in the coral than that it is far;
Take your finger away from the map of wherever-we-are,
For we lie in the map of the chart of your elderly hand;
Do not hasten the future; in agony too there is time
For the growth of the rose of the spirit astir in the slime.

For aside from ourselves as we are there is nothing alive
Except as it keeps us alive, not tomorrow but now,
Our mail-day, today of the blood of the sweat of our brow,
The year of our war to the end. When and where we arrive
Is no matter, but HOW is the question we urgently need,
How to love and to hate, how to die, how to write and to read.

KARL SHAPIRO

★ ★ ★

First Lieutenant Robert Dean Bass served with A Company, 324th Engineer Battalion, 99th Infantry Division. He wrote this letter home during the Battle of the Bulge.

Belgium,
Friday 5, January 1945

Dearest Mother and Dad:

This is the second letter that I've written in almost a month now. I've really tried to write but just haven't been in a place where I could, except when I spent the night in a Belgian home a few days ago. I did write you from there.

Dad. I received a letter from you today written December 24, the day before Christmas. I was in a fox hole, when you wrote that letter, as I had been for ten days previous and four days afterward.

I imagine that you all have been reading the newspapers about the big German counter-offensive. If I were a novelist, I could write a magnificent tale about a bunch of soda jerks and grocery clerks. After all, that's what all these American soldiers are. They're not professional military men but just a bunch of guys over here doing a job, and a darn good one, and proving themselves much the superior soldier to the German, who has spent the better part of this life pursuing military training.

I'm going to tell you a little of what my battalion has done in the last three weeks. Not just my outfit, but every outfit on the Belgian front did the same thing.

As I've told you, my division moved up to the line in early November. We were in a quiet sector though and not much was happening. My battalion moved into a little village and took the place over. We quartered all our men in houses and things went pretty smoothly. We went out every day and built roads, bridges and performed other engineering tasks in our division sector. But at night we had a house to come home to. We even had a couple of picture shows a week shown in our mess hall, the old Belgian beer garden. Remember, I've told you all that in my letters before.

During the second week in December, we were called out to build a supply road and several bridges to one of our front line

First Lieutenant Robert Dean Bass

Our location was ideal, even though it was unnoticed before this. We were in a valley, with one lone house and barn in the near vicinity. The hills on both sides were covered with pines, with the exception of a field here and there which was sowed with some sort of grain, possibly wheat. A small stream ran by the house and barn and it was full to the banks for we had had quite a bit of rain of late. In fact, it was slightly raining this day, but almost enough to be forgotten for we were used to it.

Our church was in a barn on the second floor in the hay loft. The men had to use a home-made ladder to gain access to the hay loft, and one at a time went up the ladder until the place was full and none left in the rain except the chaplain and me; then the chaplain followed me up the ladder. I didn't feel right wearing my pistol to church so just to satisfy my own feelings, left it downstairs with a friend. Most every one else took their weapons with them.

The inspiration of good feeling came to me when I sat down on that hay and the chaplain started his service with a word of prayer. I looked around me and out the window I could see this stream of water going by. I looked at the ceiling and saw a roof that had stood years of wear, made of large timbers which had evidently been cut by hand, and every here and there a light would shine through. I looked at the wall which was made of stone and it, too, was evidently layed by hand, for it was crude and with a hole here and there, especially two small apertures, probably windows.

All this time the small portable organ was playing softly and the chaplain was talking. It was then it dawned on me, the natural surroundings we were in, for from my childhood school lessons I recalled that this was like the birthplace of Christ. I thought of our church at home and of the many expensive buildings, with thousands of dollars spent to make a place beautiful to worship God. I considered all of that well and good, but I don't believe any place erected, regardless of the cost, could have meant more to me that day.

We had such little room that when it came time for Communion the chaplain suggested a plan of passing by him, dipping a wafer in the wine and uttering a word of prayer if you so

[January 27]
My travels had taken me all over France, Belgium and Luxembourg, and in these travels I had always been so busy I hardly knew which day of the week it was. As a result of my ignorance of the time and due to the nature of my work, I had never attended any of the church services that our chaplain was able to hold.

On the occasion of which I'm writing, the tactical situation was static. We were able to pull men from the front lines and give them a shower, some hot meals and afford them a chance to write a few letters in a semi-peaceful setting. It was one of these days I was assisting the chaplain in affording the frontline men a few comforts, when someone called my attention to the fact that it was Sunday and that church services would be at a certain time. I decided at once to take time, regardless of the situation, and attend.

Lieutenant Edward Hitchin

Officers sorting mail at regimental headquarters in New Georgia

clothes off for a week, lying in muddy fox holes, going without food for 24 hours, having diarrhea, cowering to the ground at every whistle of a shell—nerves that jerk at every explosion, shadows that look like Japs—being scared. Everyone goes through it. I've had enough to last a lifetime. I'm feeling fine now, and the worst is over for the time being. We are licking hell out of the Nips.

Yours,

Kermit

★ ★ ★

*A*t the time of writing, Edward Hitchin was serving as a lieutenant with the 1st Battalion, 109th Infantry Regiment, 28th Infantry Division. The following is extracted from a letter he wrote to his mother in Beaver, Pennsylvania. The church service that Lieutenant Hitchin describes took place at a point where the boundaries of Germany, Belgium, and Luxembourg meet.

several Japs and a gun. You shell a gully where you know Japs are located, but don't know whether you hit any or not. It takes a night attack on your perimeter to put the fighting on a personal basis. Killing becomes an intimate and personal matter.

The last 20 hours I spent in action were the worst. I had no sleep for three days. We got caught in an isolated position and were under constant artillery and mortar fire for the whole 20 hours. During the night hundreds of Japs hit the perimeter about 200 yards from my position yelling Banzai. There was nothing I could do during the night except listen to the fighting. The next morning, however, I had the experience of crawling over scores of dead Japs and tossing a few grenades. One of my company officers was in a fox hole on the other side of a high road embankment where the Japs hit the force. I yelled "Frank, are you OK?" (There were 26 dead Japs around him that we counted later). "That you, Kermit? There's a couple of Japs got me pinned down with a machine gun. Drop a grenade on 'em." He told me where, so I heaved a grenade. "That's a little over." I heaved another. "That's a little short." A dough-boy tossed me another grenade, and I bracketed the third toss. "That got 'em!"

That officer was hit by a mortar shell a few hours later, but we got him out OK. And he'll live. My nerves stand up all right under fire so far. My radio operator was a psycho-neurotic after four days—he had two of his buddies killed in his fox hole the first night, and he couldn't get over the experience.

After I got out of this last 20 hours of action and had got my wounded to the aid station, I had a terrific let down. It was all I could do to keep from sitting down and bawling. We got over 300 Japs in that raid—but it cost something.

The boys were surprised to see me walk into the company one day after 24 hours on a forward observation mission. Another forward observer named Stewart was reported dead, and they thought the obvious.

After writing all the above, I have a horrible feeling that I've rather over-dramatized myself. I assure you I've done nothing heroic, and that my experiences have simply been the same that everyone goes through on the front lines. Not having your

*L*ieutenant Kermit Stewart* wrote the follow-
ing letter after his outfit, the 169th Regiment, 43rd Infantry
Division, attacked Lingayen Gulf, Luzon, Philippine Islands,
on January 9, 1945.

The Philippines
21 Jan. 1945

Dear Guy and Janice:

I've had two nights of sleep in the same fox hole and haven't
been under fire for 36 hours, so I'm about back to normal again
and only look five years older instead of fifteen. I've even had a
bath and a shave—saw my feet for the first time in seven days
and have on clean clothing. Life is good. That I am alive is a
combination of pure chance, the fact that I can dig like hell, and
that I can dive to the ground faster than gravity can pull me. I
say "pure chance", because when you have seen men hit on
every side of you, Sam Johnson's words "There, but for the
Grace of God . . ." come to one rather forcibly. I've seen sights
that I'd like to rid from my memory, but they are too vivid. I'll
never talk about them. The things that high explosives and tear-
ing metal can do to human flesh discourages one to try to express himself.

For eleven days and nights I was under fire a good part of the
time. I've lain in a slit trench and watched leaves drift down on
me clipped by bullets—Jap's bullets. Two nights I heard the Japs
start shouting in a hysteria and then charge our perimeter yelling "Banzai." It's not a pleasant experience.

I've directed cannon fire that has burned a good many Philip-
pinos out of their homes. The trouble was, there were Japs occupying them at the time. The smell of burning flesh is
sickening. Firing cannons is an impersonal sort of a thing. You
see a pill box burst to pieces and think of it as a pill box—not as

---

* Other letters from Lieutenant Stewart appear on pages 211, 236, and 246.

yards from us when our artillery finally began hitting all around them. Dad, remember about the terrific barrage that I told you about when I was at O.C.S. at Fort Sill, layed down by 109 artillery pieces. Well, that barrage was child's play compared to the barrage the good old American artillery put on those attacking German Tiger Tanks. I can't tell you how many tanks or Germans that were knocked out in front of our positions that night, but they were really stacked up. What few German tanks that weren't knocked out, turned tail and fled. All night long we could hear the wounded Germans out in front of us hollering "surrender." This is one English word they all learn before they are sent on the line.

We were in these positions for about ten days. During that time, we drove off the spearhead of two major German thrusts and several smaller ones. Our boys fought like veterans. I have two .30 calibre machine guns in my platoon, and I'd wager that during those ten days each accounted for a company of German infantry piled up in front of it. My boys had never seen any actual combat before, but every one of them did a job that I'll never forget.

On Christmas Day we got out of our fox-holes, one squad at a time, and walked down into the valley behind us and had a hot turkey sandwich brought up to us by our cooks.

I certainly want to thank you for the nice fruit cake and two cans of nuts. People have been very nice to me this Christmas. I received packages from the Everitts, Entrikens, Dickie Bass, Juda Shipley in addition to all those I mentioned in my last letter.

Juda Jane sent me a swell identification bracelet with my name and serial number on it, and Elaine sent me a "Saint Christopher, Protect Us" medal to wear around my neck.

It's about time I'm getting some sleep, so I shall write again soon.

I love you all dearly,

Bob

★

First Lieutenant Bass was killed in action on February 7, 1945.

right back up on the line. This time, however, we tied right in with an infantry unit on our right and one on our left. We were told to dig in defensive positions and get ready for an enemy armored attack.

Sure enough, we had only been in these positions a day and then came the German tanks followed by their infantry. Their main thrust was in our own sector. Our own small arms fire stopped the infantry, but those tanks kept coming. There was an artillery forward observer with us and he was trying to adjust his fire on these tanks. I don't imagine a bunch of engineers ever said quite so many prayers as we did in those few minutes, when the German tanks were almost upon us before the artillery observer could get his fire on them. The tanks were less than 200

Men of an infantry division in the Hürtgen Forest near Zweifall
in Germany opening packages that have just arrived from home

infantry battalions. It was just a three or four day job, and then we were to return to our little village and go on as before.

While we were building this supply road, the big German counter-offensive began, but we didn't know it. We could hear small arms and artillery fire on both sides of us but just imagined it was the normal thing, since the infantry battalion we were supporting was making an attack.

Finally, we got an order for our whole battalion to retire to a little town in the rear and re-organize as an infantry battalion. We moved back, dropped all of our engineer tools and equipment, left our trucks, put our machine guns and rifles on our backs, and after dark marched up into the line as infantry. We were supposed to have tied in on our right and left flanks with the infantry units of our own division. But we never saw another American unit. For two days and two nights we sat on the side of a hill waiting for a German attack. We could hear fighting on both sides of us and in our rear, and we couldn't figure out what was going on. We still didn't know the Germans had opened a counter-offensive. Finally, since we had no communcation with anyone, nor had we for two days, and since we never could find our own infantry units which we were supposed to tie into, our battalion commander (whom you know) led us out of this hole down through a valley and on to the rear. The Germans never knew that we were on the side of that hill. They had us practically surrounded, and if they had known we were there, it wouldn't have taken much to fix us. We hadn't had one bit of food in over two days and had just enough ammunition to fill our guns. We had to march up there and therefore couldn't carry much with us other than our weapons. We were supposed to have been supplied, but no one knew where we were.

The division had given our battalion up as lost, and, as we came marching through a small American-held town, a Chaplain rushed out and asked what unit we were. When my company commander said "The 324th Engineers," the Chaplain said, "Thank God."

We marched on for a day and finally reached the little village where we had been staying. There for the first time, we found out about the enemy offensive. We ate our first meal in three days, received a new complement of ammunition, and were sent

in the wrong place. One of the crew opened the hatch, and after a dying run by the plane, Smitty, Vic, and Stan disappeared through the hole—just like that. Joe Lukitsch and I swung our legs into the hole and looked down. With a full moon the tumbled hills far below looked eerie; the fires looked small and distant—they were, about 2500 feet. Suddenly the green light blazed and the bell rang on the wall of the ship, and I dropped through, Joe right after me. The chute opened with a crack, but I had a bad spin and the shroud lines were twisting rapidly—if they twist enough, the chute collapses. I fought for about 1000 feet before the twists came out.

Then I looked around. With the night breezes Joe sailed past like a shot out of a cannon. Below, there was nothing but hill, woods, and rocks. It looked like a trap. I was sure it was when I landed—between two wicked spikes of limestone, doing a couple of back somersaults down a gully into some saplings. There wasn't a person around, just complete silence. I cut my way out of the chute and got out my automatic. For twenty minutes there wasn't a sound. Then I made for a low, bare hillock nearby, and in a little while the others came up. It was 2 a.m. The fires were phony all right. Smitty had landed near them and had seen a man running away.

About 700 yards away a fire shone on the side of Mount Pala, but we couldn't find the path; which was lucky as the fire came from a house the Germans were burning, we found out later. They were too drunk to pay any attention to the drop.

We hid in a deep swale until dawn, and then I went to a farmhouse to ask questions. By noon we had made contact with some local partisans and later were on our way back into the mountains. We felt that we had been granted a miracle. The whole operation was in full sight of Nazi observation towers in the plain below, and the lack of reception and the hideous rock pile we landed on should have made us all casualties and easy prisoners. Aside from cuts and bruises we were okay. It took the Nazis a week to start chasing us.

On August 12 I started out alone for the Cadore, about 30 miles from Ovasta, crossing Lavardet Pass: made contact with the partisans around San Stefano, and started work. The Cadore

out of Nazi hands in Albania; 1st Lt. Joe Lukitsch of Cleveland, a paratrooper who came over on the boat with me: Sgt. Victor Malaspino from New Jersey, interpreter, who worked for me when I was chief instructor in the Spy School in the mountains outside Algiers; 1st Class Seaman Stan Sbeig from Bridgeport, radioman.

Smitty was to organize and direct partisans in Carnia, and I was to do the same in Cadore, having also the mission of closing the Cortina road. Once inside German-occupied territory, we were entirely on our own, as autonomous as soldiers of fortune in a Chinese war or banana republic revolution. But I guess General Devers and General Alexander had faith in us because they okayed the deal. Of course it wasn't as easy as that; the project had to be drafted as carefully as a case before the Supreme Court; and the preparations were as detailed as an expedition to Everest; maps, sleeping bags, foreign money, climbing gear, radio ciphers, medicine, and just about a thousand damn things—all weighed and triple-checked.

Finally, the night of August 1, we gathered under the wing of a big four-motored Lancaster at Brindisi airport. We had on "strip-tease" suits, against the cold at 10,000 feet, and looked like Eskimos. We sweated rivers—and froze later over Udine.

The ride was painful, for we were cramped in among the containers of our supplies, and the roar of the engines was overwhelming—also, naturally, the prospect of a parachute jump into enemy territory at night, or any other time, is none too comforting.

At Brindisi we did not know just where we'd drop. A couple of places I'd been counting on were ruled out in the last two days because of Nazi troop movements. We climbed up through the small hole in the bottom of the plane and found we were bound for Mount Pala in the foothills of the Alps of Carnia, bad news for me, as it was some 85 miles from the Cortina area. Smitty and I squabbled for the privilege of being "first out" in the jump, but he outranked me. We nearly did not make it, as the pilot could not find the right pattern of ground fires in the right place. Jerry was, aside from shooting at us with flak, apparently lighting a few signals to decoy us. Finally the word came back over the intercom that the right fires had been spotted, but

Well I'm an old Vet now I fought with the krauts already. Don't think I wasn't scared shitless either. It was Germany at the crack of dawn. We attacked and drove them back then advanced over another ridge and shot the shit out of a hell of a lot of them. Their artillery was hell. It is all over and gave us hell at the time we were up there. Well we met with some enemy tanks and one got my tank. He got us twice on the right and knocked us out. Well I fired 5 or 6 rounds back at him and hit him or scared the shit out of him. Anyway he didn't fire anymore. We couldn't move the tank so we dismounted and the artillery was falling. We covered each other getting out. Germans all over the place. A couple of the other guys took a prisoner behind the lines. Me like a dopey bastard got into another tank and kept going with them. Just after that our leader's tank got knocked out by a bazooka. It wounded 34, we others were OK. All of us in our tank got out OK and no casualties. The next day we took another town and pushed the krauts out. We killed a hell of a lot of them and took five prisoners. There were more tanks and A.T. guns. A lot of our tanks got knocked out by mines.

Soldiers relax in an orchard and write letters home during an interlude between operations inside Germany.

Hey Joe can you imagine me fighting those bastards. It's hard to believe but let me tell you I was there and I know. (Phew) enough of that stuff I'll change the subject.

Holland is quite the place. Nice people and good beer. It makes you piss like hell but it's OK. The beer in Germany is better.

Don't say anything about this when you write home. I don't want Mom to know OK Joe . . .

Take care of yourself. God bless you.

As ever,

Jack

★

Corporal Bange was killed in action on February 28—the day the 8th Armored Division crossed the Roer River in assault boats at Hilfarthe, the Netherlands.

★ ★ ★

*R*obert *Coakley served as a sergeant with Headquarters Battery, 927th Field Artillery Battalion, 102nd Division. He wrote the following letter to Jean Clarke, who lived in Clifton Forge, Virginia.*

Germany
15th Feb. 1945

Dearest Jean:

I rec'd your letter of Jan. 15 and Jan. 16, a valentine dated Jan. 21 and a birthday card of the same date yesterday.

The letters I mention having rec'd were written earlier than any number of others I got, so on such issues as the entertainment they came as an anti-climax as I already know the end of the story. It was happy anyhow. But the letters are interesting

must have communicated itself in my letter—although I remember very little of what I said. I hope people didn't think I was trying to dramatize myself. My role has been just that of any other infantry officer—and not in the least heroic. One of my boys did a fine job one day—and I've put him in for a Silver Star. One of the tank drivers was killed and we were trying to pull out of a position where we were under heavy fire. I yelled for an assistant driver—he stuck himself out of a hole and asked what I wanted. "Can you drive that tank out?"—then I noticed a huge bandage over his arm. "Jesus, are you hurt?"—"Just a scratch."—"Can you drive?"—"Sure!" So he hustles a hundred yards under fire—climbs into the tank—and drives it five miles one handed—and it was piled full of wounded men. The guy is still in the hospital with a cut to the bone through his biceps. I hope he gets a medal—"Just a scratch!"

I don't care what you do with any of my letters—read or print—if they will help people to realize what the men go thru. I just don't want to be thought of as trying to emphasize my part in this hell of a war.

We've been fighting again—I don't know how many days. I've had a lot of responsibility. I directed my cannon fire today —hundreds of rounds—and most of the time firing within one to two hundred yards of our own men. The least slip, and maybe twenty of your own men get killed. When you've sat thru 300 rounds—nerves like fiddle strings till each round hits—well, that's one thing that makes an old man of you.

You have to admire the guts of these little Japs sometimes. Our men were attacking a ridge. Thru my glasses, 2,000 yards away, I suddenly saw a dozen Japs' head and shoulders above the ridge, rifles ready, like tin soldiers in a toy shop. I put a round of 105 right in the middle of them. They ducked, and came up again. That happened 5 or 6 times. —Guts—Finally we got tired of that—so I adjusted time fire about ten yards over their heads and laid in a barrage. Fox holes or trenches—they couldn't have lived thru that—and we saw no more of them. We located a pill box near there and adjusted fire on it. The third shot knocked off a corner of it—and eight Japs—looking like animated dolls thru our glasses—came running out. Our infantry was a hundred yards away—and they mowed them down with rifle fire. Our next shot was directly on the box and threw logs sky-high. It burned for an hour. That's just one example of what is happening time and again in my job. And, of course, the Japs shoot back. Fortunately, they have no heavy guns in this position, and I'm personally fairly safe in this campaign—so far. The worst worry I've had is not to hit our own men—and so far we've been lucky—or rather, the GIs have been lucky.

I sometimes reflect with amazement on my role in this war. I used to be a music teacher—I was a pacifist—talked about the infinite value of the human personality—how barbaric it was to kill a man because he was in another color uniform. But here I am—and when we make a direct hit, we smile grimly at each other and phone a "well done" to the gun crew. One day a Jap who had been bypassed nearly killed one of my sergeants. He was in a hole in a river bank. I, and some of my boys, covered the sergeant (he got the honor) while he crept up and threw two grenades into the hole. Then the men dragged out the Jap, and poured a whole magazine of tommy-gun into him. After that it's my job to search the body for documents. And it doesn't bother me! Do you wonder that I say I'm sometimes amazed at myself? I'm more of a pacifist than I ever was, but as long as there are vermin like Japs and Nazis, they have to be exterminated—and it is hellish work. The cost in human lives, material and labor simply can't be estimated.

My love to Janice and Prudence—and thanks for your good letter.

Yours,

Kermit

At the time of writing, Corporal Kenneth Connelly's* outfit—the 333rd Infantry Regiment, 84th Infantry Division—was in defensive positions along the Rhine.

---

* Other letters from Corporal Connelly appear on pages 63, 270, and 277.

Germany
March 11, 1945

I met a Jew in the streets of a town in this vicinity. I should like
to elaborate on him because I think that every American would
profit by meeting him. I was walking alone down a street in a
large city which had just passed into our hands, making my way
from one headquarters to another on business. It was a thor-
oughfare in the heart of town and here and there in the rubble
left by Allied bombers stood some stubborn pillar or sign that
indicated that it had once been a glamorous, prosperous street.
It was as deserted as a new-world plain. There wasn't a soul to
be seen in any direction and the effect was weird and discon-
certing. That is, there wasn't a soul except one fellow standing
in front of a building that had been strangely spared by the air
attack. He was a sturdy, blond-haired lad of twenty-five maybe,
dressed jauntily in a trench-coat and looked like a synthesis of
the Nordic God Siegfried and Al Capone. His hands were stuffed
in his pockets and an inner voice told me that his fingers were
probably sweatily toying with a Luger trigger. If he's out to murder me, I thought to myself, there's no reason why he shouldn't
be brilliantly successful. I decided to walk by him with absolute
unconcern, but he stopped me with a well-mannered sentence
in splendid English. "Fellow," he said, "I've been waiting for the
Military Government for two hours. You don't know where the
town major is, do you?" He pointed to the surviving edifice.
"This building was Gestapo headquarters and is full of files that
will mean life or death to many people. Your Military Government should have guards here and not leave the records unprotected. Why, I am all alone here and I am a citizen of Germany."
He apparently read bewilderment in my face. How could he, I
wondered, army-age and obviously a physical specimen, have
escaped the Volkssturm or even the Storm Troopers? Who was
this Aryan creature telling me that the American Army wasn't
cautious enough in dealing with Germans? "I am a Jew," he
said. At last I had met one of the people in whose name we are
waging this war—if we are waging this war in the name of
justice. Here was the persecuted, the tortured and hunted. Here
was the man that had set the world in armed conflict. Here was

a living symbol of a philosophical stand, the stand that all men are brothers.

"I have been hiding in this town for six and one-half months," he said. "In a basement. I formerly worked in Dresden but when the order of September 15 came out, I decided I'd have to go into hiding, preferably near the border." What the order of September 15 is I do not know but I assume it was a Mass Execution Order demanding the death of anyone tainted with a fluid ounce of Jewish blood. "There used to be three thousand Jews living in this town. Now I'd be surprised if there are fifty alive. They have been imprisoned and tortured and murdered for many years now. I am lucky to be alive."

"It is inconceivable that these people one sees on the highways, these gray-haired, kind-faced Hausfraus and beer-bellied Paps could be so cruel," I said.

"It was like a flame—a flame of intense hate that spread over Germany. The Nazis looked for some segment of the population on which to heap the blame for the sins of the world and they settled on the Jews. With each mistake the Nazis made, with each National Socialistic failure a new 'Purge' would be started. Our homes were burnt and our books. Our stores were looted and our synagogues destroyed," he said.

"How could it happen—how could such insanity seize a whole nation—"

He looked very squarely at me and asked, "Can you honestly say that the same thing could not happen in the United States? If what anti-Semitism that is there were given political direction do you think that such a program would be impossible in America?"

I remembered a thousand and one remarks that I had heard passed at cultured dinner parties, in class rooms, and among business men—and I didn't want to look that boy straight back in the eye.

*C*aptain James Richards served with the 863rd Field Artillery Battalion, 63rd Infantry Division. He wrote this letter to his wife, an Army nurse, the day before the division penetrated the Wees Wall and attacked near Saarbrücken, Germany.

14 March 1945

My darling:

Tonight there isn't time for news. There hasn't been a letter from you for a couple of days either, so I'll come to what's on my mind. Dear, while I know it will worry you to get this, until you hear from me again, I couldn't go out on the attack we're making knowing I might have written once more and didn't. We're starting something big and I know in a few days you'll be reading about it. While I shall be careful, there is a job to do, and I want you to know, dearest, that you are filling my thoughts tonight, as always. I will write when I can again, and perhaps the war will be much nearer its end for this night's work.

While I want terribly to come back to you, and that soon, there is a grim thrill to being in on something like this. Having a limited attack a while ago, I know a bit what this will be like, but this time it's a steamroller.

Tonight we saw the long silent files of Infantry moving up alongside the road, while in the middle the interminable motor columns groaned and crawled along. In the distance we could hear our planes bombing, and see the spark—like bursts of the flak in the clear night sky. It was mindful of a distant summer storm coming up in a July night, except for the purposeful plodding of those troops in the gloom. A storm of human making is brewing and we are a part in the making of it.

Even when this is over and I can talk to you, I doubt if I can describe all the impressions I am receiving at this time. The war drags along for weeks and while busy with routine matters, it is hardly a war of manhood and courageous deeds, more a drab struggle for existence. Then this comes along; the senses quicken and the mind springs into supersensitive awareness of men, objects and actions. My inside life—the love for you that carries me thru so much springs into yet sharper focus, and at the same time a tremendous sense of my responsibilities here seems to settle on my shoulders. I have not been afraid yet, and do not expect to be hurt or frightened. I am glad I can do my job and hope you will be as proud of me as I am of you for what you are doing and the way you are taking it. We both are doing what we were trained to do, and our reunion will be that much stronger by virtue of it . . .

I love you my dearest,

Forever, your husband

Jay

★ ★ ★

*H*arry Towne, who served as a corporal with *I Company, 3rd Battalion, 28th Regiment, 5th Marine Division, wrote the following letter.*

Corporal Harry Towne

March 19, 1945
Central Pacific

Dear Mom:

I don't know if you have heard that I was wounded or not Mom. I asked a Chaplain to write to you, so you probably know about it.

I am coming along fine now and expect to be in the States before long. I was wounded quite badly, Mother, but the Navy Medical Corps will fix me up like new again. In a year or less I shall be able to walk just as before.

Don't let this be a shock to you, Mother, I will be in almost as good shape as before now that they have these new artificial limbs. Yes, Mother, I have lost my right leg, but it isn't worrying

*A soldier reading his first letter from home
after arriving at Iwo Jima*

me a bit. I shall receive a pension for the rest of my life and with the new artificial limb, you can hardly tell anything is wrong . . .

I lost my leg on the front lines of Iwo Jima on February 27, but have been moved around so much I couldn't write. I would like to write to Alma, but somehow I can't force myself to do it. You write and tell her, Mother. I'll try to write to her later on.

Don't worry, Mom, the war for me is ended and I should be seeing you by fall.

Love,

Bill

★ ★ ★

Charles Cavas,[*] *a private with the 1st Battalion, 417th Infantry Regiment, 76th Infantry Division, wrote the following letter to a childhood friend in Providence, Rhode Island. At the time of writing, the 417th Regiment was in defensive positions along the Rhine.*

Pvt Charles Cavas 31386553
Hq Co 1st Bn 417th Inf
APO # 76 c/o PM, NY, NY
March 23, 1945

Dear Bob:

For the past few days we have been enjoying a well earned respite, sort of catching our breath, and believe me it is a grand feeling. However I'm afraid it will be all too brief and then we shall be off again, not knowing when or where we will stop again . . .

You may wonder how it is to be in an enemy country meeting people with whom you are fighting and taking over their homes if they haven't been destroyed by our fire. It is strange but you might say I haven't any feeling about the matter. Perhaps it may be that I've been here for some time now and have

---

[*] Another letter from Private Cavas appears on page 253.

seen too much. Whatever it is I feel nothing when we take a town and if I ever do feel the slightest sympathy you can be sure that I shall overcome it and ignore it. Some of the people make attempts to be friendly either by smiling or a wave of the hand, when that happens we usually turn our backs to them. It sounds hard I know, but it's the only way to deal with them. For example let me tell you what has happened several times we've been in towns where we caught civilians, supposedly natives of the town and in most cases they are, who by some means or other, usually by a hidden radio, they send information to their army who of course start shelling the hell out of us. We've lost men and equipment because of such practice, is it any wonder that we've learned to treat these people the way we do? It seems they want to learn the hard way and we are willing to oblige. . . .

    As always,

                       Charlie

A soldier looks over remains of a sack of mail that will never be delivered. The division abandoned supplies and equipment when overrun by Germans.

★   ★   ★

Lieutenant Kermit Stewart* wrote this letter after a month of fighting in the Zambales Mountains.

The Philippines
28 March 1945

Dear Guy and Janice:

. . . We are now enjoying a bit of rest after a month of fighting nearly every day and night. It is good to relax from the strain of action and gun-fire, although reports, inspections, unanswered letters, and other harrassments do not let us emphasize the "rest" angle of this break. There are still thousands of Japs to eliminate. We will be back on the job soon.

Most of the time during the past month I have been in a fairly safe position, tho' I have been able to do considerable damage to Jap installations and give our boys a lot of close support. We were constantly in demand and fired thousands of rounds. I'm becoming something of an expert at mass killing. Great accomplishment. The time came, eventually and inevitably, for me to stick my neck out. About a week or ten days ago my platoon of thinly armored open-topped self-propelled howitzers was assigned a mission of cleaning out a pocket in front of our lines in what looked like a cul de sac—I worked up a good case of nerves over it as I made extensive reconnaissance and formulated a plan of maneuver. Finally we went in with a handful of foot troops to protect us from suicide ground attack, blasted out a score or more caves and pill boxes, received only some harmless sniper fire, and came out both successful and unscratched. The Colonel was pleased. That was bad. Two days later we were sent in again—only much further. And therein hangs a tale.

Since the first mission had been so easy, a lot of officers and men volunteered to go in with the handful of foot troops we

---

* Other letters from Lieutenant Stewart appear on pages 211, 220, and 236.

took in the first time. You couldn't have paid me to go in there, but it was largely my show—and orders are orders.

Our tanks crawled through a pass thru the mountains (Jap territory) looking down on us from both sides. There was practically no cover. The foot troops spread themselves thinly about us for our mutual protection. Behind us on a high OP I could see our observers watching us with their glasses—like a second gallery in an opera house. We moved slowly down the valley, stopping often to blast cave mouths and possible emplacements—often from a dangerous range of 75 to 100 yards. One cave mouth was large enough to accommodate a jeep. When we fired into it, dust billowed out of four or five caves as much as a hundred yards away. That will give you some idea of how those bastards are dug in.

We finally reached a slight turn in the valley and paused to blast a few places and to make further plans. The Japs had waited until we were within point blank range of their well-concealed guns.

Suddenly they cut loose with machine guns and rifles, cross fire from above, the front and our flank. Men dropped all over the place. All was confusion. Bullets cracked past our heads and rattled on our armor like a popcorn popper. We fired back, but couldn't see much to shoot at. We maneuvered our tanks to protect medics and stretcher bearers as they worked over dead and wounded. A truck driver took terrible risks while picking up wounded and evacuating them. I yelled for an officer on the ground, a vague wave from a pale figure on a stretcher—shot in the guts! I dressed my wounded radio operator's arm while he continued to operate the radio. I had to give him a direct order to evacuate. He was protesting that he was needed.

Terse conversations with the Colonel on the radio:

"What's the situation out there?" (He could see us in his glasses a half mile back.)

"Heavy MG fire. —dead I know of. —casualties. No, I see two more. Over."

"Stay out there. Shoot back. Over."

"Roger. We *are* shooting back, Out."

It went on like that. I fired my carbine into cave mouths

where I thought I saw movement. Wounded men crowded our space in the tank. The floor became red—not a pleasant red. Good blood mixed with dirt, grease, cartridges, the litter of aid packs.

Finally we got the order to withdraw—after we had collected all casualties. More maneuvering. Our machine guns far to the rear shot over our heads. Artillery gave us wonderful cover. It was actually good to see that stuff burst barely a hundred yards ahead and to hear the sing of shrapnel.

We raced back thru the pass and into the peculiar hush of the take-off point. It was with a sense of unreality that I climbed from the tank—my knees wobbly from bad nerves and cramps. With a strange sense of detachment I watched medics lift bodies from tanks and trucks and rush them to ambulances. Blood transfusions on the spot. I reported to the Colonel. The mission was in a sense accomplished. We couldn't take the objective by that approach. I was one of three officers still alive. The friends I had joked with two hours before—both dead. One died as I helped lift him into the tank. I felt old and tired.

I don't like war. There is no beauty in a gaping wound. The dead lie on their faces. A live body has personality. A dead body becomes a shrunken mass of rumpled clothing. I can tell when a man is hit, even if he does not fall. His shoulders stoop. His arms and hands tremblingly protect his face and chest, a dazed look of shocked hurt comes into his face and eyes. I can tell now when a man is dying by the gray pallor which changes the healthiest skin. There is no beauty in a war. There is heroism at times, but the desperate heroism of desperate necessity.

We read of our battles in news magazines: "A series of counter attacks were easily repulsed." Why do they have to use that word "easily?" To flatter our vanity? If a single man suffers fear, wounds or death, it is not *easy.* I hope this damned war is over soon. Love to Janice and Prudy.

Regards, Guy.

Kermit

or any other, will still treat the wounded enemy well—but that's where it will end. This Medic was merely acting like many others not within gunshot range—or likely to be targets. Some of them don't seem to know what it's all about and forget that the enemy is not their friend—and would do them in the first chance they got.

On the lighter side, I've been telling Doc, when my packages arrive I'll have plenty of mayonnaise (a favorite item around here)—in fact, I figured I'd have at least 4 jars before the month is out. He said I wouldn't and insisted on betting $5.00 I wouldn't. Sounds silly but this went on over a period of a day. Now I'm sweating out packages for mayonnaise. If it has been put in all the packages your letters say they were, I'm in for sure. The money means nothing—the satisfaction—plenty! These foolish little things help lighten a day.

With all my heart,

Your own Keith

★　　★　　★

*P*rivate Charles Cavas,* who served with the 417th Infantry Regiment, 76th Infantry Division, wrote the following letter. Private Cavas' regiment had crossed the Rhine on March 26 and 27.

Pvt. Charles Cavas 31386553
Hq Co 1st Bn 417th Inf
APO #76 c/o PM, NY, NY
April 20, 1945

Dear Bob:

Since crossing the big river we have been moving so fast that I haven't had much chance to do anything of my own. I'd like to tell you that we made the now famous crossing in the still of a moonlight night, stealthily rowing across with everyone holding their breath expectantly but I'm afraid it wasn't so. We did

---

* Another letter from Private Cavas appears on page 244.

cross at night however but it was on vehicles and on a bridge which the engineers (God bless 'em) had put up in record time. So I'm afraid that I will have to tell my grandchildren that their grandfather crossed the Rhine on a jeep with his ears glued to a radio. However don't think we weren't nervous for although it was only a matter of a few minutes in making the other side it seemed like hours and we expected anything to happen . . . but nothing did, we didn't even hear a single shot.

In taking and going through the towns we are finding a lot of Russians, Poles, French etc. who had been used as slave labor and at times it looks like a parade going by for the streets are lined with these people cheering and waving to us. One town especially where there were even more Poles than Germans. I never saw anyone so glad to see anybody, hell they waved and cheered and surrounded us in an attempt to press our hands. One woman dashed to our jeep, grabbed my hands and if I didn't quickly withdraw them I know she would have kissed them. I'm telling you all this to give you an idea of how they look upon us here, they look upon us as liberators and several times I've thought when witnessing such scenes God help our country if it fails to do its share in maintaining and establishing a world peace at the end of the war.

When we approach a town we look for white flags which may be showing and if we see any we send our troops in but sometimes we do not see anything resembling white flags and since we have learned that SS troops when in a town prevent the people from surrendering we immediately open up on the town with everything we've got including tanks, and it isn't long before every house and building is displaying something white. That's the way we have been working, we don't wreck the town unless we have to for our own protection.

Bob, there are a lot of things I'd like to tell you but unfortunately I have neither the time nor the space. Some day when this is all over we'll have a good old fashioned bull session with plenty of beer (or should I say Four Roses?) about all this . . . that's of course after I have been home for a while for there are a few things that need my immediate attention . . . you follow me I hope???

In one town we liberated an underground factory and as a result we are all wearing clean underwear and socks. And I might add that both wearing apparel is much fancier than anything we have worn in a long time. After we helped ourselves to what we needed a bunch of Frenchmen and Russians came rushing in and they finished emptying the place. I think it is safe to say that the Germans are the only ones in that town walking around in worn underwear and socks.

Sometimes I think that it won't be long before I will be home and all this will be far behind me and it is then that I feel good and my spirits are high and then there are times I feel as though this thing will drag on and even when it is over we will be sent elsewhere (there is still another war on the other side of the world) and then I feel lower than low. I'm tired, Bob. I'm tired with things I've seen and I'm tired of always moving, of going to sleep and being awakened and told we are moving immediately. Of going all day without a bite to eat and for days without washing, can you blame me when I say I'm tired of it all? Through all this the thing that carries me on is thoughts of what I have waiting for me at home . . . each day I say to myself "It shouldn't be long now, it can't be, it's got to end sometime." I've often wondered what makes men go on the way they do and then I think of myself and I know that they too think the way I do with something and someone waiting for them.

I hope you don't think I've gone corny after writing the above but it's the first time I've written anything like that and I know it will be kept between you and me.

Adios,

Charlie.

★ ★ ★

*C*aptain Robert Neelands served with the 18th Photo Intelligence Detachment, Fourteenth Air Force, in Kunming, China. The incident described in this letter took place in what was called Chihkiang, a forward air base to which Captain Neelands was assigned at the time.

April 21, 1945

Dear Dad:

. . . Yesterday, we were standing outside the photo lab when one of the boys noticed a B-25 coming in for a landing. He said half to himself, "You're too damned high, boy—take her around again." We couldn't see the end of the runway, so we just stood and waited to see him go around again. Go around or . . .

When we saw the characteristic black oil smoke begin to roll up, we went down to it in our jeep. The plane was smashed at the bottom of a 100 foot drop at the end of the runway, the usual twisted mess that is a crashed plane. We went down to see if there was anything we could do. The heat was terrific and the plane was white hot from it. It looked like the inner mazes of Hell. Then, we heard a man screaming from the plane, "Help me, please, won't somebody help me." Someone standing near me muttered all our thoughts, "My God, there's someone alive in there." Then we could see him, partly hanging out of the side of the plane and almost indistinguishable from the wreckage. The flames were blowing away from him, and several of us ran up to try to get him out. The ammunition was exploding in the guns and the gas was continually going up in a tremendous "whoosh." No one knew at what moment the bombs would go off. He was stuck in the wreckage, and it was impossible to pull him out. He kept screaming for us to keep trying to get him out. Someone started to cut off his trapped leg with a pocket knife, but couldn't. It only made him scream louder. I never could stand a man screaming.

When the heat drove us away, the Colonel, that is C.O. of the base, borrowed someone's .45 pistol. He is a young lad, big and good looking. He walked as near as he could to the man and raised the pistol. The boy screamed, "Please, Colonel, for the love of God, don't shoot me, please, please, please." The colonel dropped his hand, shook his head and turned away. All of his men were standing behind him, waiting for him to do what he must do. Again he raised the pistol and we could hear the boy scream, "Please, oh God, please let them try just once more." The colonel shouted to him, "I have to boy, you'll burn alive. I'm sorry." The boy watched the colonel as he sighted the pistol and fired—once, twice. The boy in the plane seemed to be kicked twice by an invisible foot. His eyes kept watching the colonel for what seemed an eternity and then his head rolled slowly toward the fire as if in unbelief that he should die. The colonel stood staring into the plane, seeming only then to realize that he had shot a man. His hand dropped to his side slowly. It seemed minutes before he even seemed to remember that he had the gun. Then he threw it with all his strength into the burning plane, turned and walked a few steps, buried his face in his hands and cried in long, shaking sobs. It was an old corporal that put his arm around his shoulders and led him away. I wanted to be sick, but I couldn't. I wanted to forget it and couldn't. I slept, or tried to sleep, with it last night. I have been living with it since.

They picked him out this morning. He didn't look human, of course, and you couldn't tell which was his head and which his feet. They layed his identification bracelet on top of him— it had fallen off. . . .

Bob

★   ★   ★

*M*ajor General Andrew Bruce* wrote to the widow of Ernie Pyle, the war correspondent who had spent more than three years in combat areas in Europe and the Far East. His eyewitness accounts focused on the experiences of the GI.

APO 77, C/O POSTMASTER

SAN FRANCISCO, CALIF.

30 April 1945

Dear Mrs. Pyle:

I know you have received thousands of letters but perhaps you should like to have my story of the last few days of his life. He was present at several of our press conferences in the evening. One night I missed him and found that he had gone to Sick Bay

---

* Another letter from Major General Bruce appears on page 168.

with a cold. A few days later I visited him and we had quite a chat. I am so glad I told him when he lived how much he meant to the men and how his presence inspired them. Too often we wait until too late to let people know what they do.

On the morning of the 18th, I issued some orders for the continuation of the attack and Ernie came up and we discussed how long it would take to capture the island. We both came to the same conclusion. When he left me, several soldiers flocked around him to get his autograph. He did not tell me where he was going. Things happened very fast and messages came piling in. Suddenly I heard, "My God, Ernie Pyle has been killed." I instantly directed that a verification of this statement be made. It was difficult to get an exact statement through several relays, since Colonel Coolidge and others that were still with Ernie were pinned down by the same machine gun; hence, the reason for my sending "standing beside Colonel Coolidge" instead of saying "in a ditch beside Colonel Coolidge." As you have probably been told, they were fired upon while in a jeep and all jumped out and jumped into a ditch. As I now understand it, he raised his head to look around and was struck in the temple and instantly killed. I give you this detail of why I made the error in sending the following message:

Ernie Pyle with sailors aboard an aircraft carrier in the Pacific

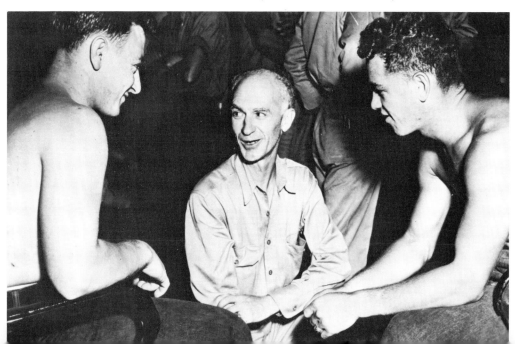

From: CG 77th Div
To: CG Tenth Army
Regretfully report Ernie Pyle, who has so materially aided in building morale of foot troops, was killed instantly by surprise Jap machine gun fire while standing beside regimental commander of foot troops, 77th Infantry Division, Lt. Col. Coolidge on outskirts of Ie Shima town about 1015 today.

Among other things, while it was fresh in our minds, I wrote an inscription to be placed on a temporary marker at the exact spot where he was killed, so that a more suitable marker can be placed there later. The inscription was:

AT THIS SPOT
THE 77TH INFANTRY DIVISION
LOST A BUDDY
ERNIE PYLE
18 APRIL 1945

That night I issued a statement to the press as follows:

It is hard to tell how much Ernie Pyle meant to the men of our services. I have seen units buck up and be thrilled when they knew Ernie Pyle was around and would give them their just recognition for a dirty job they have to do. The Jap machine gun sniper hid within our lines caused the death of a buddy of the 77th Division. We shall never forget Ernie Pyle.

Later on in a broadcast, I made the following statement:

In the short time he was with us, Ernie Pyle made many friends among the officers and men of the 77th Division. We did our best to honor him in death. The memory of Ernie Pyle will help us in the hard battles that lie ahead.

Please call on us if there is anything further you wish to know or to have done.
With deepest sympathy,
    Sincerely,

A. D. BRUCE
Major General, U.S. Army
Commanding.

A drawing on V-Mail stationery
by Sergeant Samuel Greco to his mother

★   ★   ★

Mitchell Sharpe served as a private first class with the 346th Infantry Regiment, 87th Infantry Division. He saw active service in the Rhineland, Ardennes-Alsace, and Central Europe campaigns.

2 May 1945
England

Dear Mom:

I couldn't possibly feel any worse if you had written one of the immediate family had died. Neal's death has hit me pretty bad for I know how he must have gone. I keep thinking of him like that kid with his M1 stuck in the ground with his helmet on it (a sign of death) lying off the path looking as if he were asleep. I see him lying on his back arms overhead with eyes and mouth open as if asking, "God, why?" To the people at home killed in action means one ceases to exist. Here it is different. One may be for days in a perpetual attitude of some form of physical expression—fear, sleep, laughter. I keep remembering all the letters from him. He had planned many things—"As soon as we get home." If you could only see us kids killed at eighteen, nineteen and twenty fighting in a country that means nothing to us, fighting because it means either kill or be killed not because you're making the world safe for democracy or destroying Nazism. Kids that have never had a crack at life. Some have

Private First Class Mitchell Sharpe

never worked and earned money and felt proud, never finished their quest or insatiable thirst for knowledge, never felt the temporary exhilaration of being drunk, never slept with a girl. Each one of them has something just as precious to go back to at home—a slum district in New York, a farm in Kansas, a small town in Arkansas. Each one has so many dreams and plans. There's no *"if* I get home" it is always *"when* I get home". I'm convinced of one thing—Neal didn't go "like a quarry slave at night scourged to his dungeon" but he went proudly. Mom, Neal was proud of being a buck sergeant. At first he had the same position I have, but he looked down on it. He wanted to be first scout. He was made a buck sergeant assistant squad leader. He wrote me and I could tell he was full of pride at being made a sergeant. He took a special pride in fulfilling his duties because he was conscientious. He made me ashamed of the petty jealousies and quarrels that went on in our platoon. His death has made me despise the self-centered mundane, little creatures who because of their positions as officers assume, and state, "I'm God" attitudes. It has made me see what a hopeless and senseless mockery this war is. What we have now will never compensate for the thousands of Neals buried from Normandy to Munich. It will all have to be done again in fifty or so years. . . .

Write soon, love

Mitchell

★ ★ ★

This is the first letter that Captain Ted Bellmont wrote to his parents following the Germans' surrender in Italy. Captain Bellmont served with the 3rd Battalion, 349th Regiment, 88th Infantry Division.

Foothills of the Alps
May 3, 1945

Dear Mother and Dad:

We all received the word of the cessation of hostilities in Italy with a spirit of exhaustive happiness. Yesterday afternoon we had just completed a tiring foot march over the mountain trails toward the Alps—15 miles in hot pursuit of a disgracefully disorganized and weary enemy—and we were too tired to celebrate.

It is such a blessing to have the opportunity of sitting down for a few hours in a cozy building of a picturesque Austrian village in Northern Italy. And I am even more grateful for the privilege of writing my loving family—my first letter in weeks —to inform you that I am healthy and well, although quite tired from 18 days of relatively precarious and exhausting experiences in routing the Germans from Italy.

The relation of my experiences since D-Day, April 15, will certainly remain prominent and numerous in my memories. Any limited descriptions of the offensive will be far too inadequate in words and vividness, but I will attempt in the space below to tell you some of the highlights of my life the past three weeks . . .

From our position high in the Appenines on April 14 (one day prior to D-Day) I witnessed an allied air assault on German positions which demonstrated the power and might of our great Army. For hours thousands of planes roared through the clear skies—heavies, mediums, fighter bombers, and Rover Joe's— the pursuit planes with their close bombardment and strafing support. The mountains literally shook with the impact from their bombs. I witnessed two planes falling with their crews parachuting to the earth. Smoke from fires and explosions blotted out the vision of the observers—it was a destructive, yet thrilling, sight.

H-Hour came at 2300 hours April 15. I was in a position from which I could observe most of the preliminary fireworks. For a solid hour the sound of our mighty artillery deafened our ears—50 calibre guns . . . mortars . . . tracer bullets . . . everything conceivable was hurled into the Kraut positions before the troops jumped off. The Kraut winter defenses withstood it all and the enemy fought our troops with the keenest vigor and stubbornness. The first two days saw our men advance yard by yard and casualties were relatively heavy. Later—a mountain fell to us—and after four days it was a mad race for the Po. I stepped on a Kraut trip wire which fortunately only had a flare on its end. Our attack through the mountains and towards the

Po was in full swing. The sunny morning of April 21 saw the morale of the troops rise as they stepped in to the smooth flatlands of the fertile Po River Valley. It was like a table-top. To accompany and witness the striking power and might of our forces as they poured from the mountains into the valley was an inspiration . . . tanks, armor, vehicles, men . . . thousands of men . . . were attacking furiously to rout the enemy. Contrary to our anticipated conception, the natives in the valley received us in a relieved spirit of reverent happiness and glory. They were all happy. They filled the streets and fields, waving flags, serving "vino", throwing flowers, and even kissing us . . . we were their liberators. An elderly woman in one place we stopped for a few hours had 7 dozen eggs which she had been saving for the allies . . . she fried eggs for hours and gave them to the troops. Resistance then was spotted and in small groups . . . casualties were light on us . . . speed was imperative—and you know how the Infantry travels. Twenty or twenty-five miles a day meant nothing . . . morale was good, and prisoners were being taken by the thousands . . . for two weeks my Battalion alone averaged over a thousand a day! The weather was beautiful . . . Rover Joe was over in force dive bombing and strafing to our immediate front. In one day I personally saw at least 1000 Krauts' vehicles, carts, and artillery pieces which our supporting Air Forces had destroyed. We were moving incredibly fast . . . Kraut prisoners were not only Infantrymen but Quartermaster, Artillery, Finance, and everything. We took German hospitals intact—complete with staff. Fires started by our aircraft generated smoke which partially covered our advance on one windy day. Tanks —German tanks—were afire—many exploded nearby. Civilians were fleeing in desperation only to rejoice at the sight of our troops . . . homes were burning; horses and cattle were strewn about dead. It was an exhaustingly thrilling sight. The enemy was running—on foot and on stolen bicycles. We had come so fast that they could not even get their vehicles and equipment across the Po river. They were already licked. The Italian Partisans took up arms—aided generously in routing the defeated foe. We struck through their settlements like lightning, and they "mopped up". Dressed in every colorful uniform conceiv-

edly puttering in the vicinity of the station telephone when it rang the Battalion signal. For lack of anything better to do he listened in. His face took on light. "The Russians are here," he yelled. Without further ado I ran to the Chaplain, hastily muttered something about Russians and we made a fast exit knocking a few innocent bystanders flat on their backs (more or less). It was a bumpy frantic few minutes over the impossible road to the River Crossing. For three or four days thousands of terrified Germans had been coming to the Elbe bank to be ferried into captivity by our own Division Engineer boatman. And some wounded Wehrmacht men wrapped in blood caked bandages had come across—the result of Russian artillery. It was an unorthodox situation to say the least and certainly a pertinent commentary on the attitude of the German people toward the Americans and Russians respectively. The great columns of German troops surrendering daily, passing through by the thousands were evidence that the Russians weren't far off. To get back to the River front. I wheeled up to the bank and made for a motor-boat I saw heading across the Elbe. After I had nudged my way in I learned it was the first to go across—a fact that I have made much of to my friends who only made second or later boats.

The Elbe is quite an impressive stream according to European standards and makes a respectable sister for the Rhine. The crossing seemed to take a good bit out of eternity but eventually we approached the flat shore-line and were on the verge of living the most Hollywoodian moment of the war. Our boat touched ground where three stocky Russians awaited us with broad grins on their faces. They were clad according to the best tradition with flared Cossack coats and those Persian wool-looking hats that go with them. There was a moment of self-consciousness; hand-shaking seemed a little obvious and too sedate but that's what finally sealed our meeting. I took a strong Russian paw in hand and yelled ecstatically. Everyone was genuinely elated and I experienced a feeling of tremendous relief. "This is it," I said to myself. "No more ducking from 88 shells in Europe." A Soviet tanker, with a face like that of a Garfield High quarterback and a corresponding smile, came up and slapped me on the back and after much mutual admiration he motioned for me to follow him and ran over a hill on the river-bank. On the other side I saw a large concentration of Russians, and it was a fascinating sight. I was surprised to see so many horses, maybe two or three hundred of the finest and most beautifully groomed I've ever seen. The tanker was quite contemptuous of the horses though and led me to the tank he commanded, and explained it to me part by part in excellent Russian. With my mechanical aptitude I'm confident I learned as much as if he had delivered the discourse in standard English. The tanker and I then had our picture taken together with arms about one another in the best brotherly fashion. The Soviets are intrigued by cameras and take photographs very seriously. To be frozen semi-permanently in black and white is about as much immortality as their state allows them to hope for. The soldiers not in the picture were consumed with envy. But it was neither the Russians nor the Americans that would have caught a novelist's eye on that shore. It was the thousands of Germans silently sandwiched between the Russians and the water—praying that through some miracle they could cross the Elbe and surrender to the Americans. There were columns of Wehrmacht men in the melancholy green; there were distraught civilians with their pathetic bundles of clothes and black-bread and perhaps a few pictures from the family album; there were mothers with new born babies weeping bitterly and begging for mercy. Before the Russians had reached the river-bank the wife and daughter of a German Major-General had stripped and swum the river. At one point we saw fifteen Germans drown trying to escape the vengeful forces of the U.S.S.R. Tearful men and women were pleading with any American soldier that would listen to them and threatening suicide if they couldn't surrender to the Americans. One hard, fanatical SS soldier begged to be killed. A German lad asked me if they were going to the Russians. When I told him he was he reached into his knap-sack and pulled out a camera and handed it to me. "Here," he said, "I would rather an American had it."

★ ★ ★

*K*enneth Board* *served as a sergeant with the 20th Squadron, 2nd Bombardment Group, Fifteenth Air Force. He wrote this letter from Foggia, a town south of Rome, to his wife in Detroit, Michigan.*

> Sgt. Kenneth Board
> 20th Bomb (Squadron)
> 2nd Bomb. Group
> APO 620 c/o PM
> New York, New York
> Tuesday 8 May 1945

Dearest Leona:

Well, this is it honey—VE Day is here. I'm sure I don't have to tell you what kind of bedlam has been going on around here, because you probably had just as much if not more but somehow the day has put me in a very somber mood instead of the conventional hilarious rejoicing one. I keep thinking of all the people I have heard talk about this moment in the past two years—after the war, apres la guerre, doppe la guerra, no matter what language they said it in, it was always with that same wistful tone of hope, and the few people that I have met must be just a fraction of the millions who are hoping for great things from the period which has now begun. These people have no grand plans in mind, they just hope that somehow there will be peace, jobs, reasonable prices, ample commodities, in short the opportunity to live, laugh and have fun. These wants are so fundamental and so simple that I often think we make a bad mistake to tolerate a class of professional politicians and diplomats who are liable to lose sight of these basic wants because they themselves have them provided for them. Yes honey, it's kinda frightening to think of all the millions of people who are hoping so very much for a successful reconstruction period. The problems involved are staggering, and I think it's by far the most difficult period of

---

* Another letter from Sergeant Board appears on page 187.

the entire war. At least in the fighting the objectives are very clear cut—to beat the enemy army—but from now on the path is beset by cross currents and undertow, and with everybody concentrating on just getting home and relaxing, it's a fine opportunity for these groups who desire another war to start laying the groundwork for it. . . .

Ken

★ ★ ★

Stephen Skalitzky served as a private with the 8th Infantry Regiment, 4th Infantry Division.

*Private
Stephen Skalitzky*

May 8, 1945
V-E Day
France

Dear Marion:

How did I celebrate it, well Dear when the whistles blew, I was loading a machine gun belt and without pausing said a quiet prayer of thanksgiving. Though tonight I went to a sermon and benediction in the Cathedral, after which I walked the streets. There is a big dance going full blast in the market square and the streets are jammed with people. I did try to buy champagne but too late, it was sold out, anyhow I prefer water to anything offered tonight . . .

I suppose the people in the States are really whooping things up, especially those who did everything possible to slow up the day. I've a clipping concerning that which I'm bringing along with me . . .

It's nearly time for me to sleep, it's almost midnight so darling sweet dreams although it's just starting evening.

Always yours,

Stephen

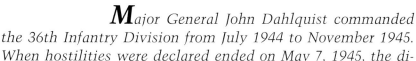

*M*ajor *General John Dahlquist commanded the 36th Infantry Division from July 1944 to November 1945. When hostilities were declared ended on May 7, 1945, the division had reached the area of Kufstein, Austria.*

Somewhere in Austria
9 May 1945

Dearest Ruth:

Well V-E Day is here. We completed our job yesterday afternoon. For two days previous I had held my troops while we negotiated the administrative arrangements for the surrender of the remaining German Troops in front of the 36th Division. We had the strength to push on but did not want to risk any unnecessary casualties.

I am waiting now for General Stack to bring in our biggest catch of the War—Reichmarschall Goering. Early yesterday morning two German Luftwaffe officers came to my CP, the emissaries from Goering. I sent Stack and a reconnaissance group to receive him. Late yesterday he had not yet shown up so I drove to the rendezvous and saw Stack. Goering and his party had left for the rendezvous hours before but had not arrived. I sent Stack to look for him. Apparently about 1:30 this morning they came in. I had sent Peel back with some cars. He was back at breakfast and had seen Goering. I also sent a Texas flag down and got a picture of Goering with the flag for home consumption . . . The German troops who have surrendered and are in our midst seem to be very docile. They all salute as I pass —a good many giving the "Heil Hitler" salute of the upraised hand which I just ignore. It is time I got back to work.

Loads of love,

John

Field Marshal Hermann Goering with Major General John E. Dahlquist, commanding general, 36th Infantry Division (left) and Brigadier General Robert I. Stack, assistant commanding general (right), on the balcony of the Grand Hotel in Kitzbühel, Austria, after the field marshal's capture by General Stack.

★

10 May 1945

Dearest Ruth:

Just a note to enclose with some pictures of von Rundstedt and Goering. Goering spent about an hour and a half with me. I gave him lunch before I shipped him off to 7th Army. He is a big fat slob and looks just like his pictures. He talked very freely and spent his whole time telling me all about it. I asked him few questions because he apparently needed no prompting. He was quite nervous, naturally, and did a lot of sweating. He was also hungry. I believe his fork hit the chicken before the plate touched the table. When I came to my suite—Stack had brought him there—and was introduced to Goering the first thing he asked me if I was a Swede. Goering's first wife was a Swede. He tried to talk to me in Swedish but we got along much better in German. It was an interesting experience nevertheless. . . .

Loads of love to you all,

John

*C*orporal Kenneth Connelly* served with the 333rd Regiment, 84th Infantry Division.

Germany
May 10, 1945

We now have an abundance of luxuries—including our own radio which is currently tuned to Radio Hamburg. Not so very long ago Radio Hamburg meant the cold sharp voice of Anna, the English speaking Nazi, who by every device known to man and the devil tried to break our morale with false news reports, threats of terror, subtle philosophical lectures, tear-jerker dramas, etc., etc. I had the greatest admiration for her art which was highly developed indeed—and she would have been dis-

---

* Other letters from Corporal Connelly appear on pages 63, 238, and 270.

heartened if she knew how many of my lonely evenings on the
Rhine and Siegfried Line she lightened with her broadcasts.
Now a calm English voice holds forth over Radio Hamburg.
Perhaps Anna's greatest feat as far as the 84th is concerned took
place just after we had returned to the North from Belgium. The
move was made in dead secrecy. All markings were removed
from our equipment and vehicles; before we received our mail
the address on the envelope had to be burned before an officer.
We moved in motor convoy in the night, and "stole" into position. We had been on line for a day or two when Anna nonchalantly came on the air and cooed, "Welcome back, Railsplitters!

Home again

We're so glad to have you and promise you a BIG SURPRISE when you try to cross the Roer." The next day the enemy shot over shells loaded with papers which were decorated with our insignia which we had removed scrupulously from our clothes. The papers read, "Dear Hatchet Men! Why did you take off your pretty patches? Are you ashamed of them? We know you must miss them so we are sending some over." Anna also loved to give us OUR SECRET password about sun-down. All in all a remarkable woman. I'd love to meet her.

The first page of a letter written by Private First Class Andrew Sivi, who served with the 179th Infantry Regiment, 45th Infantry Division. He and three other GIs entered Adolf Hitler's house in Munich on May 1, 1945, and stayed there for approximately three weeks.
The day before Private Sivi left he took the opportunity to use Hitler's desk and personal stationery to write his sister a letter.

★ ★ ★

*A*ndrew Balogh served as a technical sergeant with the 209th Combat Engineers in the Central Burma Army Command from 1944 to 1945. He wrote the following letter to his wife.

June 10, 1945
Burma

Hello darling:

Sunday has rolled around again and as usual I am working today just like any other day. I haven't been to church since I arrived at this place. Perhaps if I tried hard enough, I could get out of the office for a few hours, but somehow or other I don't get around to doing it.

I never forget the fact though that I am in need of spiritual guidance and I do feel quite bad about the whole thing. I never knew that a place could get as hot as this place is now. It is almost unbearable and when they tell me that it is going to get worse, I really get worried about it. It isn't the heat alone, but the humidity is what gets us down. I have never sweated so much in all my life and I keep wondering where all the water

Technical Sergeant
Andrew Balogh

comes from in the body. I tried to take salt tablets, but I threw them up when I tried. The old area was much cooler than this place and in most respects it was a better place to be. Oh well, what is the use of complaining, it certainly won't do me any good, but when I gripe to you in these letters, they make me feel a little better.

I took off for a few hours today and rode down to a native village with a sergeant friend of mine. We were invited into a native home and the native woman served us some tea. The tea was very good and we stayed for an hour. She knew how to speak English and I was surprised to hear her talk about the Baptists in Burma. Her whole family is Baptist and from what I found out, most of the natives around here are Baptist. Before the war the American missionaries were doing wonderful work here and they did a lot by teaching these poor natives about religion. It is very surprising to see a Bible in a native hut. They also told me about the Japs and the way they tortured these poor people. The Japs would come into the village and kill all the women that were around. They took particular delight in bayoneting pregnant women. They would throw the small babies into the air and then shoot them. Of course the Americans chased all the Japs out of this place and now the natives are very grateful.

Rather gruesome isn't it, darling? Perhaps I shouldn't write about these things but it will give you an idea what this place had to go thru. If everyone at home could see the effects of war like we do over here, they would do everything in their power to speed this war along to a final victory. Seeing nothing but shell holes and fox holes for miles around isn't exactly a pretty sight. With all the buildings torn down by shell fire and seeing bullet holes in everything around you a person gets a very vivid impression of warfare. To see the American cemeteries around here is no fun at all. Things are quiet around here now, darling, so don't let this letter alarm you. I know that this is the first time that I wrote about this to you, but I know that you are interested in everything I see or do.

This is about all I can write tonight, darling. I'll close this one more letter to you by saying that I love you more and more every day. I never forget you for a minute darling, and I am hoping that you never forget me. I love you with all my heart and I will always love you, darling, as long as I live. Kiss my little son for me and tell him that Daddy loves him too. Have your folks drop me a line and I want to send them my best regards. Keep praying for your very homesick husband darling and perhaps it won't be too long before I get home to you and Billy. Again darling, I love you very very very much.

Always yours,

Andy

* * *

*D*avid Mark Olds went to Britain in 1944 *with the 3255th Signal Service Company, a radio intelligence company assigned to the XII Corps. He landed at Omaha Beach on D-Day plus 30 and followed the route of the XII Corps and Third Army across France, into Luxembourg for the Battle of the Bulge, and then across Germany. At the war's end his outfit was on the German-Czechoslovak border.*

*Second Lieutenant
David Mark Olds*

Rosenheim
July 12, 1945

Dear family:

Beaucoup letters from you to answer. Two V-mails (July 3 and 5), a letter from Dad and two letters from Mimi, including one late effort of July 5. Not bad! Not bad! Dad, you ask for my opinion and reactions and those of the GI in general about several things, including the San Francisco conference. Naturally we read about these things in the paper. We even try to get some discussions going in the weekly or semi-weekly 'Army Talks' periods. As a general rule several reactions show up. For one thing everybody is mostly concerned with getting his own skin back to the States and home, regardless of what he leaves here and in what condition it is. I think this is a pretty universal feeling anyway—leave it to the next fellow or the politicians to worry about the world. I wanna go home and get some small measure of happiness out of life. There are many of us who feel that not much good will be done with all these noble efforts. First of all, the death of President Roosevelt was almost a mortal blow. Second the regrowth of national selfishness which we can plainly see in France, where we are no longer the saviors but annoying foreigners who interfere with their life. Thirdly, the turmoil in England, and finally the pathetic shortsightedness of those who keep hinting at and whooping up talk of war with Russia. Everywhere we hear how terrible the occupying Russian forces are, how barbaric, how savage, how primitive, etc. etc., and I blush to say, many who say this are wearing the American uniform, men who should realize that without Russia's help we would have surely been beaten. In addition to this, the non-fraternization policy is a farce. Whether rightly or wrongly, it is almost impossible to enforce, and what is worse, it is not followed by high ranking officers, which infects the lower ranking officers and so on, until the soldiers don't give a damn, as long as they are not caught. Do not misunderstand. It is not real 'fraternization' they seek, i.e. being friendly with the Germans, living with them, sympathizing with them, etc. Mostly it boils down to getting a woman, or getting laundry done, or getting film developed etc., but because there is the beginning wedge

283

made by, say, giving a German girl some cigarettes to sleep with her, or making a deal with a family to do your clothes, sooner or later there will be a growing more intimate contact, where the disarming friendliness and cleverness of the Germans will make us doubt if they are so bad. 'After all they are a civilized nation, they have great men, etc. etc.' My own solution would be to open Army supervised houses of prostitution, allow a permitted type of fraternization, such as buying items in stores, seeing movies, and the like. I would have a very liberal policy of passes so that men could get out of this accursed country say once a month or so, to breathe the freer air of the Allied countries. Let them change the occupying personnel every six months or so. Let the German PWs be kept in the Army and used as labor of all kinds, farm, factory, etc., instead of discharging them here while we poor bastards have to sit and sweat in the Army in a foreign hated land. I would crush every vestige of military or industrial might in Germany. Let them be a pauper nation. They deserve it. Let the Russians take over, they have shown how to handle them—be rough with them. Of course

A returning soldier leaps from the plane to greet his wife and daughter.

some innocent and some helpless will suffer—too bad—in the Army you learn callousness. It is impossible I know, but I would love to personally shoot all young Hitlerites, say between the ages of 10 and 30, and have a rigidly supervised program of education for the young. I don't know if that gives you any better idea of how I feel, certainly it will not be a clear picture of the GI reactions, except perhaps in parts, but it should help some.

You also asked about the concentration camps and the mass grave victims. It is hard for me to convey all of it to you. You drive through the surrounding towns where there are happy little children at play, and people going about their business, looking like any townspeople the world over, yet within two miles of them, its charged fences harsh against the plains, its chimneys belching smoke from cremating ovens—within two miles is a concentration camp whose very existence is such a horrible thought that a man may doubt that any good can exist in the same world, let alone area, with them. The humans who, though long dead, are yet physically alive with their stick like limbs and vacant faces are so terrible a blasphemy on civilization—yet the German civilians nearby either pretend not to realize them, or what is worse, see no wrong. God, how can people be like that. The concentration camp is even worse when it is empty, and just stands there, a mute testimonial to a brutality beyond comprehension. The gas chambers, as neat and as clean as shower rooms, the cremating ovens where the odor of human flesh is yet ingrained in the bricks, the pitiful barracks and grounds enclosed by the deadly barbed wire and guarded walls. I have seen soldiers get sick standing in the empty desolate chambers, thinking of the horror the walls have seen.

The mass graves and reburials are, for brutality, even worse. Is your stomach strong? Let me tell you about Volarv. The SS troopers and the civilians of the town, including some women, when the Germans were falling back in April, rounded up some 200 Jews with about 50 women in the lot. The men were emasculated, disembowelled and shot. The women were killed very simply. A bayonet was run into their reproductive organs and into their bowels. Pretty, isn't it. When they were being dug up from the ditch where they had been thrown, placed in rude but honorable wooden coffins, and being reburied in plots dug by German civilians and soldiers, American officers and men called all the people out of the town to witness the burial, to see the bodies, to touch the bodies, to have that memory printed on their minds of what a horrible thing they had done, only few of them showed either remorse or sickness. They stood there, hard and sullenfaced, muttering and obstinate. They would turn away and be forced to turn back and look. These same people would have cried in anguish had this been done to their own, to Germans, but what if it happened to inferior people, to Jews, and Russians, and Poles? A shrug of the shoulders, too bad, it had to be done. And yet how quickly these things can be forgotten here. And if the lieutenant isn't looking they will wink at the pretty German girls, and wave at them, and sneak into stores to make purchases of things with American food and cigarettes. No, I don't know if we have done much good as yet. And I'm hardly any different myself, and so I want to get out of this country while I still hate it. Forgive me if this picture seems too pessimistic—I have been here longer than I want to, and it is all getting on my nerves.

Love,

David

★ ★ ★

*B*arrie Greenbie served as a private in the 54th Field Artillery attached to I Corps, Sixth Army. He wrote the following letters to his wife while on active duty in the Philippines.

August 9th, 1945

Dear Meg:

This is the day of the announcement of the incredible futuresque atomic bomb, and the long awaited, long hoped for news that Russia is now seeing the war through with us over here too. At breakfast those were the subject of all conversation. When we got into town we saw the flowing headlines of extras selling out on all corners. At a railroading outfit where Vern and I ate chow, there were cheers throughout the camp when the radio repeated the announcements. It can't last long now, everybody declared, with the Russians in it. Vern said as we walked down Azcarrogo Street to the center of town, "Well, now we know how the Russians felt when we declared war on Germany." This new bomb still seems incredible. From the newspaper reports, it seems as if we should almost feel the concussion here. I guess everybody's reaction the free world over is the same, mingled excitement, hope, and satisfaction at the idea of winning the war quickly, a sort of awesome fear at its utterly terrible potentialities for mankind. Like getting a first hand look at hell or a preview of the end of the world. Looks like this will have to be the last war for freedom because after the next there won't be any world left to be free. Maybe it's a good thing. Maybe even the most degenerate tyrants will hesitate to commit world suicide. What Japan does now will tell that or perhaps the people of the world will be so scared that they will never put their fingers near the fuse of such power.

Private Barrie Greenbie

Well to get back to the present and our little private orbit in this cosmic world of men and matter, I feel a thousand miles closer to home tonight, a feeling shared I guess by several million men in clothes like mine. I smell the moist sea breeze coming from over Manila bay, and only have to close my eyes to see the white waves breaking over the prow of the transport, plowing straight and steadily East.

★

Friday, August 10th

Crowds of G.I.s around the bulletin board here at the Red Cross rec. hall reading the latest news. Newspapers, usually shoved under your nose by insistent little newsboys, are harder to find in Manila than American whiskey. I can't remember such excitement and hopeful speculation. I think only the ending of the war itself could bring more universal relief and exultation, and somehow there is an underlying promise in this recent spectacular news of not only a speedier end to the war but a real enduring peace. Even the hard-bitten generals of this theatre, such as Lt. Gen. Griswall of the XIVth Corps, have noted that. The bomb and the Russians occupy everybody's attention. They are all you hear anybody talking about. I can't remember any world event over here that so completely dominates conversation big and small. You get in line for coffee and doughnuts and you don't hear guys talking about their women or their outfits. You don't hear them bitching about prices or speculating on the point system. It's the atomic bomb and the Red Army that will be sending them home.

It really no longer seems pure speculation and wishful thinking to discuss being home by Christmas, at least for many of us. All this still seems incredible, beyond the wildest hopes of guys who deep in their heart couldn't help wishing for some miracle to end this dreary war. And the bomb at least seems something in the nature of a miracle.

There's much talk of our not having to make any more invasions, that the bomb will take care of Japan and the Russians China. That's carrying things a little too far I think. The War Department doesn't seem to bank on any such easy way to Victory. As they said, the atomic bomb is the only one weapon. And how ready we are to throw the rest of the job on the Red Army doughfeet? Will we be as ready to forget? And everybody says. "Jeezus, looks like this better be the last war."

This "furlough" seems to be getting longer and longer. We'll be here at least another week. What a break it is to be free and in a city again! I love just to wander or sit on the balcony outside the RD bldg here and feel immersed in the hum and stir, feel solid concrete and steel under me and the handsome shapes of city architecture all around and spreading out in geometric patterns into the hazy distance, traffic rolling, people flowing, going about their ways, G.I.s strolling and civilians in loose cool clothes moving about. People selling, buying, building. Theatres playing and restaurants with color, food, wine, and music, exciting even from the outside looking in over a barrier of pesos. You can't forget it's a scarred city, a wounded city. But it's throbbing with the life of a city, sprawling with the form of a city. At night the scars are covered by darkness, the lights sparkle, and the pulse of a metropolis beats nostalgically. A million sights and sounds and smells remind me of what I left behind, and have to come back to.

I'll never feel part of it again until I'm out of uniform. The army is so ugly sometimes, with it's sacrifice of everything that makes life warm and beautiful. No matter how exalted the end may be, the army is naked power, mechanical efficiency stripped of all color and variety, organized ruthlessly for destruction. Human beings, themselves mechanized and standardized for the Purpose, try to retain their individuality, their identity, in pathetic little ways, a picture stuck on a rack among identical racks of identical clothes. Whenever and wherever they are allowed, they wear their uniforms differently. Some leave their boots unbuckled for no good reason, some roll their pants up, some tilt their hats back or forwards, and paint names on anything and everything. It's surprising how much having the name on your truck means. It gives it a personality. In combat, where individuality shines against the really necessary organization, life can be exciting often and full of variety. It's these garrison camps like ours that are most trying. No one who hasn't been a soldier can understand the bitter resentment with which we are made to paint the names off our trucks. There isn't any Connecticut Yankee now, just U.S.A. No. 4464630. Before I nursed it, worked on it, sweated it over rough roads. Now I don't give a damn about it. It's not my truck, just the truck I drive. . . .

★

Tuesday, August 14th

"IT'S TRUE! IT'S ALL OVER!": says the enclosed Free Filipino Extra. Isn't that the most beautiful headline you ever saw? It should be framed!

No official confirmation yet, but there isn't much doubt. We could have been sure before if we'd dared. The news came this afternoon out at camp, came with a shouting and hailing but without surprise. There's not the celebrating in the streets tonight. No honking, shooting. The harbor whistles blew a while, but there's no crazy joy, just happy relief, and that's even better.

I'd like to be on Times Square, but maybe it's more appropriate this way. New York must be wild, celebration without reservation this time. Drunks can get drunk knowing doughboys are celebrating outside their foxholes and nice old ladies needn't shake their heads. With V-J Day proclaimed, perhaps tomorrow while I'm rolling north, I'll be thinking of my two girls up in the Empire State Building high over the city, on top of a world at peace at last, and my heart will float up to meet them.

I'm watching the street for the 'cease firing' news. The street is the reporter and the barometer. A Sergeant next to me looks out and says, "No excitement yet. Maybe it's better. People are just quietly happy." But I'm going out and spend my last four pesos for a couple of drinks and will drink with the first guy standing by to peace and home and family! Don't know where the other boys are, but everybody's a friend on a night like this.

The band upstairs is playing and the singer singing "Awful lonely without you, don't get around much anymore . . ." but not for long.

Love,

Barrie

★ ★ ★

*S*taff *Sergeant Willis Ward served with the 413th Regiment, 104th Infantry Division, attached to the Quartermaster Company, which was based in London. He wrote this letter to his young nieces and nephew on the day of the Japanese surrender.*

S/Sgt. Willis Ward 35558038
HQ-UK Base-QM Sec.
APO-413 c/o PM. NYC

August 15, 1945

Dear Ann, Lucy and Butch:
How about pampering your maternal uncle for just a short time by lending an ear to a few random remarks which swirl through my stream of consciousness. With close to fifteen months overseas I sometimes wonder if I ever was conscious—but today it is certain that I am for try as I might it would be nigh impossible to erase the red circle around this date on my calendar of relatively uneventful happenings. Your daddy and I along with all the peoples who live on the land masses of this good earth have turned a corner, reached the top of a hill, or what have you. It isn't a glorious miracle and unlike John's vision on Patmos none

Staff Sergeant Willis Ward

of us see "a new heaven and a new earth." Everyone is turning their lights on, having a special feast, and staying up past midnite because soon those in uniform or out will be able to live more nearly as they please than at any time in five years. And all of us sober old folks rave on about holing in and never budging from our particular home town. That is one hunk of malarkey you can burn in the incinerator. Just let some twentieth century pharaoh tell some islanders to make bricks without straw or something—from many a hamlet the howl will rise until some action has been initiated to look into the matter. The globe hasn't been immunized against war fever even by this over-strength injection but the patient will have to be more careless than in the past if exposure is to grab hold of him. If you can keep that USA address all your life then my time and your Daddy's effort will be justified to the fullest. I miss you very much and am awaiting that day when we can all have a soda together.

One of many travellers in foreign lands,

Uncle Bill

EPILOGUE

Sergeant Newton Minow